"Käsemann's study remains the point of departure for any contemporary study of Hebrews. It is a marvelous introduction to the epistle writer's hermeneutic and to his interpretation of Jewish covenantal piety and Hellenistic religiosity as encountering their telos *at the cross."*

—Roy A. Harrisville & Irving L. Sandberg,
translators

THE WANDERING PEOPLE OF GOD

An Investigation of the
Letter to the Hebrews

ERNST KÄSEMANN

TRANSLATED BY ROY A. HARRISVILLE
AND IRVING L. SANDBERG

AUGSBURG Publishing House • Minneapolis

THE WANDERING PEOPLE OF GOD
An Investigation of the Letter to the Hebrews

This is a translation of *Das wandernde Gottesvolk: Eine Untersuchung zum Hebräerbrief,* 2nd German edition, copyright © 1957, Verlag Vandenhoeck & Ruprecht, Göttingen. Translation from German with the approval of Verlag Vandenhoeck & Ruprecht, Göttingen, © Vandenhoeck & Ruprecht in Göttingen.

Library of Congress Cataloging in Publication Data

Käsemann, Ernst.
  THE WANDERING PEOPLE OF GOD.

  Translation of: Das wandernde Gottesvolk.
  Bibliography: p. 241
  Includes indexes
  1. Bible. N.T. Hebrews—Criticism, interpretation, etc.   I. Title.
BS2775.2.K3313   1984   227'.8706   84-20523
ISBN   0-8066-2121-4   ISBN 0-8066-2316-0 pbk.

Manufactured in the U.S.A.   APH 10-6941

      2   3   4   5   6   7   8   9   0   1   2   3   4   5   6   7   8   9

Contents

Abbreviations

Commentaries (cited only by the author's last name)

Gyllenberg   Gyllenberg, R. "Die Christologie des Hebräerbriefes," *Zeitschrift für Systematische Theologie* 11 (1934), pp. 662-690.

Michel   Michel, O. *Der Brief an die Hebräer.* 1936.

Preuschen-Bauer   Preuschen, E. & Bauer, W. *Griechisch-deutsches Wörterbuch.* 1928.

Riggenbach   Riggenbach, E. *Der Brief an die Hebräer.* 1922.

Seeberg   Seeberg, A. *Der Brief an die Hebräer.* 1921.

Strathmann   Strathmann, H. *Der Brief an die Hebräer.* 1935.

Weiss   Weiss, B. *Der Brief an die Hebräer.* 1897.

Windisch   Windisch, H. *Der Hebräerbrief.* 1931^2.

Wrede   Wrede, W. *Das literarische Rätsel des Hebräerbriefes.* 1906.

General

ET	English translation provided by the translators
KJV	King James Version
G.C.S.	Schmidt, C., ed. *Die Griechischen christlichen Schriftsteller der ersten drei Jahrhunderte.* 1905.
TDNT	Kittel, G., ed. *Theological Dictionary of the New Testament, Vol. I-III*, translated by G. W. Bromiley. Grand Rapids, 1964-65.
RSV	Revised Standard Version
ZNTW	*Zeitschrift für die Neutestamentliche Wissenschaft*

English Editions of Texts Used in Translation

Apostolic Fathers: *The Apostolic Fathers* I, II. The Loeb Classical Library, trans. by Kirsopp Lake. Oxford, 1912f.

New Testament Apocrypha: *New Testament Apocrypha, Vol. I & II*, ed. by E. Hennecke & W. Schneemelcher; trans. by R. McL. Wilson et al. Philadelphia, 1961, 1965. All translations are from vol. II (indicated by H.-S.) unless indicated thusly: *H.-S. I*

Odes of Solomon: *The Odes of Solomon,* ed. & trans. by James H. Charlesworth. Missoula, 1977.

Philo: *Philo's Works.* The Loeb Classical Library, trans. by F. H. Colson & G. H. Whitaker. Oxford, 1929ff.

Testaments of the 12 Patriarchs: *The Apocrypha and Pseudepigrapha of the Old Testament, Vol. II,* ed. by R. H. Charles. Oxford, 1913.

Translators' Preface

The Wandering People of God is the second major work from the pen of a scholar who has spent his life swimming upstream. (The first was his *Leib und Leib Christi, Eine Untersuchung zur paulinischen Begrifflichkeit,* 1933.) In the 1950s, Ernst Käsemann reopened the "quest of the historical Jesus." In opposition to the contention of his former teacher, Rudolf Bultmann, that such inquiry was motivated solely by the desire to legitimize faith, Käsemann insisted that the quest was nothing but the church's acknowledgment of the sovereignty of God who in Jesus had set the time and place within which faith became possibility.

In treatises of the 1950s and 1960s, Käsemann opposed his 19th-century liberal inheritance with the assertion that it was apocalyptic which gave expression to the fact that in Jesus ultimate promise had broken into the world.

Subsequently, Käsemann's studies led him to split one lance after another with the regnant "theology of facts," which he believed rendered the German theological scene a "jungle," maintaining that the *theologia crucis* of the Reformers comprised the heart and core of Scripture (cf. *e.g.,* his "Die Heilsbedeutung des Todes Jesu nach Paulus" of 1967). If Julius Schniewind could write of Bultmann that he alone of all his generation held to justification as the article on which the church stands or falls, it can be said of Käsemann that he, if not alone,

11

then certainly more than most, if not all, has focused on the task of theology as an explication of the cross.

In addresses to the German *Kirchentag,* Käsemann excoriated the Christian community for its service to civil religion and summoned it to struggle for freedom and liberation. In 1937, his summons was answered by his arrest and imprisonment after his attack on National Socialism and the "German Christians" during a worship service. He later gave a daughter to that struggle in Argentina.

Of all Bultmann's students the least influenced by his teacher's philosophical presuppositions, Käsemann drew contemporaries to his lectures at Mainz, Göttingen, and finally at Tübingen, like moths to the flame. Faculty and students from all university disciplines jammed the Neue Aula at Tübingen to hear this brilliant, polemical, fiery man hammer away at the idols and ideologies of his age. After a fall from grace among those who had come to embrace revisionist doctrines of the old liberalism, Käsemann has lived to hear his motions seconded again and again, many through translation of his principal works, most noted among them his magnificent study on the Epistle to the Romans.

In reflection on that period of his life from which this volume comes, Käsemann wrote:

> Long enticed by my teacher Bultmann and his Marburg School to accept the notion of the "redeemed Redeemer" as Richard Reitzenstein had depicted it for us, I believed that the Christology of Hebrews should also be viewed from this perspective. This was bound to have effects even for ecclesiology, which were then reflected in the book, *The Wandering People of God,* appearing in 1938/39. In three years of work (an arduous task for the pastor of a large, blue-collar congregation), I gathered the material with which, during a four-week imprisonment in 1937, I was able to compose the first draft of the version which

was completed the following winter. The war denied me a wider response. When it did come, the situation of the Nazi period was already past, so that my religious-historical sketch more or less veiled the theological concern which was important to me. By describing the church as the new people of God on its wandering through the wilderness, following the Pioneer and Perfecter of faith, I of course had in mind that radical Confessing Church which resisted the tyranny in Germany, and which had to be summoned to patience so that it could continue its way through endless wastes (*Kirchliche Konflikte*, Vol. I [Göttingen: Vandenhoeck und Ruprecht, 1982], p. 17).

The value of this work lies first of all in its refraction of a period of intense struggle within the Christian community in Germany. But its worth surpasses that immediate occasion, despite dependence upon presuppositions which later scholarship has challenged, leading Käsemann himself to hesitate over its reprinting or translation. It remains the point of departure for any contemporary study of Hebrews. It is a marvelous introduction to the epistle writer's hermeneutic, to his interpretation of Jewish covenantal piety and Hellenistic religiosity as encountering their *telos* at the cross. Many of the themes and motifs taken up by Käsemann in later life are earliest struck in this book, above all, his abiding concern for the church of Christ.

In a labor of love, we have striven to provide as literal a translation as possible of Käsemann's often difficult style, and we hope that this early work of a master of biblical interpretation will delight old friends and enlist admirers from a new generation of readers.

Roy A. Harrisville
Irving L. Sandberg
July 1984

Preface to the Second German Edition

Material for this book was gathered during brief holiday weeks in 1936. A first draft followed in the leisure of a prison cell in autumn of 1937. The book took final shape during the following winter when the daily tasks of a pastor to miners had been completed. This story will explain the defects in the study and the deficiencies in the use of literature. But it should also refute the judgment of one of my critics that I had attempted "to shed new light on the history of the Hellenistic-oriental tradition and the Gnostic myth." To the extent such actually occurred, it merely served a theological idea most current at the time, which still seems to me to be constitutive for understanding the theme of our epistle.

The work was quickly bought up, and due to the confusions of the time was not very well known outside our country. Again and again I delayed yielding to the request for a new edition. New commentaries, monographs, and, in addition, the discovery of the Qumran texts in recent years seemed to require treatment at the fundamental level as well as corrections and supplement in particular. In view of other tasks, I lacked time and energy for both. Moreover, even scientific pursuits have their *kairos*. It appeared to me a lighter task to rewrite the book rather than to patch and improve on it, since I

---

* Numbers in the margins refer to the pagination of the second German edition.

feared ruining the wholeness of the sketch through revision. I finally decided upon another edition in the old form, since I found that in contemporary discussion my concern was only superficially taken note of, and I did not want to give the impression that I too had abandoned it.

Thanks are due the publisher for assisting me toward this end. If out of shy respect I once dared to note indebtedness to my teacher in a mere foreword, I now deem it proper to hand down the clear confession of a thankful pupil on behalf of a man about whom there has been much dispute, a confession which despite all the criticism aroused in the meantime has become only more clear and vital. [Translators' note: The reference is to Rudolf Bultmann, to whom the first edition was dedicated.]

The Wandering of the People of God as the Principal Motif in the Letter to the Hebrews [5]

A. Hebrews 3:7—4:13 as Point of Departure for the Presentation of the Motif

The motif of the wandering people of God is discussed thematically in the section 3:7ff. From this starting point, therefore, the interpretation will attempt to clarify the structure of the motif.

1. Wandering as the Form of Existence of the Bearer of the Revelation

Hebrews intends to show the Christian community the greatness of the promise given it and the seriousness of the temptation threatening it. For this reason, it sets before its eyes the picture of Israel wandering through the wilderness. From such a type the possibilities of Christian existence can be perceived. This assumes that type and antitype share a basic posture. Such a common posture does in fact exist in both, insofar as in both there

17

is issued a λόγος τῆς ἀκοῆς which summons to wandering, and both must hold fast this Logos precisely in their wandering (4:1f.). The context makes clear what is to be understood by this "heard Word." It is God's historically manifested revelation, distinguished from the ῥῆμα of creation (cf. 1:3), of which Christians have now been deemed worthy to be εὐηγγελισμένοι (4:2, 6), as was Israel long ago. It is that living Logos which, by way of an image no doubt already handed down to the author,[1] is described as a sharp, two-edged sword (4:12f.). In contrast to human words which are so often ineffective, this Logos is a fully life-giving and creative power. It does not recoil from opposition, as do these human words, but

[6] continually presses toward its goal.[2] Just as it possesses a penetrating eye, so it allows no darkness to exist before it. It is not judged, but is and remains "the critic" of our heart and impulses. In it is revealed an objective "power that seizes us and to which we have surrendered without opposition."[3] For this reason, this "Word" does not merely appear as an agent for handing down a particular set of ideas, nor can it be connected merely with a message of salvation or judgment, though at times both aspects may certainly be conveyed by the Logos, conceived in almost personal fashion and most probably equipped with mythological attributes. In 3:14 the work

---

[1]Cf. the commentaries *ad loc.* In any case, derivation of the λόγος τομεύς from Philo cannot be directly demonstrated. Philo indeed may have modified in psychological fashion a common tradition that carries forward the doctrine of the eschatological sword of God in Jer. 27:1; 34:5; 66:16; and Isa. 21:3, and that penetrates Rev. 1:16; 2:12; and 19:15.

[2]Cf. the *Odes of Solomon* 12:5f.: "For the subtlety of the Word is inexpressible, and like His expression so also is His swiftness and His acuteness, for limitless is His progression. He never falls...."

[3]Windisch, p. 35.

of the Logos is described as ὑπόστασις; in 4:1 as ἐπαγγελία. Conversely, the reference in 4:12 has an unmistakably ominous character. There is no static quality inhering in the gift of the Logos. The gospel that it proffers is at the same time task, and it in turn does not fulfill this task as though such were the end of its activity. Since the Logos presents this task, its recipients must render a decision and come under judgment to the extent they now hold the first ὑπόστασις firm to the end (3:14), or forsake the promise ahead of the goal (4:1). From these possibilities of decision it is clear *that the Logos grants no final revelation. It calls to a way*, the goal of which it points out by way of promise, and which can only be reached in union with the Logos and its promise. Israel was rejected since it, of course, received the gift of the Word, but did not allow itself to be bound in faith by it. To that extent, Israel failed to recognize the character of the Logos as a promise hastening one on the way. Only obedience that achieves this wandering beneath and together with the Word to the end is evidence that acceptance of the Word has actually occurred. The basic presupposition of our text is that one possesses the εὐαγγέλιον on earth only as ἐπαγγελία. But then it follows *that the form of existence in time appropriate to the recipient of the revelation can only be that of wandering.* Only in this way may holding the initial ὑπόστασις firm to the end be spoken of in meaningful fashion, and only in this way may beginning and end be spoken of at all. Only in this way can the danger of forsaking the promise loom up. The existential necessity of wandering for the bearer of the revelation allows Israel, wandering through its wilderness, to appear as antitype of Christianity. It permits the goal common to both to be described as entry

[7]

into rest, just as rest appears as promise only after the toil
and restlessness of a sojourn. Finally, ἀποστῆναι must
be viewed here as a characteristic temptation (3:12).

Should it be deemed methodologically perverse to allow our investigation to proceed from a section so bound
to tradition, since the tradition utilized here from the
outset imposes its scheme on the exegesis? The very appropriation of this tradition in such an emphatic manner
and in such a prominent passage makes clearer than all
the details that in Hebrews the basic posture of the bearer
of the revelation should, in fact, be described as a wandering.

2. The People of God as Bearer of the Revelation

This tradition also illumines another element that is
constitutive for the entire letter: The existence of the
bearer of the revelation is not only determined by wandering under the sign of promise, but also by *incorporation into the fellowship of the people of God.* Moreover,
the term λαὸς τοῦ θεοῦ (4:9), which does not appear by
accident in the summary of our section, is also clearly applied to Christianity.[4] Characteristically, the "heard
Word" in both of its historical manifestations applies
precisely to a fellowship.[5] Further, in both instances it establishes a fellowship that, according to its nature, is best
compared with a people. From this fact the expression
μέτοχοι τοῦ Χριστοῦ (3:14) first obtains its full weight.
Conversely, the latter phrase makes clear that the people

---

[4]Cf. also 2:17; 11:25; and 13:12.
[5]Thus already in A. Schlatter's *Die Theologie der Apostel* (1922[2]), p. 473.

of God does not involve an earthly social structure, but a
fellowship of Christ established by and derived from revelation, and claiming revelatory character.[6] This people
does not exist of itself and is not intrinsically identifiable.
It exists and grows out of its king. Insofar as the revelation encounters the individual as such, this results
through the medium of the company; it encounters the
individual as a member of a people. But what is fundamental is solely the people of God as bearer of, and as
creature of, the revelation. Hebrews emphasizes this element so strongly that, in contrast to Paul, it never arrives
at a real anthropology. With a certain naivete, Hebrews   [8]
seems to explain Christian existence by way of an illumi-
nation of existence as in fellowship. Only in union with
Christ's companions is there life, faith, and progress on
the individual's way of wandering. As soon as a person is
no longer fully conscious of membership and begins to be
isolated from the people of God, that person must also
have left the promise behind and abandoned the goal.[7]
The former possibility of rejecting the entire people will
not be repeated in the New Covenant. Now danger continually threatens only the individual member, as it finds
pregnant expression in the repeated "lest any of you"
(3:12f.; 4:1,11). To remain among Christ's companions
and to preserve the initial firmness to the end is one and
the same condition which can in no way be severed (cf.
3:14). *The Logos points the individual to the fellowship
established by Christ, and only in this fellowship does the
individual persist in hearing and preserving the Logos.* If

---

[6]Windisch, p. 32, rightly concludes from 1 Cor. 10:4 that Israel could already be considered as the company of Christ. This is clearly shown in
11:25.
[7]This fact gives meaning to the admonition in 10:25.

one no longer holds to the Word, then one is at the same time παραρυόμενος, that is, "drifting away" (2:1) from the people of God, or one goes astray and thus suffers the fate of Israel which retreated from the promise. This means that existence in the form of isolation is peculiar only to disobedience and that such a form demonstrates that disobedience is under the divine curse. Apart from the people of God there is neither revelation nor a bearer of the revelation, nor is there a wandering oriented to a goal, but only the solitude of an existence left to itself and the hopeless and aimless erring of a world becoming wilderness. In this sense we may deny to Hebrews any "private Christianity,"[8] and describe faith as well as obedience as the true attitude of the community.[9]

B. The Unfolding of the Motif of the Wandering People of God in the Conclusion of the Letter

The motif of the wandering people of God is un-folded clearly and with emphasis in the closing section of the letter, beginning with 10:19. This is so easy to see that a mere entering upon all the details to be cited here is un-necessary. Otherwise no less than the entire context of the last chapter would have to be worked through, al-most section by section, and this would only produce an obvious result. It is enough merely to examine the text

[9]

---

[8]Strathmann, p. 80.
[9]Gyllenberg, p. 687.

for its *verbs of motion*[10] to obtain a clear picture of the
conspicuous position of our motif in these chapters. Just
as 10:9f. summarizes what precedes in the idea of the
New Way that Jesus opened to those who believe in him,
so the high point of Chapter 13 summons to going outside the camp with Jesus. This is established by the sentence that applies to the entire letter: "We have no lasting
city, but we seek the city which is to come" (13:13f.). In
the midst of this is set that broad description of the
"cloud of witnesses" whose activity is decisively and
continually described as a wandering toward the city of
God (11:8ff., 13ff., 24ff.), the description of the Christian attitude under the figure of running in an ἀγών,[11] and
the sight of the goal of faith's wandering on Mount Zion
(12:18ff.). By this means the people of God as bearer of
such wandering is constantly kept in view, just as a "we"
is addressed throughout, and just as the Old Testament
witnesses appear expressly under the title of people of
God (11:25).

But more important than setting forth these individual data is the evidence that our motif not only erupts directly in the text with constant freshness, but that it also
appears as the conception that controls the close of the
letter with a logical consistency, and indeed both from

---

[10]Cf. προσέρχομαι in 10:22; 11:6; 12:18, and 22; ἐξέρχεσθαι in 13:13;
ἀναστρέφεσθαι in 10:33 and 13:7; running in the ἀγών set before us in
12:1; strengthening weak knees and making straight paths in 12:12f.; and the
κομίσασθαι τὴν ἐπαγγελίαν construed spatially in 10:36; 11:13, and 39. In
addition, there is an abundance of related verbs in Chapter 11, where the
motif of alien existence on earth and seeking the heavenly homeland (in vv.
13f.; cf. vv. 8,15f.) dominates, and where Israel's exodus in vv. 22,27 is interpreted in terms of Enoch's being "taken up" in v. 5.

[11]To 12:1,12f. corresponds the image of ἄθλησις in 10:32f., and of παιδεία
in 12:5ff.

the standpoint of the terminology used as well as from the train of thought expressed. At the same time, for the sake of clarity and completeness, we cannot entirely avoid encroaching on the remainder of the letter. How might this occur, provided we are correct in our initial thesis that the motif of the wandering people of God forms the hidden basis of Hebrews?

[10]   ## 1. The Concrete Situation of the Community

Only from the letter's concluding portion can we ascertain the aim of the whole, since it is here that the doctrinal expositions predominant elsewhere come to a head in a concrete and personal way. Unfortunately, this insight has often enough produced no practical conclusions. The old prejudice that Hebrews represents a more or less historically conditioned dispute with the Jewish religion would otherwise not be held to with stubborn tenacity, and in the most diverse variations and abridgments. This prejudice has given rise to so much exegetical confusion that its final burial would be equivalent to liberation from a sinister ghost. It is a product of fantasy to read from our letter a Judaizing disintegration threatening the Christian community or the danger of apostasy toward Judaism. It merely closes off understanding for this most unique writing of the New Testament and cannot be confirmed by enlisting the advocates of this thesis, however great.

Where its absoluteness is concerned, the revelation of Christ must obviously be distinguished from that of the Old Testament. In what sense this occurs in Hebrews at first remains to be seen. Naturally, in the individual instance, such fundamental distinction may be occasioned and determined by concrete Judaizing tendencies in primitive Christianity. *But in general, any concretely conditioned orientation of an anti-Jewish character on the part of Hebrews must be roundly contested.* In the entire closing section nothing of this can be observed with any clarity. Verses 13:9f. are still too obscure to furnish the basis for such broad interpretations.[12] On the other hand, what danger actually threatens the community is perfectly clear: Behind it lies a struggle for faith, and, like the Christian struggle of faith in every age, it has been waged in suffering. If that struggle first summoned to joyfulness in endurance, fellowship in love, and growth in knowledge, then its further progress suffered a setback manifest in *the weariness and weakness of faith.* One wishes an end to the time of distress, neglects the admonition to [11] faithfulness in worship, and in practice more and more neglects the ὁμολογία τῆς ἐλπίδος (10:23). If in the beginning the certainty of a better and abiding good in heaven following the loss of earthly possessions (10:34) was a comfort and spur to perseverance, now this very certainty gradually retreats in face of present tribulation. This creates a situation that renders intelligible a comparison with the Old Testament wilderness generation and calls faith a παράκλησις (13:22). But in what should such "admonition" consist than in the renewed unfolding of just that wavering homology of hope, and in a summons to complete the wandering of faith?

---

[12]Though sectarian impulses may play a role, this does not yet prove their Judaizing tendency. Asceticism and cultic food regulations were rife in antiquity. Even if one wanted hypothetically to concede a Judaizing tendency to these verses, still the narrow limits to food regulations drawn here dare not be exceeded, and from that point the threat of a menacing relapse into Judaism superimposed on the entire letter.

2. *The Meaning of* ἐπαγγελία

Hence, we must first inquire into the content of hope in Hebrews. Christian hope is always encountered as bound to the revelation of God, thus as the reflection of the divine promise. With this fact corresponds the signal role of the concept of ἐπαγγελία in Hebrews.[13] Its interpretation is indispensable for understanding the entire letter and particularly the hope manifest in it.

We have already encountered the striking fact that in Hebrews εὐαγγελίζεσθαι and the reception of the ἐπαγγελία are identical (4:2,6). This means *that in a constitutive and fundamental way the divine revelation in Hebrews bears the character of promise and thus is purely eschatological in nature.* Now this is true of the entire New Testament message, insofar as the Christ event in the New Testament is always viewed eschatologically. And it is also peculiar to the entire New Testament proclamation that the data of eschatology are, as it were, divided into two stages: What began in Jesus' incarnation, death, and exaltation will be completed at the end of earth's time. Which of the two stages receives the accent spells the difference at any given time. Hebrews is thus no stranger to the idea that the eschatological event [12] already took place in the past. But if for Hebrews God's address occurs in the arrival of the Son 'επ' ἐσχάτου τῶν ἡμερῶν τουτῶν (1:2), or ἐπὶ συντελείᾳ τῶν αἰώνων (9:26), then Christians also have tasted the heavenly gift or Word of God and the powers

---

[13]Cf. 4:1; 6:12,15,17; 7:6; 8:6; 9:15; 10:36; 11:9,13,17,33, and 39; cf. also ἐπαγγέλομαι in 12:26. Substantive use is perhaps to be assumed for 6:13; 10:23; and 11:11, in which God would then be construed as "Giver" and "Donor" in terms of the Hellenistic records. Cf. Preuschen-Bauer, col. 436, and Schniewind-Friedrich, *TDNT* II, 578, 581.

of the coming age (6:4f.). And yet the orientation is quite
obviously governed by an expectation of the future, as
the accent on the concept of ἐπαγγελία precisely shows.
There is thus a tension here that will be worthwhile to
pursue for an understanding of the latter idea.

It is characteristic that in the passage 6:4f. just cited,
the ῥῆμα ϑεοῦ is viewed as the primary eschatological gift
and the heavenly powers are viewed as if merely its ac-
companiment. As creation (1:3) and salvation history
(1:1) have been set into motion by the working of the divine speaking, so also the eschatological Christ event has
begun with a new Word of God.[14] This latter takes its peculiar stamp from the fact that it is a last word, final and
once-for-all.[15] Of course, this word had its first attestation in Jesus' speaking, and was subsequently strengthened and "confirmed" by the apostles (2:3). But this
earthly activity has not annulled its eschatological once-
for-all-ness. To this word also corresponds the promise
issued to the Old Testament wilderness generation, and
the context of 3:7ff. actually makes clear the identification of the new Word of God with the Old Testament
promise.[16] But again, this does not blunt its eschatological
once-for-all-ness. For just as the Old Testament promise
was likewise oriented to the one eschatological goal of

---

[14]The difference between λόγος and ῥῆμα is that while either can appear as a
concrete historical manifestation of the revelation, λόγος describes more the
power of salvation or judgment operating independently, and under certain
circumstances construed in almost personal fashion, whereas ῥῆμα describes
more the agent of the execution and transmission of the divine will.

[15]According to 12:26f., what is yet to follow it will no longer be Word, but
altogether an evidence of the divine power.

[16]Cf. Schniewind-Friedrich, *TDNT* II, 585, n. 67.

"rest," so even in the old covenant, according to Hebrews, Christ was the norm of this orientation (11:26). As the Old Testament people of God are the antitype of the people of Christ, so also their promise was merely an antitype and prolepsis of the Christian promise. They thus take their light from the Christian promise and finally, in union with it, reveal the same eschatological bond. The Word of God in Christ is new solely for the reason that its fulfillment can no longer be menaced or broken as before, but has become irrevocable. And it is [13] unique despite its varied earthly activity or attestation, and despite its prolepsis in the Old Testament, since in Christ it not only reveals anew the one eschatological salvation, but also conclusively guarantees the realization of this salvation. As such it is already present and perceptible in history, yet not other than as promise, that is, as orientation and direction toward a future still to come. As surely as the ῥῆμα ϑεοῦ must itself be called an eschatological and heavenly gift, *the less does it already embrace all of eschatological salvation.* Only the one willing to be guided by the Logos toward the future completion rightly understands the presence of the Logos. In this sense we could apply Paul's statements concerning the *pneuma* to the ἐπαγγελία in Hebrews: It is only guarantee,[17] and it unites with itself in order then to point away from itself to something other and greater. Those who are grasped by it are regarded as μαρτυρηϑέντες (11:2, 4, 39), and from that point themselves acquire the character of μάρτυρες (12:1), precisely because the promise remains μαρτυρία, a witness to the better possession in heaven. In the earthly present this μαρτυρία is

---

[17]Cf. 2 Cor. 1:22 and 5:5.

still such a transcendent event and pure testimony that originally only the Holy Spirit is regarded as its bearer, and humans may be such only in derived fashion.[18]

This in no way reduces the ἐπαγγελία to an empty pledge or an uncertain consolation, as usually adheres to human promises. It rather has a fixed content, a clearly outlined goal, a guaranteed realization, and is thus qualitatively superior to every earthly promise. Schniewind's observation is of importance at this point, that the nuance of meaning "to proclaim" is peculiar to the entire ἀγγελ-stem.[19] Hebrews most strongly underscores this perception in respect to the derivative ἐπαγγελία.

It is, of course, not accidental when in 12:26 an ἐπήγγελται λέγων continues and parallels the χρηματίζοντα. This parallel expresses the element of solemn announcement and proclamation.[20] And it is no more accidental that the divine promise in Hebrews is connected with the celestial taking of an oath,[21] as occurs elsewhere only in Jesus' installation to his high priestly office (7:20f., 28). According to the clear statement of the text, Jesus' installation occurred in enthronement forms, and was accompanied by a solemn proclamation. The oath confirms the proclamation as an inviolable legal arrangement.[22] We may then

[14]

---

[18]With the exception of the complicated idea in 9:14, the Spirit in Hebrews, described in 10:29 as πνεῦμα τῆς χάριτος, has only the one task of bearing witness; cf. 2:4; 6:4; 9:8; and 10:15.

[19]Schniewind, *TDNT* I, 56ff.

[20]χρηματίζειν (cf. 11:7) was originally used of the inspired word of the oracle. Cf. Preuschen-Bauer, col. 1411.

[21]6:13ff.; the annulling of the promise is connected antitypically with an oath in 3:18.

[22]If, according to 6:16, the oath gives βεβαίωσις, then Preuschen-Bauer already referred to the term as derived from the legal. Cf. col. 218. Even Schlier, *TDNT* I, 603, calls εὐαγγελίζεσθαι a legal act which, according to

assume the same sense for the taking of an oath and the issuance of the divine ἐπαγγελία. This means that the promise is distinguished from the uncertain sphere of mere earthly pledges to the extent *it was constituted only on the basis of a heavenly act of proclamation revealing God's future will*. From this perspective, then, it is entirely probable that the description of God as ὁ ἐπαγγειλάμενος, in accord with ancient parallels, is a technical term, and is used as title for the "donor" in Hebrews. Above all, the factor of correspondence—for so long not sufficiently taken into account—indeed, of Hebrews' partial identification of ἐπαγγελία and διαθήκη,[23] now at last becomes clear. In our letter, διαθήκη is the divine legal arrangement[24] on which our salvation is built. Everything depends on correctly recognizing and preserving the juridical character of *diathēkē* in Hebrews. It is inevitably misleading to distinguish the juridical concept, as it emerges with full clarity in Greek literature and thus usually connotes "testament," from a "religious" use.[25] This is unfortunate because the religious in no way excludes the legal, and in our context actually presupposes it.[26]

[15]   The ἐπαγγελία is more than an expression of the divine good will. *That is, it is a statute of the future order of*

2:2ff., is ratified by signs—a definition thoroughly in harmony with legal form respecting the issuing of ἐπαγγελία.

[23]If in 8:6 the *diathēkē* is based on promises, then in 9:15 the *diathēkē* is the presupposition for the reception of the promise. Both terms allow what are obviously only different aspects of the same thing to emerge as indissolubly united. On *diathēkē*, cf. in addition 7:22; 8:8; 9:4, 16f., 20; 10:29; 12:24; and 13:20.

[24]Cf. Behm, *TDNT* II, 131f.; Preuschen-Bauer, col. 285, and Windisch, p. 67.

[25]Contra Behm; cf. above.

[26]Thus in 9:16f. only the meaning "testament" is possible.

salvation and thus establishes the way of faith on an un-shakable ground, anchored, as it were, by divine right. This is the conclusion to be drawn from the intimate con-nection between promise and *diathēkē* in Hebrews. God has bound himself to his people in solemn procla-mation and thus guarantees to them eschatological salva-tion in himself as the Word construed as eschatological gift.[27] But just as in heaven an oath accompanied the proc-lamation and appeared as inviolable, so on earth miracu-lous signs and powers of the future world accompany this Word and thus assure us of the legal power and validity of the Word, which its character as promise in no way robs of its surety and saving power. Rather, according to Hebrews, both aspects are always combined in the ἐπαγγελία: On the one hand, the act of proclaiming the divine statute occurring in the past, or its earthly procla-mation in the present, through the λόγος τῆς ἀκοῆς; and, on the other hand, the future fulfillment of the divine statutes, insofar as the former guarantees the latter as in-violable, and the latter finds its beginning in the former. This achieves the union of the two eschato-logical stages in the concept of ἐπαγγελία. *As promise it furnishes the basis, as object of the promise it furnishes the goal, of the wandering people of God.*

But now the object of the promise must be more ex-actly determined. What kind of σωτηρία[28] actually awaits the Christian in the future? To this Hebrews first answers in the formal concept of μισθαποδοσία (2:2; 10:30, 35; 11:6, 26), and in it pursues the Old Testament-Jewish ex-pectation of the end[29] which sees the eschatological future

---

[27]Cf. the ἐμεσίτευσεν ὅρκῳ in 6:17.
[28]Cf. the terminology in 1:14; 2:3, 10; 5:9; 6:9; and 9:28.
[29]Cf. Gyllenberg, p. 663.

as under God's judgment or forgiveness. All eudaemonism is from the outset excluded, because the recompense can consist either of reward or punishment. Neither is dependent upon our choosing, but expresses the divine righteousness which does not heedlessly pass over the character of earthly life as involving decisions.

The positive content of the recompense is paraphrased once more in the Old Testament-Jewish sense through the term κληρονομία,[30] so that the recompense of punishment consists in exclusion from this "inheritance." But what does κληρονομία mean as regards content? Behm has pointed out that it includes the component of an "apportioned possession,"[31] and Foerster[32] has amply demonstrated by his investigation of the Septuagint concept that what occupies the foreground there is not so much the juridical idea of inheritance as that of taking possession for the duration. This is no doubt also true of Hebrews to the extent that its statements regarding κληρονομία reveal a striking spatial tendency.[33] In stating this, of course, we must exclude a few passages. *Righteousness* in 11:7, *blessing* in 12:17 and the *promises* in 6:12,17, and 11:9 still form the object of the "inheritance." Gyllenberg also proceeds from this point. In conjunction with the Old Testament citation in 10:37ff., he chooses to derive reward and promise in the positive

[16]

---

[30]κληρονομία in 9:15 and 11:8; κληρονόμος in 1:2; 6:17; and 11:7; cf. 11:9; and κληρονομεῖν in 1:4, 14; 6:12; and 12:17.

[31]Behm, *TDNT* II, 131, n. 102.

[32]Foerster, *TDNT* III, 777.

[33]We must interpret 9:15 from 11:8, where the inheritance consists of a τόπος. The thought is of possession in "rest." In 1:2 Christ is the "heir of all things." The inheritance of salvation in 1:14, the intimate connection between σωτηρία and οἰκουμένη μέλλουσα in 2:5, must be kept in mind, as with Riggenbach, p. 36.

sense from the ζήσεται and περιποίησις ψυχῆς formulas, and in the negative sense from the οὐκ εἰς ἀπώλειαν.[34] Schniewind-Friedrich[35] proceed still further, when in reliance on 8:8ff. and 10:16ff., they find the content of the promise described in the divine assurance of Jer. 31:31ff. According to them, "the Law written on the heart, perfect knowledge of God and fellowship with Him, and the full remission of sins" constitute salvation. Gyllenberg, of course, already recognized that a careful exegesis does not manage only with such tracing of motifs, and that it meets with "complications." Alongside the first concept of salvation, he thus sets a second, which "by way of cosmic and metaphysical ideas" widens and makes specific "the eschatological doctrine of salvation in Hebrews."[36] "Thus," he writes, "we find that God's promise, the inheritance, eternal life, signify participation in—or, perhaps, still better—entrance into the invisible, heavenly world."[37]

A new tension thus emerges where it is necessary to fix more precisely the content of the promise. *But this content appears to increase twofold*, since it not only embraces the fulfillment of the imminent expectation in the Old Testament and Judaism as expressed in Jer. 31:31ff., but also assumes a peculiar metaphysical coloration and consists in the spatial entity of κατάπαυσις as the heavenly world. Does it suffice with Gyllenberg to link both aspects, so as to characterize the latter as a widening and particularizing of the former? This question must be answered in the negative. It does not take into account the

---

[34]Gyllenberg, p. 664.
[35]Schniewind-Friedrich, *TDNT* II, 584.
[36]Gyllenberg, p. 665.
[37]*Ibid.*, p. 667.

[17]   factor of the fulfillment of Jer. 31:31ff. in the Christ-
diathēkē . That is, in Hebrews we can and must distinguish promises already realized from those still outstanding, though of course there is no external criterion for
such differentiation.[38] According to 11:33, the Old Testament witnesses of faith already obtained the promises.
These obviously do not denote mere promises for the future, but the realization of such assurances already
occurred and concretely preserved for the earthly present. According to 11:9, Abraham could in fact already
live in the earthly land promised to him, though as a for-
eigner. So also the promises of 11:17 and 6:13ff. were fulfilled in Abraham in earthly fashion, as the ἐπέτυχεν in
6:15 indicates (cf. also 11:33). Now the ἐπαγγελίαι in
8:6 must be set in this series and more closely defined in
8:8ff. and 10:16ff. In the forgiveness of sins, in the
knowledge and fellowship of God natural to the brethren
and children of Jesus (cf. 2:10ff.), consists that very
Christ-*diathēkē* which came into force in precisely this
form when the old *diathēkē* passed away (8:13). In
these passages the ἁγιαζόμενοι have already undergone
perfecting,[39] so that they, redeemed and freed from dead
works, may serve God with a pure conscience (9:12, 14,
and 26). So it is not accidental that in 8:6 the new
diathēkē rests on the promises,[40] while conversely in
9:15 the new *diathēkē* is the presupposition for the reception of the promise. The assurances in 8:6 are those of
Old Testament expectation, and with the establishment

---

[38]The concept in the singular cannot simply be reserved for the future promise (cf. 6:15 and 11:9), and the plural cannot simply be reserved for the
promise already fulfilled (cf. 11:13, 39).
[39]Cf. the τετελείωκεν of 10:14 in the very context under discussion.
[40]ἐπὶ κρείττοσιν ἐπαγγελίαις νενομοθέτηται.

of the new *diathēkē* they are already fulfilled, while the promise of 9:15 is still outstanding. But what is true of 8:8ff. and 10:16f. is no less true of 10:37ff. Together with righteousness, the people of Christ are also given the ἐκ πίστεως ζήσεται and the περιποίησις ψυχῆς, indeed, not as an earthly possession ready to hand, but as an eschatological gift, and for that reason a gift outlasting earthly time. Due to their eschatological nature, the promises that give assurance of this gift are also "better promises" (8:6). If one should object that the realization of these blessings contradicts the idea of promise since it renders the Christian's status one of having rather than of waiting, then we must answer that this *"having" as a possessing of eschatological blessings occurs in no other way than through the proclaimed Word*, and thus on earth can still be lost once the Word is forsaken. Such an objection would not have grasped the paradoxical character of the Christian ἐπαγγελία, which in the Word already gives a share in salvation and in perfecting to the extent it is infinitely more than a promise which only gives hope for the future, that is, a firmly guaranteed divine ordinance. On the other hand, this ἐπαγγελία of course gives a share in salvation and in perfecting only in the Word, and in this promise the Word must thus also point to a state of a total perfecting in salvation. [18]

This opens the way toward understanding what Hebrews regards as a promised blessing still awaited, and thus as an acutal κληρονομία. It is precisely what Gyllenberg describes as the widening and particularizing of the Old Testament-Jewish eschatology as cosmic and metaphysical ideas, or, *briefly put, as the κατάπαυσις or οἰκουμένη μέλλουσα.* To this corresponds the definition of κληρονομία as an "apportioned possession," as well

as of κληρονομεῖν as a "taking possession for the duration." Where righteousness or blessing are described as
the object of inheritance (11:7 and 12:17), characteristically enough the Christian hope is still not at issue. That
this hope consists of heavenly rest is amply demonstrated
by the fact that the ἐπαγγελίαι of 11:13 and 39 are quite
clearly construed in spatial fashion,[41] and according to the
context of 11:14f., have the heavenly πατρίς as their
content. Thus, according to 4:1, "promise" and "rest"
are just such correlative concepts as we were able to establish for "inheritance" and "rest." In addition, further
observations that give Hebrews its peculiar cast belong
here. There is not merely an unmistakably spatial tinge in
the reference to the προκειμένη ἐλπίς as the blessing of
hope,[42] or in the reference to the κλήσεως ἐπουρανίου
μέτοχοι (3:1). Not only the heavenly homeland (11:14,
16), but also the city built and firmly established by God
(11:10, 17; 13:14) as the goal of faith's wandering, emerge
with full clarity. Just as these lie spatially before the eyes
of the "witnesses," so they may be referred to as seen or
greeted from afar (πόρρωθεν ἰδεῖν, ἀσπάσασθαι,
11:13), and they are reached only through a
προσέρχεσθαι (4:16; 7:25; 10:22; 11:6; 12:18, 22) or a
μετάθεσις (11:5) in the literal sense of a change of
place.[43] So too that passage in 12:18ff., extraordinarily
important in the framework of Hebrews, takes on the
significance it deserves as a broadly descriptive revelation
[19]   of our inheritance. "The way into the sanctuary" (9:8)
leads to the heavenly Jerusalem and to a share with its in-

---

[41]From this perspective the analogous κομίσασθαι τὴν ἐπαγγελίαν of 10:36
is also to be understood.
[42]6:18; contra Riggenbach, p. 175.
[43]Thus according to 11:8, also Abraham's inheritance is a τόπος.

habitants. As given through revelation,[44] it is an ὁδὸς πρόσφατος καὶ ζῶσα (10:20), and as a way to the heavenly city it is an εἴσοδος τῶν ἁγίων (10:19).

Analysis of the concept of ἐπαγγελία in Hebrews has disclosed to us the eschatological orientation of this concept and the ideas comprehended in it. At the same time, it has taught us to understand more precisely the eschatological tension that the concept implies between the act of promise and completion, between the already fulfilled and yet to be fulfilled reality of the promise. By means of this tension our analysis has explained why the attitude of faith can only be described as wandering, and finally, in the heavenly world and its Jerusalem, has concretely revealed the ultimate goal of such wandering and the final consummation.

3. The Meaning of πίστις and ἁμαρτία

The way of God's people was already set under the theme of πίστις. Now we must demonstrate not only the rightness of this approach, but also develop in detail what it means. Chapter 11, in which faith at the outset is also defined as ἐλπιζομένων ὑπόστασις, πραγμάτων ἔλεγχος οὐ βλεπομένων, gives clear justification for this approach. It is clear that, in contrast to Paul, the concept undergoes a shift in meaning here. To some extent, of course, Hebrews shares the Pauline concern for the ὑπακοὴ πίστεως,[45] thus for obedient subjection to the revealed Word, as was shown in 3:7ff. The precise concern

---

[44]Cf. the πεφανερῶσθαι of 9:8.
[45]Rom. 1:5.

of that passage was also the coordination of faith and
Word and the constancy of their union (4:2). Thus, by
treating in parallel the ἀπιστία of 3:12, 19 and the
ἀπείθεια of 3:18; 4:6, 11, and by linking παράβασις
and παρακοή in a hendiadys in 2:2,[46] Hebrews no less than
Paul describes the nature of faith as obedience. But it is
nonetheless characteristic of that shift in meaning that has
occurred over against Paul that, in the same section in
3:7ff., the admonition to the obedience of faith is replaced by the formula: "Hold fast our first ὑπόστασις to
the end" (3:6, 14). There is no doubt that this formula expresses nothing but what is meant elsewhere in Hebrews
by μακροθυμία[47] or ὑπομονή (10:36; 12:1). Also, these
[20] concepts are used in correlation to faith and appear identical with it.[48] It is therefore quite correct when
Strathmann[49] views *pistis* as related to the faithfulness
"which one shows to God and his promise by holding
fast to what was once seized, and by allowing it to be nor-
mative for one's behavior. The concept contains both aspects: Assent to the divine promise, and the persistence
with which this assent is maintained in assurance of the
future. Marked stress on this second aspect alongside the
first characterizes the uniqueness of Hebrews' conception of faith." But this becomes really clear only where
we see that the Pauline obedience of faith as such is preserved in face of the σκάνδαλον of the cross of Christ
present in the Word,[50] while in Hebrews we can at best

---

[46]According to 11:8, Abraham, by believing, is obedient to the divine call.
[47]Heb. 6:12; μακροθυμεῖν in 6:15.
[48]Cf. 6:12 and the context of 10:35ff.
[49]Strathmann, p. 124.
[50]Cf. A. Schlatter, *Der Glaube im Neuen Testament* (1927⁴), p. 259, according to which there is no reference here, as in Paul, to our guilt or to the divine
righteousness by faith revealed in Jesus' death, for which reason faith does

speak of a scandal in view of the delay of the consummation. Further, in Hebrews the obedience of faith is fulfilled when, in trusting the divine promise, one is willing
to be led patiently through the present time of suffering
into the heavenly future. For Paul, the paradox of faith
lies in the witness of the word of the crucified as salvation; for Hebrews it consists in the choice of a transcendent future over earthly delight for the sake of the Word
alone, despite the waiting and suffering attached to that
future in the immanence of the present. Here πίστις is in
essence also ἐλπίς,[51] and to that extent also μακροθυμία
and ὑπομονή. It is faith only as hope which takes its concrete orientation from the Word and is made sure of its
object. In Paul, on the other hand, hope remains alongside faith insofar as faith is basically directed toward the
salvation event as past and made contemporary in the
Word, while hope awaits the final act of God already decisively revealed in the past through Christ. We agree
with Michel that "for early Christianity there is no faith
without hope; hope is established by faith."[52] Yet at times
we must ask how this is the case. At this point Paul and
Hebrews—both of whom refer faith primarily to the
Word—part company by modifying the character of the
Word. It is not by chance that for Hebrews the word is
promise and portent of the divine future, nor is it by   [21]
chance that for Paul Word and sacrament move in series,
to the extent the Word is essentially a contemporizing of
grace already become effective. As surely as this aspect is
also given its due in the *diathēkē*-idea of Hebrews, and

---

not appear "in its union with Christ, but as the movement of our soul toward God."
[51]Cf. 11:1 and the parallels in 6:11 and 10:22.
[52]Michel, p. 158.

as surely as Paul allows hope to await its consummation, in both the accent is shifted. Just as for Riggenbach[53] the concept of faith in Hebrews has more strongly preserved "the Old Testament coloration," so Bultmann[54] traces the unity of faith and hope in particular, together with the substitution of ὑπόστασις for ἐλπίς in 11:1, to the Old Testament usage or the Septuagint. Of course, we will not be able to overlook the Hellenistic impact registered in Hebrew's characterization of the future as a sphere of what is not visible here and now. *The future of faith may in no way appear as a continuation of the earthly present.* Just as creation occurred through the Word, and in it the will of God that shapes all things came to light "that we may not remain with the visible,"[55] so also creation is not recognized with the eye but by faith (cf. 11:3), as conversely *pistis* on principle has nothing to do with the world of appearance. *Pistis* rather belongs to the sphere of signs and wonders (11:33ff.); it is an eschatological posture, and its future is ushered in by God as relief from and the end of, indeed as the catastrophe (cf. 12:26ff.) of, the earthly present. How should it be otherwise, when world time is stamped by changeableness, but the divine world of rest by unchangeableness? There is no human leap or possibility of appropriation by the senses leading from one to the other. With the πραγμάτων ἔλεγχος οὐ βλεπομένων in 11:1, an insurmountable barrier is erected between faith and the possibilities of this aeon.[56] Whoever holds to the one not only loses connection with the other, but still more comes into opposition and hostility to

---

[53]Riggenbach, p. 338.
[54]Bultmann, *TDNT* II, 531.
[55]Schlatter, *Glaube im Neuen Testament*, p. 527.
[56]*Ibid.*, p. 530.

it. *Conflict, suffering, and death separate faith and world,* as the destiny of the "witnesses" makes shockingly clear: "Believers die in the world."[57] Perhaps we will also venture with Strathmann[58] to see in faith's perseverance in the face of death the connecting thought in the list of the patriarchs. To be sure, death in itself is not yet a mark of faith, and as a result of hate for the world it could derive from a merely immanent opposition. It is a mark of faith only where it includes hope of resurrection, where one thus trusts God's will and work more than earth and by that trust rejects it.[59] By allowing oneself to be led willingly even into death, one gives evidence of despising the temporary delight of sin (11:25), but also of grounding the future no longer in one's own performance, but in the divine deed. But this makes it clearer that even wandering toward the divine rest is not carried out as an earthly activity on one's own power,[60] but that one is led in the unity of faith by the Word from God. There is no other way from changeableness to unchangeableness than through faith—bound to the Word—which marks the only bridge between the two worlds. [22]

Even while on earth, a possibility of access is disclosed to *pistis* from the Word. This access is of an almost sensual, but in any event quite certain, type, as is clear both from the πόρρωθεν ἰδεῖν and the ἀσπάζειν of 11:13, and above all from the term ἔλεγχος used to describe faith. This expression, which does not denote, say,

---

[57]W. Loew, *Der Glaubensweg des Neuen Bundes* (1931), p. 93.
[58]Strathmann, p. 128, 2.
[59]Cf. the κατέκρινεν τὸν κόσμον in 11:7.
[60]According to 11:29 the Egyptians fail by their own power.

a subjective conviction, but the objective state of being apprehended,[61] is at first puzzling. In regard to it Windisch spoke of the accent upon the intellectual element in the concept of faith peculiar to Hebrews.[62] We can hardly term this formulation fortunate. Bultmann describes the actual situation: "The certainty of trust in a divinely given future is underlined, and the added ἔλεγχος...emphasizes further the paradoxical character of this hoping trust, to the degree that it cannot count on controllable factors."[63] The Word that awakens faith is, and also gives, a share in the unchangeable heavenly world. For this reason it is so βέβαιος that it creates absolute certainty concerning the future, and indeed an objective certainty, since it does not derive from the human. *As echo of the objective and divine Word, faith is consequently a certainty that is objectively established and in its surety towers above all earthly possibilities;*[64] but it is such only for the sake of the Word and in face of the heavenly world, which is otherwise not accessible on earth. Thus [23]   to accent its paradox even more strongly, we may call it a "certainty of the uncertain, a seeing of the invisible."[65]

Now in this passage, the concepts of πίστις and παρρησία in Hebrews also move closer together. The less we can detail the history of the latter concept here, the more controversial is its use in our letter (cf. 3:6; 4:16; 10:19, 35). B. Weiss[66] states that "it is obvious that παρρησία denotes neither freedom nor authorization,

---

[61]Büchsel, *TDNT* II, 476.
[62]Windisch, p. 106.
[63]Bultmann, *TDNT* II, 531.
[64]Cf. Schlatter, *Glaube im Neuen Testament*, p. 526f.
[65]Gyllenberg, p. 667.
[66]Weiss, p. 262, n. 1.

nor a guaranteed certainty, but a joyfulness like that which Christians as such possess and can only be exhorted to hold fast." With this Michel of course agrees: "It is the joyfulness of approaching God, the certainty that hope and promise stand firm; it is trust and confidence in God's Word."[67] Still, this purely subjective interpretation requires a supplement. We concede that it is justified to the extent παρρησία describes a Christian attitude (cf. 4:16; 10:35). For that reason, it belongs in a series with faith and hope. But we may well note that *pistis* as ἔλεγχος also appears as an objective positioning of the Word that encounters us from without, and as such is identical with ὑπόστασις, a term that Schlatter for good reason chooses to translate as "firm stance."[68] Thus παρρησία, when most closely linked, for example, to καύχημα τῆς ἐλπίδος (3:6), also has a peculiarly objective character, just as καύχημα here is something objective. One "has" (10:19) παρρησία, not merely as a subjective attitude, but as an appropriation of something already given. One holds it fast, not merely by holding on as a believer, but by clinging to the presupposition of faith in the promise. As ἐπαγγελία is more than mere promise, so also παρρησία is more than mere subjective trust. *That is, it is the joyful enlistment in a cause already guaranteed by God in an objective* ἔλεγχος.[69] Here the eschatological dialectic of Hebrews is again disclosed. The view is directed wholly forward to the divine future toward which the promise points. But it may and can do so only because this future is no longer an occasion for sor-

---

[67]Michel, p. 44.
[68]Cf. the excursus in Schlatter's *Glaube im Neuen Testament*, p. 614ff.
[69]Only in such fashion can Riggenbach, p. 312f., weigh the definition of "authorizing" or "empowering."

row, questioning, or uncertainty, but already lies before us as though visible and is secured by God's present activity in the Word of promise. Because God has shown himself to us, the invisible future is already revealed to us.

[24]   *Faith thus becomes a confident wandering.* Since the past of the *diathēkē* and the future of the consummation stand firm for it, it finds the power to overcome the earthly present. Again and again it overcomes the earthly present by an ἐξελθεῖν (11:8, 22). And since it hearkens to the divine call by going out (11:8), it stands under a blessing. Isaac, Jacob, and Joseph, who in dying bow over their staffs as a symbol of wandering,[70] transmit this blessing and with it prepare for the blessing of the children of Israel under Moses. Following Abraham's story, the story of Moses then forms the second fully detailed δεῖγμα of the nature of faith (11:23f.). It was already explained that in every age faith's wandering must be a march through a zone of conflict and death, and it is again clearly shown in the example of Jesus (12:1ff.). Indeed, the visible and invisible do not confront each other in static fashion, but rather as powers contending with each other. Viewed from the world, the church must appear as a band of deserters when it forsakes encampment in an existence where all else is intent on solidarity and total union. So the world's fate will also overtake the church in all its severity. But that God's people traverse this zone of conflict and death for the sake of the Word is taken for a sign of victory (cf. 11:11f., 19, 29f., 33f.) and sonship, which paradoxically enough, and yet with inner

---

[70]Cf. Michel, p. 177: "Not even Joseph could find rest in the land of his political power, but in dying thought of the impending exodus from Egypt."

necessity, embraces as παιδεία the divine instruction in the present distress (12:7ff.).

The above result is antithetically confirmed by an *analysis of the concept of ἁμαρτία*. Apparently, Hebrews mentions sin only in a context paled by way of formula, that is, in an obviously cultic and liturgical context. Thus there is reference to the καθαρισμὸν τῶν ἁμαρτιῶν (1:3), taken up by the ἱλάσκεσθαι (2:17), ἀφαιρεῖν (10:4), and περιελεῖν (10:11) ἁμαρτίας. And they are, of course, individual sinful deeds[71] which as such are called ἀνομίαι (10:17), and whose expiation the sacrifices prescribed in the Old Testament were supposed to effect (cf. 5:1, 3; 7:27; 9:28; 10:6, 8, 12, 18, 26; 13:11). To be sure, the συνείδησις ἁμαρτιῶν (10:2) cannot be purged by this means. Rather, by this means their very ἀνάμνησις (10:3) arises.

It is evident that, from all these statements, the nature [25] of sin cannot be clearly grasped. Such is possible only where there is particular reference to the power of ἁμαρτία (3:13; 11:25; 12:1, 4) concealed behind the individual ἁμαρτίαι. In such instances, the sphere of cultic usage preserved elsewhere in stereotype is broken through, and an independent view of sin can be recognized. In saying this, we must again proceed from 3:7ff., where ἁμαρτία is characterized as ἀπείθεια[72] identical to ἀπιστία. We could plainly contrast 3:7ff., as the genealogy of unbelieving disobedience, with the cloud of witnesses in Chapter 11. And of course it is the method of sin to ensnare its prey in ἀπάτη (3:13), thus to harden it against the promise (3:13f.; 4:1), and bring it to the goal

---

[71]This is what the plural ἁμαρτίαι obviously means.
[72]See 3:13; cf. the parallelism of sinning and not obeying in 3:17f.

of apostasy from the living God (3:12). To this extent only the bearer of the promise can be made really guilty of sin, since only the bearer is capable of an ἀποστῆναι, a παραπίπτειν (6:6), an ἐκουσίως ἁμαρτάνειν (10:26), a παράβασις construed as παρακοή (2:2). Here, just as with the concept of *pistis,* the idea of wandering is assumed to be fundamental. This is clear from the term ὑποστολή (10:39), identical to ἀποστῆναι, in which the attitude of ὑπομονή and ὑπόστασις is abandoned. How this occurs is made clear in 11:25 and 12:1ff., where the deceit of sin is more precisely described: The one who is on the way to the heavenly homeland is said to be ensnared or burdened while on earth by the visible, with its pleasures or menacing pursuits. An ὄγκος (12:1) imposed by the εὐπερίστατος ἁμαρτία is said to delay him. *Just as faith finds its own true character in perseverance, so sin finds its own in slackening.* Just as ὑπομονή is the eschatologically oriented persistence under the earthly load, so ὑποστολή retreats before this burden and leads to drooping hands and weak knees (12:12). Michel thinks that "our letter does not reckon with a sharpened concept of sin," and supports his statement by the fact that in Hebrews sin is first of all a human act of yielding and falling into temptation.[73] But this does not appropriately describe the actual situation. At bottom, Hebrews does not look to the universal human condition, does not reflect on sin's lordship in the world, in short, on the nature of original sin, which according to New Testament teaching is stripped away from the baptized. On the basis of assumptions having to do with the care of souls,[74] Hebrews

[26]

---

[73]Michel, p. 57.
[74]Cf. Schlatter, *Der Glaube im Neuen Testament,* p. 529.

is concerned with the possibilities open to the bearer of the promise. But for the people of God, sin can only be apostasy, so that we must inquire in detail whether this apostasy, thus this aloofness or disobedience toward the promise, occurs unconsciously[75] or consciously.[76] And since the focus is exclusively on the bearer of the promise, sin must be traced to ἀσθένεια (4:15; 5:2; 7:28). According to the unanimous message of the New Testament, the world does not sin out of weakness, but is continually qualified by sin at the very outset. Weakness is not "for Hebrews a particularly characteristic mark of humankind in general"[77] which both natural and Christian existence share. It is solely the condition of the one who bears the promise in this world. While the natural person is always regarded as having fallen prey to sin, the existence of God's people and its members is defined by the reality of πειράζεσθαι (2:18; 3:7ff.). For this reason, we cannot say that ἀσθένεια approximates the meaning of "sin."[78] *Just as in Paul, weakness is that capacity for being tempted inherent in the existence of the bearer of the promise,* and out of which sin strives to become actual. But since sin "is the essence of opposition to God which prevents access to the throne,"[79] or "apostasy from the community and from the faith,"[80] the bearer of the promise may not engage in it and must perceive the danger in the weakness, lest a wanton act of ὑποστολή result. Such wanton apostasy would destroy God's salvation history and establish the ἀδύνατον (6:4) which cuts

---

[75]The ἀγνοεῖν of 5:2.
[76]Cf. the wanton sinning of 10:26.
[77]Michel, p. 56.
[78]Stählin, *TDNT* I, 492.
[79]E. Lohmeyer, *Kyrios Jesus* (1928), p. 81.
[80]Gyllenberg, p. 688.

off conversion and surrenders Christ once more to public shame (6:6). The question raised by Windisch[81] here of a once-for-all repentance, understood in terms of the later history of the church, is not up for debate. The intention is rather to take the character of faith with utmost seriousness as ὑπομονή. Through wanton apostasy faith is shattered, precisely because it is "perseverance." When this actually occurred can never be determined by external means. It is sufficient to entertain this possibility by the example of the wilderness generation or of Esau (12:16f.). It must be seen that even the existence of the bearer of the promise still consists of decision, that such existence, after all, consists only of an absolute, eschatological decision resulting in μισθαποδοσία. The decision is for πίστις or ἁμαρτία, that is, for obediently abiding under the promise and wandering with the people of God already begun, or disobedience toward and apostasy from the promise, from wandering, and from the people of God.

[27]

4. *The People of God as a Cultic Fellowship*

It goes without saying that cultic reflection in Hebrews plays a greater role than in any other New Testament writing. But it is necessary to see that it is not merely the high priestly motif and its Old Testament antitype which gives rise to this cultic reflection. The idea of the people of God[82] is also culticly defined. The peculiar "collective" language of our letter is best explained from this perspective, since it is precisely from the cultus that the individual as active or passive always appears as member

---

[81]Windisch, p. 52.
[82]Thus also the Old Testament λαός is by its nature a cultic community.

of a collective fellowship. To be sure, at issue here is not an active cultic act on the part of persons or the people of God which, of course, does not constitute or maintain itself, but rather receives its basis and union in the heard Word. But even this λόγος τῆς ἀκοῆς, as the formula as such already indicates, is of a thoroughly cultic nature. This becomes even clearer from a separate treatment *of the section in 12:18ff., which is of decisive importance for Hebrews.*

At first glance it is surprising to find a relatively fixed tradition here.[83] This naturally first applies to the description of the Sinai revelation, for which Philo offers good parallels, above all in his *On the Decalogue,* Chapter 44. Yet Michel is correct in his opinion that he can detect "a lofty and solemn speech, a deliberate mode of expression and definite rhythm"[84] also in verses 22ff. But more important than these rather superficial observations is one having to do with content, namely, that both the revelation on Sinai as well as that on Mount Zion are clearly portrayed in the colors of an epiphany. According to the rabbinic tradition, no doubt adopted here,[85] angelic powers are manifest in the frightening natural phenomena of the first revelation. In the same connection, Philo clearly speaks of an epiphany: ἔδει γὰρ θεοῦ δυνάμεως ἀφικνουμένης μηδὲν τῶν τοῦ κόσμου μερῶν ἡσυχάζειν, ἀλλὰ πάντα πρὸς ὑπηρεσίαν συγκεκινῆσθαι.[86] But then we must interpret the corresponding revelation on Mount Zion in the same way. This revelation preserves its special cultic   [28]

---

[83]Cf. the commentaries *ad loc.*
[84]Michel, p. 209.
[85]*Ibid.,* p. 207, n. 2.
[86]*On the Decalogue* 44:"For when the power of God arrives, it must needs be that no part of the world should remain inactive, but all move together to do Him service."

character by the fact that in it is manifest the heavenly
πανήγυρις (12:22), thus the festal gathering of the in-
habitants of heaven publicly praising God. It is not clear
how we should understand the "assembly of the firstborn who are enrolled in heaven,"[87] or "the spirits of the
just men made perfect."[88] We recall that in general the
highest ranks of angels bear the title "first begotten."[89]
The πρωτότοκοι as a special ἐκκλησία would then be distinct from the countless other ministering angels referred
to in 1:14.[90] They would be followed by another group,
the "spirits of just men made perfect," also named elsewhere.[91] If we may press the term οὐρανοί, then, follow-

---

[87]On account of the ἀπογεγραμμένων, which in their view is to be referred
only to humans, Michel, p. 210f., and Windisch, p. 113f., interpret the
phrase to refer to the Old Testament witnesses of faith in Chapter 11.
Strathmann, p. 128,10, and Riggenbach, p. 416, refer it to members of the
Christian community still lingering on earth but already entered in the heavenly books as "firstborn." But the latter are still standing before Mount
Zion, whereas πρωτότοκοι rather clearly points to dwellers in heaven. Incidentally, it is not clear why only humans should be entered in the heavenly
register. Such occurs with every citizen of the new Jerusalem as with every
candidate for citizenship there. Finally, what militates against the idea of the
Old Testament witnesses is that we would prefer to interpret them as among
the "spirits of the just men made perfect."
[88]Are these the Old Testament witnesses of faith? If so, there is a yawning
contradiction with 11:13, 39f., according to which the "witnesses" are still
not perfect. Scholars have avoided this difficulty by interpreting them of the
Christian martyrs. But elsewhere Hebrews knows nothing of such a thing.
On the other hand, 12:22ff. appears to derive from another tradition than
does 11:13 and 39. And according to the Extracts of Theodotus, Chapter 18,
Abraham and the other δίκαιοι are already in the ἀνάπαυσις, of course not
yet identified with the sphere of perfection.
[89]Just as Christ in 1:6; cf. further W. Lueken, Michael (1898), p. 38. So also
in the Extracts of Theodotus 27:3ff., the highest angelic creatures are called
πρωτόκτιστοι
[90]Seeberg, p. 138, also interprets them of angels.
[91]Above all in 3 Enoch (edited and translated by Odeberg, 1928), where the
idea of "spirits" or "souls of the righteous" is quite common; cf. II, p. 132ff.
They have "returned" from the earth, thus been made perfect; cf. Chapter
43; they share the joy of the heavenly Jerusalem and the assembly about

ing the idea generally assumed in late Judaism, these individual groups would be assigned to various spheres of
heaven. The "just men made perfect" would thus occupy
the lowest level. Be that as it may, no final definition is   [29]
given this heavenly court, but indeed to Jesus, guarantor
of the new covenant,[92] and to his sprinkled blood, conceived as personified. This blood, as that of Messiah, is
better than the martyr's blood of Abel,[93] and for this very
reason establishes the new covenant. Angels and those
made perfect may praise God, but the true role in the
heavenly cult—to be taken up in greater detail in connection with Hebrews' idea of the high priest—is reserved
for the guarantor, Jesus and his blood. We need merely
state here that in this blood there occurs a divine speaking, to be identified with the χρηματίζειν of verse 25.
In it lies the content of the revelation and the true center
of the epiphany on Mount Zion. It is striking how
strongly the idea of speaking influences our brief section
(cf. 12:19, 24-26). This becomes clear only when, re-
turning to an earlier observation,[94] we construe χρηματίζειν as a term for inspired preaching and proclamation. *As on Sinai, so also on Mount Zion a divine proclamation occurs* which, due to its heavenly character, far
surpasses the earthly.[95] If angelic powers were once the
bearers of the first, now it is the blood of Christ. But in

God's throne; cf. Chapter 48 A 3; they fly over the throne of glory; cf.
Chapter 43:2. According to 44:7, there are patriarchs among the just in
heaven, as also elsewhere men have been united with angels, cf. Chapter 22
B 4; Odeberg II, p. 78.
[92]It is, of course, a νέα διαθήκη in view of its recent establishment.
[93]Cf. Michel, p. 212.
[94]Cf. p. 29.
[95]With Seeberg, p. 139; Riggenbach, p. 412f.; and Windisch, p. 114f.; and
contra Michel, p. 213, who makes Moses—not at all referred to in the
text—the speaker on earth.

either case, God himself appears behind these bearers[96] as the proclaiming authority. The wilderness generation would otherwise not have received the true promise and actual εὐαγγέλιον at all. And the establishment of the new *diathēkē*, which is the content of the proclamation on Mount Zion and guaranteed solely by Jesus and his blood, belongs only to God. Confirmation by blood is required for every divine *diathēkē*; it confirms the new *diathēkē* on Zion as unbreakable and guaranteeing eternal salvation. To be sure, the promise is now described in verse 26 as arousing fear. It consists in God's announcement of the parousia, in which heaven and earth, as merely created and transitory, are shaken and destroyed. But then does verse 22 really contrast with verse 18? The parousia is revealed as even more disastrous than the epiphany on Sinai, and both times God appears as a consuming fire (12:29). The contrast is clear only [30] from the goal of the τῶν σαλευομένων μετάθεσις in the ἵνα μείνῃ τὰ μὴ σαλευόμενα (12:27). The destruction of what is created is necessary in order to make clear the eternal as visible to every eye. What is eternal is the βασιλεία ἀσάλευτος (12:28). As to its external appearance, the proclamation from Mount Zion actually involves an ἐπαγγελία.[97] This once more confirms what we have already learned of the heavenly πατρίς as the sole aim of the wandering of faith. But we must also note that the unshakable kingdom is already revealed to the people of God in the Zion epiphany and the heavenly Jerusalem. This finally confirms the dialectic noted earlier,[98] accord-

---

[96]The χρηματίζειν of verse 25a is clearly based on the λαλοῦντα in the same passage.
[97]Cf. the ἐπήγγελται of v. 26.
[98]Cf. pp. 30-31.

ing to which the promise is both the goal as well as the constitutive basis of the wandering of faith. The proclamation within the heavenly festal gathering has this very πανήγυρις as the content of promise. *The new Jerusalem as site of the proclamation and the* diathēkē *established and guaranteed in Jesus' blood is the primal datum of the people of God and its wandering, just as in the shape of the "inheritance" to be won it will be the final datum of the wandering people of God,* and just as Jesus is both "pioneer and perfecter of our faith" (12:2). The νῦν of verse 26 denotes the moment in time of God's decree of salvation and promise at the beginning of Christian history—the καιρὸς διορθώσεως.[99] Because this is not a moment in terms of earthly history, but rather the eschatological present since Christ, it can be referred to only by a νῦν. But again what is at issue is not a mythical datum. It is actually the present time following Christ's entry into heaven and the beginning of the Christian wandering of faith. Here, then, a concrete event is fixed through a proclamation. It is described as the establishment of a *diathēkē,* portrayed in the colors of an epiphany and contrasted with the concrete event of the Sinai revelation as the primal datum of the wandering wilderness generation. The προσεληλύθατε of verse 22 may thus not be interpreted as though this goal were achieved only during

---

[99]Heb. 9:10. It is not sufficient with Preuschen-Bauer, col. 310, to construe διόρθωσις as "proper settlement" or "order." What is meant is the establishment of the eschatological order of salvation in the new covenant, as the link with καιρός already indicates. Just as the enthronement of the Redeemer is the beginning of a new time [cf. E. Lohmeyer, *Die Offenbarung des Johannes* (1926), p. 49] so here the issuance of the *diathēkē.* According to the *Extracts of Theodotus* 35:1ff. (cf. Hippolytus, *The Refutation of All Heresies* VI, 46:3) the *Sōtēr* comes εἰς διόρθωσιν τοῦ σπέρματος [ET: "to redeem the seed"].

the Christian wandering. From beginning to end, the en-
[31] tire Christian wandering occurs in view of the heavenly
Jerusalem. The people of God have come to that place
where they were first constituted. Now they finish their
course in the immediate presence of this heavenly Jerusalem itself, holding the πανήγυρις in view and in turn
being observed from it. They have arrived at that place
just as the priest nears the altar to perform the sacrifice.
Elsewhere in Hebrews προσέρχεσθαι appears in a cultic
context (cf. 10:1, 22; 11:6; 4:16; 7:25). *Here, too, the
context is cultic.* Where the heavenly festal company is
gathered in order to hear from the utterance of the sprinkled blood the proclamation of the new *diathēkē* for
God's people still wandering on earth, there the heavenly
worship is carried on. There the earthly people of God
are called to this worship, are on the way toward the altar
(13:10) and the throne of grace (4:16), and are thus a
cultic fellowship. But then the λόγος τῆς ἀκοῆς uttered
on earth has only the single meaning of renewing and
preserving the constitutive heavenly proclamation in the
community's worship, and thus of holding together
God's wandering people as such and of strengthening
them in the completion of their wandering.

The above interpretation has assumed a fixed tradition behind Hebrews 12:22ff. The question arises whether this assumption can be proved in any way, or can be
illustrated through parallels. This can in fact be done, and
most clearly by reference to the *Odes of Solomon*, Chapter 33.[100] In that passage, grace, like a pure virgin, thus
equipped with the features of Sophia, appears "on a high

---

[100]The question of the heavenly cult is dealt with later.

peak and lets its voice ring from one end of the earth to the other." To the extent that this peak ranges above the whole world, it is the mythical mountain of earth and heaven, the idea of which also underlies Mount Zion. Just as in Hebrews 12, so in the *Odes of Solomon* 33[:7ff.], the concern is for the promise of the heavenly world and the beginning of the wandering aiming toward that point: "O you sons of men, return, and you their daughters, come. And leave the ways of that Corruptor, and approach me. And I will enter into you, and bring you forth from destruction, and make you wise in the ways of truth.[101] Be not corrupted nor perish.[102] Obey me and be saved. For I am proclaiming unto you the grace of God. And through me you will be saved and become blessed. I am your judge; and they who have put me on shall not be falsely accused, but they shall possess incorruption in the new world.[103] My elect ones have walked with me, and my ways I will make known to them who seek me; and I will promise[104] them my name." [32]

Lohmeyer[105] has cited the same Ode in his interpretation of Revelation 14. In fact, Revelation 14 represents the scheme present in Heb. 12:22f. Again, the heavenly Zion is the site of a πανήγυρις formed by angelic hosts and the community of the faithful, gathered to receive a divine proclamation. Here, too, there is reference to the imminent final judgment, the announcement of which is

---

[101]Here also a wandering is established.
[102]Just as in Heb. 12:26ff. the threat of judgment on the transitory world gives the proclamation its peculiar stamp, so this theme threads through the *Odes of Solomon* 33.
[103]Cf. the βασιλεία ἀσάλευτος of 12:28.
[104]Thus the παρρησία of Hebrews.
[105]Lohmeyer, *Die Offenbarung des Johannes*, p. 116.

described as an "eternal gospel,"[106] in striking analogy to the train of thought in Heb. 12:22. But at the center stands the epiphany of the Lamb, indeed, as "the beginning of the messianic acts extending from there over the entire world."[107] Here, the διαϑήκη νέα of Heb. 12:24 corresponds to the ῴδὴ καινή of Rev. 14:3, the content of which is obviously identical with that of the new *diathēkē*. But all of Revelation 14, just as Heb. 12:22ff., intends to show to the people of God still wandering on earth the greatness of their promise and their goal.[108] In both instances, what gives the text its peculiar character is that it discloses an eschatological event on earth. Since in either case this occurs through a heavenly cultic act, it is finally clear that the mark of a cultic fellowship is an essential component of the people of God constituted here.

5. *The Old and New People of God*

The unfolding of the motif of God's wandering people in Hebrews would be incomplete if the exegete's eye were not also trained to the relationship between Israel and the Christian community. The task that falls to us here is of course made much more difficult by the old [33]   prejudice that Hebrews devaluates the Old Testament and its cultic piety, due to concrete historical dangers.

---

[106]Rev. 14:6.
[107]Lohmeyer, *op. cit.*, p. 118.
[108]The allegory of the building of the tower in the *Shepherd of Hermas Sim.* IX:2ff., fulfills the same task. It too has points of contact with the scheme just demonstrated.

We have already rejected this thesis as misleading, but, on the other hand, we cannot ignore the fact that in Hebrews there is an actual debate with the cultic nature of the old covenant. Now we must inquire into the significance of this debate.

The relationship of the old and new people of God is *that of the two diathēkai revealed on Sinai and on Mount Zion*, thus of the twofold divine order of salvation in the course of earthly history. In 3:7ff. it is already made clear that the first *diathēkē* was voided through Israel's unbelief. This *diathēkē* thus underwent an official ἀθέτησις (7:18, 12), an annulment linked to the solemn taking of an oath (3:11, 18; 4:3). The time of its validity is past; there is no earthly continuity with the second *diathēkē*. Rather, the second replaces the first: ἀναιρεῖ τὸ πρῶτον, ἵνα τὸ δεύτερον στήσῃ (10:9). There is no room for the two side by side.

But this situation is complicated by the fact that the setting aside of the first *diathēkē* is based, not only on the unbelief of the ancient people of God, but *also on the material inferiority* of its institutions over against those of the second *diathēkē*. The first *diathēkē* was not faultless (8:7) and, as νόμος ἐντολῆς σαρκίνης (7:16), contrasts with the power of an indestructible life. Its annulment occurred due to its weakness and uselessness (7:18): οὐδὲν γὰρ ἐτελείωσεν ὁ νόμος (7:19). It possesses merely the shadow of the good things to come (10:1; cf. 8:5). It is only their ὑπόδειγμα (8:5; 9:23). Actual perfection belongs only to the future, as such called τὰ ἐπουράνια (9:23) or τὰ ἀληθινά (9:24; cf. 8:2), and which itself bodies forth the εἰκὼν τῶν πραγμάτων (10:1). In contrast, the *nomos* imposes regulations for the body

(9:10); in its service stand mere humans with their weakness (7:28) and perishableness (7:23). The true tent does not originate with the *nomos* (8:2), but rather the earthly sanctuary (9:1), or the one made with hands (9:11, 24), most closely linked to the nature of this creation (9:11). In summary, what we have found is that *the exponent of the old* diathēkē *is the* νόμος ἐντολῆς σαρκίνης which, attached to the transitory condition of this world, can only produce works which are external and do not abide. So the gifts and sacrifices to which this *nomos* summons need continual repeating (10:1f.), and accomplish nothing eternally one-for-all or final. So also the sanctification which it effects has merely to do with the purification of the flesh (9:13), but not with the deliverance of our conscience from dead works (9:14). Consequently, sins are not removed (10:4,11).

[34]

Since even the sacral institutions are still of an earthly nature, the new people of God—as comports with its character—must forsake them, must always and everywhere abandon what is earthly. Very likely, the disputed verses in 13:9ff. have this sense: The place of the Christian community is outside the camp where sacral and earthly sacrifices still occur, which thus do not effect grace. The throne of grace is outside the sphere where people still possess and perform something, that is, in that place where Christ died. Strathmann in particular has seen a real coming to terms with Judaism here: "The sacrifice of Christ corresponds to the sacrifice on the Day of Atonement.... Just as the priests could not eat of the sacrifices of the Day of Atonement burned outside the camp, so the Jewish cultic community does not share in Jesus." Share in his grace is acquired only by breaking with Judaism, by "separation from the Jewish cultic

community, its views and religious life-forms."[109] Yet
this interpretation certainly goes too far. Should this
passage actually involve debate with Jewish sacrificial us-
ages and cultic meal regulations, then it is only because
Judaism serves as the nearest example of the earthly character of all the sacral institutions of this world. It would
then be necessary to break with the Jewish cultus insofar
as it does not represent the "true" worship that alone can
aid the people of God.

We continually overlook the fact that the great diastasis
*of Hebrews is between the "heavenly and the earth-
ly," in which the Jewish cultus is seen as a specific representative of what is earthly.* For this reason we so easily
and subtly alter this contrast to that between Christian
and Jewish. But what should give us pause is that the Judaism actual in the author's time does not interest him at
all, since all his arguments are directed exclusively to the
Old Testament *nomos.* No less important is the other assertion that Hebrews clothes its message in the form of a
superceding of Old Testament statutes.[110] It is no accident that it continually speaks only of a better hope
(7:19) or *diathēkē* (7:22; 8:6), of a διαφορωτέρα
λειτουργία (8:6), of a greater and more perfect tent   [35]
(9:11), of better promises (8:6) and sacrifices (9:23). The
intention is not at all exclusively polemical, since the old
order is appraised positively as "shadow and example"
(8:5; 9:23; 10:1), as "copy" of the heavenly (9:24), and
Israel's possession is actually described "according to all
its greatness and godliness."[111] Michel correctly states
that the "Old Testament category is also appropriated for

[109]Strathmann, p. 128, 13f.
[110]Schlatter, *Die Theologie der Apostel,* p. 463.
[111]Schlatter, *Der Glaube im Neuen Testament,* p. 521.

the new salvation."[112] For this reason we cannot say that with Christ's sacrifice the cultus as such[113] is abolished or limited to the θυσίαι of the praise offering, of charity, or of the loving fellowship of 9:14 and 13:15ff.[114] Indeed, with Christ the sacral institutions of this world lose their meaning. But in place of the earthly cultus that has been abolished appears another carried out by Christ in heaven. *The relationship of the new to the old* diathēkē *is thus not simply polemical, so far as the question of ceremonial law is concerned. It is rather dialectical, since the old* diathēkē *is abolished and yet at the same time surpassed,* consequently acknowledged as "shadow" and "example." And this dialectic is required by the subject matter itself.

The meaning of the Old Testament cultus lay in the fact that by it people sought to appease God with sacrifices and gifts, and to that end were spurred on by the *nomos*. This cultus points beyond itself to the future, since by it individuals not only proved they were conscious of the divine promise, but through their activity clearly strove to hold fast the *diathēkē*. Through gifts and sacrifices they wanted to make sure of the divine grace in face of sin as the reality of their earthly existence. Just as from now on Jesus should become the surety and guarantor of the new *diathēkē* in face of human sin, so in former times the sacral institutions had to guarantee the stability of the Old Testament *diathēkē* despite human guilt. The *nomos* took care that this task was not forgotten or neglected. This concern was thoroughly

---

[112]Michel, p. 83.
[113]Grundmann, *TDNT* I, 314.
[114]Schrenk, *TDNT* III, 282.

justified and is acknowledged in the Christ-*diathēkē* to be a shadow and example, indeed, not merely of the future but also of the εἰκών,[115] already existing eternally and hidden in heaven. Moses readied his σκηνή according to the τύπος revealed to him on Sinai, thus according to the [36] heavenly pattern (8:5). Accordingly, the institutions of the Old Testament cultus are also prefigurations of the eschatological service of Christ and imitations of the heavenly patterns hidden since eternity.[116] To that extent, they actually participate in the divine revelation. Due to sin, a cultic guaranteeing of the *diathēkē* is in fact necessary for the people of God.

The Old Testament cultus was performed according to the νόμος ἐντολῆς σαρκίνης, not according to the power of imperishable life. This means that the *nomos* was so oriented to the merely sarkic and earthly sphere that it could only take its means from there[117]—mortal men as priests, with animal sacrifices, foods, drinks, and ablutions as cultic gifts and acts. But it also means that under this *nomos* only external, sarkic effects could be achieved (cf. 9:13). Here sins were not removed. In reality, then, surety of the divine *diathēkē* could not be given. The true, eternal δύναμις did not even exist in the sphere of sinful humanity and transitory worldliness. In its stead dead works had to appear. But this merely bur-

---

[115]εἰκών is not a mere formal designation (as Kittel, *TDNT* II, 395, supposes; he translates, "the thing itself"). Rather, due to the correlatives τὰ ἀληθινά and ἐπουράνια, thus the eternal and heavenly (cf. Bultmann, *TDNT* I, 250), it denotes content—the heavenly pattern.

[116]Cf. in addition Schlier, *TDNT* II, 33.

[117]According to Schrenk, *TDNT* II, 219ff., δικαίωμα not only denotes "statute" and "ordinance," but also "right act." Are, e.g., the δικαιώματα λατρείας of 9:1, called sarkic in 9:10, the means toward realizing the divine right to title?

dened the conscience and kept alive the remembrance of sins rather than purging them.

It is thus not the existence of the Old Testament cultus which is faulted. That cultus is rather an imitation of the heavenly pattern, an index of what is to come and which it prefigures in shadowy fashion. *But the manner in which it is practiced is of no use,* for it is determined by human deeds that do not suffice to vouch for the divine *diathēkē* and thus cannot annul the history of disobedience to the heavenly promise. Hence, the ἀθέτησις of the first *diathēkē* is grounded in the sinful neglect of the promise on the part of the ancient people of God and also in the fact that Old Testament cultic practice could not atone for this neglect. But just as in Christ the first [37] *diathēkē* is appropriated anew, so since Christ the meaning of the Old Testament cultus is disclosed anew and now performed in the power of imperishable life.

Now the motive and purpose of Hebrews' debate with the Old Testament sacral institutions can finally be determined. Concretely historical dangers threatening the community from the side of Judaism are not at issue. For this reason, the debate does not occur in paraenetic, but, as Chapters 7ff. indicate, in dialectic fashion. It is *not the situation of the community, but rather Hebrews' concept of revelation which gives rise to the debate.* Not earthly communities but two peoples of God stand over against each other and with them two divine *diathēkai.* It must be clear that only the Christian people of God possess the *diathēkē* that at once promises and guarantees eternal salvation. To this extent Hebrews shares exactly the concern of Romans. But in Hebrews the κληρονομία is not perceived primarily in δικαιοσύνη

but in the heavenly Jerusalem and its cultic πανήγυρις.
Hence concern for the absoluteness of the Christian revelation must not be kindled by the question of works of
the law but by the question of the Old Testament cultus.
Thus in Paul, as in Hebrews, the debate with the Old
Testament revelation has the same result. In both cases
God's revelatory will in the Old Testament is acknowledged as valid. But in both cases the miscarriage of that
revelatory will is fixed in the attitude of people oriented
to the sarkic and earthly. The cultus that takes place in
the ἅγιον κοσμικόν can no more redeem than the *nomos*
that leads to the establishing of one's own righteousness.
According to Paul as well as Hebrews, the Old Testament
people of God does not attain to the goal because it seeks
from the law and from the cultus on earth what it can only
find from heaven. For this reason also there is no earthly
continuity between the one people of God and the other.
On earth, two bearers of revelation merely oppose each
other, separated by a new act of God. The one must perish so that the other receives the promise. The righteousness in Christ is established upon the end of the *nomos*
aligned to what is earthly; reconciliation through the
heavenly high priest is established upon the cultus
aligned to what is earthly and its end.

6. The Divine μαρτυρία as the Continuity of Salvation History

Chapter 11 appears to contradict the preceding statements. Yet the Old and New Testament history of salvation are united in the "continuity of the whole revelation;

the OT demands the NT as a link and continuation."[118]
[38]   Windisch put it more emphatically: "What is indicated
here is an unbroken succession of heroes of faith..., all of
them filled with a hope that has been fulfilled for us only
in Jesus. Here there is no antithesis between an imperfect
shadow and perfect appearance, not even between apostasy and renewal, but only between expectation and fulfillment, faith and sight."[119] But such statements no longer
suffice once we have seen the dialectic in the relationship
between the old and new people of God which, for example, contrasts 3:7ff. as the history of unbelief with that of
faith in Chapter 11. In any event, for Hebrews there is no
succession of heroes of faith, in which case there would
also be an earthly continuity between the first and second
diathēkē. Chapter 11 shows precisely that the succession allegedly present there is not at all that of heroic
men. *All the witnesses of faith are described merely as objects of the divine* μαρτυρεῖν. To the extent we must actually speak of a continuity here, it is that of the divine
witness which continually creates new objects for its
concretization. In this sense Michel more exactly defined
the idea of μαρτυρεῖσθαι (7:8,17; 10:15; 11:2,4f.,39),
correctly assigned it "a peculiar ring," and called it "typical."[120] Characteristically, the term is found only in the
framework of the debate with the Old Testament revelation. Bultmann has stressed its altogether juridical sense
and in particular stressed the legally binding character of
each "witness."[121] In Hebrews the biblical word is its

---

[118]Schrenk, *TDNT* I, 761.
[119]Windisch, p. 116.
[120]Michel, p. 79.
[121]Bultmann, *The Gospel of John* (1971), p. 50, n. 5.

bearer, which legally sets a person within the series of the witnesses of faith: "Through the Scripture God acknowledges humankind and the Scripture is witness to the history which God has made with the human race."[122] At the same time, this history is established and secured "neither by a people nor a church, but only by the Word of God contained in Scripture; but it is also not a mysterious juxtaposing of illuminations and revelations, without clear connection. God's Word has its own history which is hidden but real, which transmits the blessing of the past and lays a promise in the lap of the future."[123] *Hence* [39] *the faith of the Old Testament figures is no more a quality that can be happened upon in earthly fashion than their sequence is a succession that can be encountered in historical fashion.* Their faith is an echo of the divine election and accessible only from recognition through the Scripture. *As the divine Word establishes and bears the creation (cf. 1:3; 11:3), so it alone guarantees the continuity of the history of salvation that is often enough broken off from the human side.* Precisely because the bearers of promise in Hebrews 11 do not care for their own lives (such as those in 3:7ff.), but turn from earthly things and yield themselves to death, they actualize the continuity of the heavenly revelation which from creation onward tends toward the goal of the eternal πατρίς. For they keep the faith only by turning aside from the visible and tangible to the invisible eschatological Word. In so doing they are exceptions to the Old Testament people of God, since they are also not under the νόμος ἐντολῆς σαρκίνης and its cultus. Having come into being

---

[122]Michel, p. 79, n. 3
[123]*Ibid.*, p. 157.

through the divine Word, their faith embodies the attitude of the new *diathēkē* in which God's law is written on the human heart and in which every earthly surety of salvation is spurned. Thus they also do not succumb to the ἀθέτησις of the first *diathēkē*, but symbolize its true destiny as shadow of the revelation of Christ, a destiny thwarted by the other Old Testament people of God. Of course, to the degree the first *diathēkē* did not achieve fulfillment, they did not become κομισάμενοι of the promise, but awaited the perfection in Christ (11:39). But it is precisely this that links them in turn to the second people of God, who also have not yet arrived at their goal. Thus from divine μαρτυρηθέντες they become μάρτυρες for Christianity (12:1), and by example disclose to it its homelessness on earth and point it all the more strongly to the divine promise.

It is clear from the Old Testament witnesses of faith that the *diastasis* between the old and new *diathēkē* does not spell surrender of the saving will. Rather, this will has remained the same since creation. The promise that Israel abandoned and perverted in earthly fashion is merely appropriated anew in Christ. But in this new appropriation the Old Testament witnesses are recognized as companions of salvation, as forerunners and witnesses to the way, who did not help to pervert the old *diathēkē* in earthly fashion, and whom Scripture confirms as having remained true to the promise. Their faithfulness makes manifest that obedience to the divine Word overcomes the *diastasis* of both *diathēkai*, and that as a result this Word produces the continuity of the entire history of salvation.

C. Religious-Historical Background of the Motif

The question of Hebrews' religious-historical dependence has often been discussed, for the most part by entertaining or rejecting direct influence from Philo. In fact, with his store of concepts and ideas, Philo often moves within range of our letter. Yet sober observation cannot miss the material discrepancy between the two. The difference between a cosmological, psychological philosophy and the soteriology of Hebrews is all the more evident the deeper we penetrate details that at first seem analogous. Lastly, Michel states the case as follows: "The form of its utterances is Hellenistic, but not the content.... It is this apocalyptic conceptuality that sets Hebrews in decisive contrast to the Hellenism of the Wisdom literature and of Philo. No worse error can be made than to interpret Hebrews by way of Philo. Hebrews is in sharpest contrast to Philonic teaching."[124] But no real solution to the problem lurks behind that contrast between "form" and "content." We never know where "form" ends and "content" begins, because every form, however hollowed out its shape, always carries with it a vestige of the original content, and every content only has a form really proper to it. It must be conceded without qualification that Philo and Hebrews have different orientations and that for this reason any direct dependence of the latter on the former is out of the question. But, conversely, the almost universally recognized kinship in language and sequence of ideas[125] allows us to ask

---

[124]Michel, p. 175.
[125]From a different orientation, Riggenbach, p. xxxvi f., had already recognized a kinship in "methods and in the complexes of ideas." Cf. von

to what extent both represent the varied impress of a common basic tradition. The next section will answer the question within a limited frame.

1. The κατάπαυσις-speculation

The exposition on κατάπαυσις in 3:7ff. indicates that within the context of the motif of the wandering people of God speculative ideas emerge in Hebrews that do not derive from the Old Testament, but are linked to Old Testament utterances. To begin with, the proper starting point for understanding this theologoumenon is missed where it is merely stated that "the rest of God appears [41]   both as his attribute and as the essence of human salvation; it embraces not only the possession of Canaan, but also the promised bodily and spiritual perfection."[126] It should actually be clear that the rest is a purely heavenly blessing and hence does not include the possession of Canaan. For Canaan, too, was only a way station for pilgrims on the journey toward the heavenly Jerusalem (11:9f.). Above all, it is false to refer to the κατάπαυσις as a divine attribute, since one cannot "enter into" an attribute. *The "rest" is a purely spatial entity, the name for a heavenly place.* Just as the "essence of human salvation" is conceived in Hebrews throughout as spatial, so the divine rest is nothing else than the heavenly κόσμος itself. But then nothing is gained by adducing proofs of a "religious ideal of transcendence" inherent in the notion of eternal rest.[127] As important in itself as the evidence

---

Dobschütz, "Rationales und irrationales Denken über Gott im Urchristentum," *Theologische Studien und Kritiken* (1923-24), pp. 253ff.
[126]Michel, p. 46.
[127]Windisch, p. 35; cf. also the evidence in Michel, p. 50.

may be that from remotest times rest has been awaited from eternity, this does not at all explain the curious idea of rest as the heavenly world itself, but at best indicates what motifs contribute to that idea. And when, touching that curious connection in our text (4:5) between κατάπαυσις and σαββατισμός, it is further stated that "two Old Testament passages that refer to rest are ingeniously combined,"[128] this too does not yet solve the problem *which consists in the technical use of the concept of rest and its connection with a speculation on σαββατισμός, no doubt already traditional.* A comparison of Heb. 3:7ff. with the *Epistle of Barnabas* 15 would already have forced one to face these two questions. In the *Epistle of Barnabas*[129] we encounter the same view of the Sabbath-κατάπαυσις, and recited in as much detail. We gain initial clarification of the problem from the rabbinic material compiled by Strack-Billerbeck.

In this material, the Sabbath as the day dedicated to God also represents the manifest form of the world which is consecrated and belongs to God. Thus in the Aboth of Rabbi Nathan 1, the word of Psalm 92:1 ("the day of Sabbath") is interpreted as follows: "This is the day which is wholly a Sabbath (rest) in which there is no eating or drinking, no buying or selling, but the righteous will sit with crowns on their heads and enjoy the splendor of the Shekinah."[130] Still more clearly Rabbi Hanina b. Yizhaq calls the Sabbath the likeness of the fu- [42]

---

[128]Windisch, p. 34.
[129]Cf. Windisch in the supplementary volume of Lietzmann's *Handbuch, Die Apostolischen Väter* III: *Der Barnabas-Brief* (1920), p. 382ff.
[130]Strack-Billerbeck, *Kommentar zum Neuen Testament aus Talmud und Midrasch* (1926), III, 687; on the concept as a whole, cf. in addition IV, p. 839f.

ture world.[131] The saying in Pirke of Rabbi Eliezer 18 (9d) forms the transition to Philo: "God has created seven aeons and of them all he chose only the seventh. Six aeons are for going and coming (of the people), and one (the seventh) is wholly Sabbath and rest in eternal life."[132] The idea of the aeon of rest as linked to a ἑβδομάς-speculation appears, for example, in Philo, when he says of Samuel's condition: αὕτη δ' ἡ κατάστασίς ἐστιν ἑβδομάδος, ἀναπαυομένης ἐν θεῷ ψυχῆς καὶ περὶ μηδὲν τῶν θνητῶν ἔργων ἔτι πονουμένης.[133] In this fashion, at least, Philo exegetes Hannah's song of praise in 1 Sam. 2:5, which reads that the "barren one" has borne seven children, while Hannah bore only one, Samuel. Philo writes that Hannah holds the One to be the same as the Seven, not only in the lore of numbers but also in the harmony of the universe and in the thoughts of the virtuous soul: στεῖραν, οὐ τὴν ἄγονον, ἀλλὰ τὴν στερρὰν καὶ ἔτι σφριγῶσαν, τοὺς διὰ καρτερίας καὶ ἀνδρείας καὶ ὑπομονῆς ἐπὶ κτήσει τοῦ ἀρίστου διαθλοῦσαν ἄθλους, ἑβδομάδι τὴν ἰσότιμον μονάδα τίκτειν εἰκὸς ἦν.[134] This interpretation seems totally to ignore the connection with our theme. Psychological considerations are fused with a modern appetite for abstruse numerologies and are supported by an allegorical inter-

---

[131]*Ibid.*, III, p. 672.

[132]*Ibid.*, III, p. 687.

[133]*On the Unchangeableness of God* 12: "But this condition of his implies the Seven, that is a soul which rests in God and toils no more at any mortal task."

[134]*On the Unchangeableness of God* 10f., 13: "The barren woman, not meaning the childless but the 'firm' or solid who still abounds in power, who with endurance and courage perseveres to the finish in the contest, where the prize is the acquisition of the Best, should bring forth the Monad which is of equal value with the Seven."

pretation of the Old Testament passage. Pythagorean doctrine combines the numerical value of the ἑβδομάς [7] with that on the μόνας [1] to produce an equivalence (ἰσότιμος), and perceives in this the reflection of world harmony. The fact that in 1 Sam. 2:5 seven children are to be born of the στεῖρα, while Hannah gave birth only to the one, allows Philo to rediscover this Pythagorean doctrine in the Old Testament. By a play on words, he makes the unfruitful one strong and defiant, an image of the virtuous soul from which then is born that world harmony which embraces the ἑβδομάς and the μόνας. What gives weight to this speculation is that the condition of the hebdomad which represents world harmony is characterized by the rest in God. This can occur only when the hebdomad is not merely construed in Pythagorean fashion as harmony, but also according to Jewish tradition as the seventh day devoted to rest, that is, as the Sabbath. Accordingly, the idea of Sabbath here is embedded in cosmic and metaphysical speculations.   [43]

The correctness of this assertion derives from L. Troje's investigation of Sanbat in her supplement to R. Reitzenstein's *Vorgeschichte der christlichen Taufe* (1929). There Troje states that "in Philo the ἀνάπαυσις corresponds to the seventh of the powers holding sway among humans, and of course to the only power in peculiar contrast to them all, the guiding spirit—ἡ δὲ ἑβδομὴ δύναμις ἡ περὶ τὸν ἡγεμόνα νοῦν.[135] Or it is also the first of God's immaterial creations—ἐδηλώσαμεν δὲ ὅτι παύων ὁ θεὸς οὐ παύεται, ἀλλ' ἑτέρων γενέσεως

---

[135]*On Abraham* 28-30: "But the seventh faculty is that of the dominant mind."

ἄρχεται.[136] The idea of the Sabbath is thus actually identical with Hellenistic notions of the (immaterial) divine such as the νοῦς, σοφία, and φῶς (= γνῶσις). Philo[137] interprets the φῶς, ἐν ᾧ τὰ πάντα συνθεωρεῖται as the seventh day."[138] Troje explains this speculation further: "In order for this light-equation to remain in harmony with the Genesis narrative, it is based on the equation of seven to one already transmitted in Orphic and Pythagorean thought."[139] "The result is that in the Sabbath the spiritual principle was and still is continuously given to the world—'the oldest of all created things,'[140] 'the wisdom of God which feeds and nurses and rears to sturdiness'[141] those who yearn after imperishable food."[142] "According to Philo, whoever keeps the Sabbath shares in the divine spirit."[143] Troje assigns an especially Alexandrian touch to this equation of Sanbat and Spirit of God, and concludes that[144] "behind the idea of 'the seventh' as Sabbath or God there is that code-like notion of 'the seven' as aeons in which the direction and representation of the whole...falls rather to the first in the series. Hence the persistent attempt of Alexandrians to win for the Sabbath...an essentially equivalent monad mysticism. The seventh day should also be the first."

---

[136]*Allegorical Interpretation* I, 18: "But we pointed out that God when ceasing or rather causing to cease, does not cease making, but begins the creating of other things."

[137]ET: "The light in which all things are seen together"; cf. *Aristobulus* 12:9.

[138]Troje, p. 344.

[139]*Ibid.*

[140]*Allegorical Interpretation* III, 175.

[141]*The Worse Attacks the Better*, 115.

[142]Troje, p. 345.

[143]*Ibid.*, p. 346.

[144]*Ibid.*, p. 349.

The enigmatic idea of "rest" in Hebrews has found its historical origin in the notion of the aeons, according to which the highest aeon, the realm of the divine Spirit, the Sabbath, and the ἀνάπαυσις are identical. In the single instance we need not decide how many Alexandrian theories may be assumed as known to Hebrews. At any rate, there, too, the κατάπαυσις is construed spatially, thus as aeon-like, as a heavenly sphere, and is linked to Sabbath speculation. ἀνάπαυσις and κατάπαυσις alternate. This [44] is clear *from Gnostic sources,* when for example, reference is made to the τόπος τῆς ἀναπαύσεως.[145] Familiarity with the notion of the aeons is proved from a passage in the *Acts of Andrew*[146] which personifies the "rest": ὅτε τῆς χάριτος μυστήριον ἐξήφθη, καὶ ἡ βουλὴ τῆς ἀναπαύσεως ἐφανερώθη, καὶ τοῦ λόγου φῶς ἐδείχθη,[147] καὶ τὸ σῳζόμενον γένος ἠλέγχθη. In the *Acts of Philip,*[148] the rest appears as the goal of the Gnostic wandering of redemption: θέλετε ἀναπαῆναι ἐν τῇ ἀναπαύσει τοῦ θεοῦ. This is true particularly in the *Odes of Solomon.*[149] Insofar as Christ as *Urmensch-* Redeemer and aeon for the souls of his race is himself the goal in a wholly spatial sense, he is called ἡ καταφυγὴ καὶ

---

[145]*Acts of John* 99 (Bonnet I, 200; H.-S., p. 233); cf. in addition the *Unbekanntes altgnostisches Werk* (C. Schmidt, ed. G.C.S., p. 360f.), where the Lord of glory divides the sphere of life, light, and rest from the sphere of death, darkness, and suffering. On ἡσυχία as a divine sphere, cf. H. Schlier, *Religionsgeschichtliche Untersuchungen zu den Ignatius-Briefen* (1929), p. 27.

[146]*Acts of Andrew* 18 (Bonnet I, 45; H.-S., p. 416): "But when the mystery of grace was lighted up, and the counsel of the (eternal) rest was made known and the light of the word appeared and it was proved that the redeemed race had to struggle...."

[147]Here the rest is the very last mystery of redemption.

[148]*Acts of Philip* 148 (Bonnet II, 89). ET: "Desire to rest in the rest of God."

[149]See 38:4; 25:11f.; 26:11f.; cf. 3:5 in connection with the sacrament of the bridal chamber.

ἡ ἀνάπαυσις τῶν τεθλιμμένων.[150] The *Extracts of Theodotus* 63, deserves special mention: ἡ μὲν οὖν τῶν πνευματικῶν ἀνάπαυσις ἐν κυριακῇ ἐν ὀγδοάδι, ἣ κυριακὴ ὀνομάζεται.[151] In this passage, the rest is not merely regarded as the place where departed souls are stored, or identified with the ogdoad, thus with the highest aeon; the ogdoad is also defined as κυριακή, thus as the Christian Sunday. Here, then, the Jewish tradition of rest in the Sabbath-hebdomad is given a Christian alteration. This explains the shift to the ogdoad, which is also the world of the eternal Sunday. Finally, the passage in the Pseudo-Clementine Homilies (xvii, 10), already cited by Windisch,[152] gives an excellent summary: τοῦτό ἐστιν ἑβδομάδος μυστήριον. αὐτὸς γάρ ἐστιν ἡ τῶν ὅλων ἀνάπαυσις, ὅς τοῖς ἐν μικρῷ μιμουμένοις αὐτοῦ τὸ μέγα αὐτὸν χαρίζεται εἰς ἀνάπαυσιν.

The result of our study is that the motif of κατάπαυσις, so important for the doctrine of the wandering people of God, does not derive from the Old Testament or from an allegorical exegesis of it. Reference to Old Testament quotations in Heb. 3:7ff. merely intends to anchor in Scripture a speculation already in existence. Decisive elements of the idea are already known to Jewish rabbinism. But only in Alexandria was it fully coined, and from there it found entry into Christian Gnosticism. If the idea is initially marked by its connection with the motif of σαββατισμός and the aeon-character of the

[45]

---

[150]*Acts of Thomas* 10 (Bonnet II, 114; H.-S., p. 447): "The refuge and rest of the oppressed." Cf. the *Acts of John* 109 (Bonnet I, 208; H.-S., p. 255f.).

[151]ET: "Therefore the rest of the spiritual elements on the Lord's day, that is, on the Ogdoad, which is called the Lord's day."

[152]Windisch, p. 35. ET: "This is the mystery of the hebdomad. For he himself is the rest of the whole who grants himself as a rest to those who imitate his greatness within their little measure."

"rest," later in Christian Gnosticism the rest appears as goal of a doctrine of redemption based on the motif of the heavenly pilgrimage. Philo is evidence of the age of this tradition. We cannot maintain in this connection that Hebrews is based upon it. But we absolutely dare not deny the perception that here, thus at one point of its central theme, Hebrews presupposes a doctrine of wisdom and redemption fixed in Alexandrian Gnosticism.[153] Consequently, it can no longer be dismissed as fantasizing when we draw from this result the right to inquire further of Philo or Gnosticism as to what role that motif of God's wandering people, which is decisive for Hebrews, plays in them. Moreover, we will be able to take up the question of a direct historical relation between Hebrews and Philo or Gnosticism only when a common tradition has clearly emerged.

2. The King's Highway in Philo

We may first inquire of Philo as to the motif of the wandering people of God, because he has often been set in direct proximity to Hebrews, and in particular could give valuable information regarding the κατάπαυσις speculation. With laudable clarity, J. Pascher's *H ΒΑΣΙΛΙΚΗ ΟΔΟΣ, der Königsweg zu Wiedergeburt und Vergottung bei Philon von Alexandrien*[154] informs us that this motif plays a role in all of Philo, indeed, *that it stands at the center of all his teaching:* "Thus the basic

---

[153]Even in the treatment of Heb. 12:18ff. we come upon Gnostic parallels, a fact requiring attention in this context.
[154]Paderborn, 1931.

theme, which overtly or covertly subsists in all the resi-
due of mystery in Philo, is that of setting forth on a path,
which according to Num. 20:17 is called the 'King's
Highway'[155]. ... When Abraham emigrates from Chaldea,
when Jacob flees to Haran, or when all Israel leaves
Egypt; in a word, when the note of the motif of wandering is struck, then mystery works its enchantment on
Philo."[156] The "way" described here[157] is taken by the soul
[46]   and "proceeds in three main stages—the visible world,
the spiritual world, and God." The last level proves to be
an essential and of course mystical conclusion to the
series. The more exact description of the mystical
"King's Highway" is the flight of the soul; a "journey of
the spirit to God."[158]

Of special significance is the connection between the
motif of wandering and the ever recurrent symbolism of
the name "Israel," interpreted as "seer" of the divine.
"The basic and chief characteristic of the mystical wanderer is to be seen in the fact that he is a 'visionary,' that
he belongs to the 'race of seers.'"[159] Pascher's interpretations need not be reproduced in detail at this point. It is
enough to indicate that the vision of God also establishes
sonship with God.[160]

But the question whence Philo derived this mystery is
important. That it cannot simply be the result of his
scripture-Gnosis applied to the Old Testament is most
obvious from the fact that we meet it again in his

---

[155] *Ibid.*, p. 9.
[156] *Ibid.*
[157] In particular, according to *On the Creation* 69; *On the Change of Names* 179ff.; and *On the Unchangeableness of God* 143.
[158] Pascher, *op. cit.*, p. 23.
[159] *Ibid.*, p. 24.
[160] *Ibid.*, p. 28.

allegorizing of the high priest's garment,[161] where the journey of the soul is construed in clearly cosmic fashion. According to Philo the high priest's garment symbolizes the universe. Pascher describes its allegorization as follows:[162] "On the way to God there is a preliminary stage symbolized by the cosmic garment. At this stage the mythical wanderer has the Logos as advocate for a guarantee of eternal blessedness. The securing of this high advocate is symbolized by the cosmic garment, and of course because the Logos bears the world as a covering."[163] Since by entry into the Holy Place the Logos-High Priest brings the world with him into the sanctuary of God, he appears as mediator between God and world. "Allegorization of the high priestly garment symbolizes an ascent through the cosmic elements to the Mediator-Logos and thence to the Father."[164] It is clear that it is no longer Philo's arbitrary scripture-Gnosis which is behind this cosmic speculation, but that at this point firmly existing traditions are secreted into the Old Testament by way of allegorization. Pascher convincingly derives these traditions from the Isis-Osiris mysteries,[165] though in the individual instance conceding marked Iranian influences.[166] But this is no longer of interest for our purpose.

[47]

It is enough to have seen that the motif of wandering from the world to God is found at the center of Philo's thought, and that it is set forth in terms of a cosmic mys-

---

[161]Cf. *Moses* II, 117-135; *On the Special Laws* I, 84-97, and *Questions and Answers on Exodus* II.
[162]Pascher, *op. cit.*, p. 49f.
[163]*Moses* II, 134.
[164]Pascher, *op. cit.*, p. 59.
[165]*Ibid.*, pp. 34f., 67ff., 78ff.
[166]*Ibid.*, p. 228.

tery drama. Through the agency of the Logos, characterized as high priest and mediator, the soul of the sage as-
cends to the highest stage of a vision of God and sonship
with God. But since the garment of the Logos-High
Priest represents the cosmos, and the soul of the sage is
presented to God in it, and since, further, the individual
sage is understood as Israel, that is, as member of the
"race of seers," Philo's psychological individualism hides
a collective idea of the sage as member of the people of
God, an idea that is of course no longer clearly recogni-
zable.

Thus within the narrower environs of Hebrews we have
located an analogy with its central theme, the importance
of which may not be overlooked. It is not our first concern to set off this analogy more precisely from Hebrews'
presentation of the motif. Then, of course, we would
naturally have to point at once to the fact that in Philo the
mystery of redemption is presented in philosophical garb
and in an essentially individualistic way, while Hebrews
is oriented in strictly eschatological and collective fashion; that Philo's Logos-High Priest bears the stamp of
the Stoic World Reason; and that salvation is viewed in
genuinely Hellenistic fashion as the vision of God. *All
this at once disposes of any direct dependence of Hebrews
on Philo. On the other hand, the traditions that both use
jointly will not allow themselves to be so easily dismissed.*
On the contrary, the more the speculation in Philo is un-
folded in detail, the more sharply we repeatedly encounter striking parallels to particular motifs in Hebrews.

First, we must incorporate here what we already observed, that for Philo as well, the highest level of the
King's Highway denotes an attaining to rest. For "that
which is unwaveringly stable is God...so that he that

draws nigh to God longs for stability."[167] As in Hebrews, this also *marks the return to the heavenly* πατρίς
construed as πόλις, while the bodily-earthly life is viewed
as an ἀποδημία. Egypt is the symbol of those who hide
from God within themselves[168] and in general of everyone who dwells in the body and in the mortal γένος.[169]
Conversely, the one who is beloved of God regards all of
bodily life as an alien land and longs ἐν πατρίδι καταμένειν.[170] "The men of God are priests and prophets   [48]
who have refused to accept membership in the πολιτεία
of the world and become citizens therein, but have risen
wholly above the sphere of sense perception and have
been translated into the κόσμος νοητός and ἐγγρα-
φέντες and dwell there in the commonwealth of ideas
which are imperishable and incorporeal."[171] If in Philo
the φαῦλος is ἄπολις and ἄοικος, then the sage is by
contrast πολίτης.[172] This corresponds with the idea that
πολίτης is a πάροικος and παρεπίδημος on earth.[173]
Thus all whom Moses calls wise are introduced as so-
journing: αἱ γὰρ τούτων ψυχαὶ στέλλονται μὲν
ἀποικίαν οὐδέποτε τὴν ἐξ οὐρανοῦ, εἰώθασι δὲ ἕνεκα
τοῦ φιλοθεάμονος καὶ φιλομαθοῦς εἰς τὴν περίγειον φύσιν ἀποδημεῖν.[174] The continuation of this

---

[167]*On the Posterity and Exile of Cain* 23.
[168]*Allegorical Interpretation* III, 37ff.
[169]*Ibid.*, III, 42.
[170]*Who is the Heir* 82.
[171]*On the Giants* 61.
[172]*Allegorical Interpretation* III, 2f.
[173]Cf. especially *On the Confusion of Tongues* 79-82, modified in *On the Cherubim* 120f., where the world appears as a strange city in which we are aliens and strangers while God is its only true citizen.
[174]*On the Confusion of Tongues* 77: "Their souls are never colonists leaving heaven for a new home. Their way is to visit earthly nature as men who trav-el abroad to see and learn."

passage is especially clear: ἐπειδὰν οὖν ἐνδιατρίψασαι σώμασι τὰ αἰσθητὰ καὶ θνητὰ δι' αὐτῶν πάντα κατίδωσιν, ἐπανέρχονται ἐκεῖσε πάλιν, ὅθεν ὡρμήθησαν τὸ πρῶτον, πατρίδα μὲν τὸν οὐράνιον χῶρον ἐν ᾧ πολιτεύονται, ξένην δὲ τὸν περίγειον ἐν ᾧ παρῴκησαν νομίζουσαι. τοῖς μὲν γὰρ ἀποικίαν στειλαμένοις ἀντὶ τῆς μητροπόλεως ἡ ὑποδεξαμένη δήπου πατρίς, ἡ δ' ἐκπέμψασα μένει τοῖς ἀποδεδημηκόσιν, εἰς ἣν καὶ ποθοῦσιν ἐπανέρχεσθαι.[175] Vulnerability is thus a ruling necessity for them.[176] Of interest here is the use of the passage in Exod. 33:7, according to which Moses pitches his tent outside the camp. In this fashion the God-loving soul must put off the body and all that belongs to it; its πῆξις, βεβαίωσις, and ἵδρυσις must be among the ordinances of perfect virtue.[177] That is, the body is to be compared to a camp which, filled with war and its misfortunes, knows no peace. For this reason the sage lives outside it in the tent of wisdom[178] which is with God, and in any case is an ὀπαδὸς τοῦ πανηγεμόνος θεοῦ.[179] We need merely note here that the goal of the soul is occasionally also viewed as a kind of πανήγυρις, with sun, moon, and the host of stars as participants.[180]

---

[175]Ibid., 78: "So when they have stayed awhile in their bodies, and beheld through them all that sense and mortality has to shew, they make their way back to the place from which they set out at first. To them the heavenly region, where their citizenship lies, is their native land; the earthly region in which they become sojourners is a foreign country. For surely, when men found a colony, the land which receives them becomes their native land instead of the mother city, but to the traveller abroad the land which sent him forth is still the mother to whom also he yearns to return."

[176]Allegorical Interpretation II, 56ff.

[177]Ibid., II, 55.

[178]Ibid., III, 46.

[179]On the Migration of Abraham 175: "Attendant on the All-leading God."

[180]On the Special Laws I, 207.

Where the life of the sage is defined in this fashion as a journeying toward heaven, it is (no less than the way of God's people in Hebrews) set beneath ἐλπίς, described in more detail as the προσδοκία κτήσεως ἀγαθῶν παρὰ τοῦ μόνου φιλοδώρου θεοῦ.[181] Further, in Philo just as in Hebrews, ἐλπίς and πίστις are identical: "For the soul, clinging in utter dependence on a good hope, and deeming that things not present are beyond question al- [49] ready by reason of the sure steadfastness of Him that promised them, has won as its meed faith, a perfect good."[182] The essence of *pistis*, the τελειοτάτη ἀρετή,[183] is that it trusts God's promise and does not doubt: περὶ δὲ ὧν ὁ θεὸς ὁμολογεῖ, τί προσῆκεν ἀνθρώπους ἢ βεβαιότατα πιστεύειν.[184] And of course one believes God when one sees that elsewhere everything changes, but that God alone is unchangeable.[185] Whoever sets heart or soul on the corporeal and external brings it to ruin because such things are wholly unstable; but whoever in contemplation of the virtues seeks after God, goes a way that is absolutely certain, because there is no possibility of deception here. Whoever trusts the former ἀπιστεῖ θεῷ, as conversely whoever believes God mistrusts the former.[186] Here too, then, *pistis* sets itself in opposition to the sphere of visibility, and does so with complete certainty. ἀπορεῖν is an affair of the doubter, but μηκέτι

---

[181]*The Worse attacks the Better* 138: "Expectation of obtaining good things from the only bountiful God." Cf. *On the Posterity and Exile of Cain* 26.
[182]*On the Migration of Abraham* 44.
[183]*Who is the Heir* 91: "Most perfect of virtues."
[184]*On Abraham* 275: "And when they have God's promises before them what should men do but trust in them most firmly?"
[185]*Allegorical Interpretation* II, 89.
[186]*On Abraham* 269.

ζητεῖν is the attitude of the believer who has firmly grasped the divine ὑποσχέσεις and trusts that he will be a κληρονόμος σοφίας.[187] Thus, the paradox of faith in Hebrews, which views what is tangible in the world as uncertain and what is invisible and divine as absolutely true to its promises, is to a certain extent already prepared for in Philo. This is not true in a Christian sense, of course, since in Philo the human spirit—as if it were an agent of control—recognizes and evidences the instability of the cosmic and the unchangeability of the eternal, but at bottom only of what is spiritual.[188] In any event, it is characteristic that for Philo, as for Hebrews, *pistis* is understood as an inerrant type of access to the eternal: μόνον οὖν ἀψευδὲς καὶ βέβαιον ἀγαθὸν ἡ πρὸς θεὸν πίστις...ψυχῆς ἐν ἅπασι βελτίωσις ἐπερηρεισμένης καὶ ἐφιδρυμένης τῷ πάντων αἰτίῳ καὶ δυναμένῳ μὲν πάντα, βουλευομένῳ δὲ τὰ ἄριστα.[189]

Accordingly, here too persistence and constancy are an essential element of true *pistis*, as Philo often states: τοῦ δὲ βεβασανίσθαι καὶ δεδοκιμάσθαι σημεῖον τὸ πεπηγέναι,[190] or ἵνα...τὴν ἀρετὴν ἀφικόμενος βεβαίως ἱδρυθῆς.[191] There must be such stress on this constancy *because the King's Highway, like the wandering of the*

---

[187]*Who is the Heir* 101f.
[188]This is to be noted where, as for example in Bousset's *Kyrios Christos* (1970), p. 200f., the relation between the concept of faith in Hebrews and Philo is accented. On the subject as a whole, cf. Schlatter's excursus in *Der Glaube im Neuen Testament*, pp. 575-581.
[189]*On Abraham* 268: "Faith in God then is the one sure and infallible good...all around betterment of the soul which is firmly stayed on Him who is the cause of all things and can do all things yet only wills the best."
[190]*On the Sacrifices of Abel and Cain* 80: "The sign that it has been tested and proved is its solidity."
[191]*Ibid.*, 90: "That...(thou) mightest there find a stable resting-place."

people of God in Hebrews, appears as a struggle: ἦν ὁ
ἀρχαῖος ἀσκητῶν θίασος διήθλει, τὰς τιθασοὺς τῆς   [50]
ἡδονῆς γοητείας ἀποστρεφόμενος, ἀστείως καὶ
αὐστηρῶς χρώμενος τῇ τοῦ καλοῦ μελέτη.[192] This struggle is necessitated by opposition between the senusal-
visible and the spiritual-invisible which dominates
Philo's world view: "All flesh destroyed the perfect way
of the Eternal and Indestructible, the way which leads to
God. This way, you must know, is wisdom."[193] Still more
clearly: "Those who are members of that race endowed
with vision, which is called Israel, when they wish to
journey along the royal road, find their way διαμάχεται
ὁ γήινος ᾿Εδώμ...μετὰ σπουδῆς καὶ παρασκευῆς τῆς
πάσης εἴρξειν ἀπειλῶν τῆς ὁδοῦ καὶ ἀτριβῆ καὶ
ἀπόρευτον αὐτὴν κατασκευάζειν εἰσάπαν.[194] Thus the
wanderers must allow the question[195] whether they can let
lie everything beneath and beside them that belongs to
the world of appearances and is reckoned as earthly
good; whether anything that hinders their forward
march can be arrested or brought to a standstill. They are
warned that "the φαῦλος is an exile without home or
city or settlement, so also is he a deserter."[196] They are
summoned not to step out from the divine τάξις but, as
required, to stand bravely in it and not desert to coward-
ly and reproachful pleasures.[197] The danger of apostasy is

---

[192]*On the Posterity and Exile of Cain* 101: "The philosophy which the ancient
band of aspirants pursued in hard-fought contest, eschewing the soft en-
chantments of pleasure, engaged with fine severity in the study of what is
good and fair."
[193]*On the Unchangeableness of God* 142f.
[194]*Ibid.*, 144: "Contested by Edom...who threatens to bar them from the
road and render it such that none at all shall tread or travel on it."
[195]*Ibid.*, 149.
[196]*On the Giants* 67.
[197]*Ibid.*, 43.

acute and must be discussed because the dangers and
seductions of earth seem almost overwhelming:[198]
χαλεπὸν γὰρ ὥσπερ τοὺς δρομεῖς ἀρξαμένους ὁδοῦ
τῆς πρὸς εὐσέβειαν ἀπταίστως καὶ ἀπνευστὶ
διευθῦναι τὸν δρόμον, ἐπειδὴ μυρία ἐμποδὼν πάντι
τῷ γενομένῳ.[199] As in Hebrews so in Philo, Israel mur-
muring in the wilderness is taken as a warning: "We left
the country in the hope of freedom, and yet we have no
security even of life. Our leader promised us happiness;
in actual fact, we are the most miserable of men. What
will be the end of this long, interminable journey? Every
traveller by sea or land has set before him some goal to
come to, market or harbor for one, city or country for
the other; we alone have before us a pathless wilderness,
painful journeying, desperate straits."[200] So then it is necessary to count the cost:[201] ἄμεινον ἐνταυθοῖ
καταμένειν τὸν θνητὸν βίον ἀλητεύοντας, ὡς τὸ
πλεῖστον ἀνθρώπων γένος, ἢ πρὸς τὸν οὐρανὸν
ἐξάραντας ἑαυτοὺς ὑπὸ ἀλαζονείας ἀνατραπῆναι.

Without endurance all comes to nothing, for which
reason then ὑπομονή plays a preeminent role in Philo.
[51] Further, just as in Hebrews *the peril of the way is explained from the need for divine instruction:* ἄνευ γὰρ
τοῦ δυσωπηθῆναι καὶ περὶ ἐνίων ἐπιπληχθῆναι
νουθεσίαν ἐνδέξασθαι καὶ σωφρονισμὸν ἀμή-

---

[198]*On the Unchangeableness of God* 150f., 180.

[199]*On Husbandry* 177: "For it is difficult for the runners, as we may call
them, after starting on the way to piety, to finish the whole course without
stumbling, and without stopping to draw breath."

[200]*Moses* I, 193f.

[201]*On the Migration of Abraham* 171: "It is better to stay where we are,
roaming, with the bulk of humankind, through this mortal life rather than
lift ourselves heavenward and incur shipwreck as imposters."

χανον.[202] The wise one leans on discipline as a staff and thus gives firmness to the confused tossing of the soul.[203] βελτιώσεις are an occasion for rejoicing. We would otherwise have to scold parents and teachers who reprimand and at times even thrash their children, though they act from love and good intention.[204] But we may be comforted by the fact that help is near: As God himself raises the rational creature from the nether world of passions to the Olympian region of virtue, and of himself says, τὴν εἰς οὐρανὸν ἄγουσαν ὁδὸν ἀνατεμὼν λεωφόρον ἱκέτισι ψυχαῖς, ὡς μὴ κάμνοιεν βαδίζουσαι, πάσαις ἀποδέδειχα,[205] so also the Logos appears as θεῖος ἄγγελος ποδηγετῶν and removes obstacles before the feet that one may walk without stumbling along the high road:[206] οὐκοῦν ὅτι καὶ πρὸς βοήθειαν δύναμις ἀρωγὸς εὐτρεπὴς ἐφεδρεύει παρὰ θεῷ καὶ αὐτὸς ὁ ἡγεμὼν ἐγγυτέρω πρόσεισιν ἐπ' ὠφελείᾳ τῶν ἀξίων ὠφελεῖσθαι, δεδήλωται.[207] This help from the Logos is detailed elsewhere in Philo, but need not be pursued further here, since first of all the intention behind our analysis of Philo has been achieved and we are now able to summarize our results.

---

[202]On the Posterity and Exile of Cain 97: "For there is no way of taking to heart warning and correction, unless for some offences one is chastized and brought to a sense of shame."

[203]Allegorical Interpretation II, 90.

[204]On Joseph 74.

[205]On the Posterity and Exile of Cain 31: "I have laid down the road that leads to heaven and appointed it as a highway for all suppliant souls, that they might not grow weary as they tread on it."

[206]On the Unchangeableness of God 182.

[207]On the Migration of Abraham 57: "So far it has been shown that there is waiting ready and equipped at God's side strong help to come to our succour, and that the Sovereign Ruler will Himself draw near for the benefit of those who are worthy to receive His benefits."

The boundaries separating Philo from Hebrews are vast. Wisdom speculation and the Christian message continually part company, even though a doctrine of redemption clearly appears back of Philo's wisdom speculation. This is especially true where we compare only individual texts. The same concepts and spheres of ideas are at odds in respect of content. To this point, then, drawing upon Philo for the exegesis of Hebrews has been in essence unfruitful. *But this treatment of our problem by comparing individual texts is too simple.* It can never explain how there may be any analogy at all in the so-called external form. Such derives solely from the context as a whole. At the center of Philo's and Hebrews' speculation there is the motif of a highway leading through the cosmos to heaven, traversed by a people of God who sojourn on it, or by a race of seers which symbolizes this people. Philo and Hebrews anchor this motif in biblical [52] thought by an exegesis of the Old Testament, a motif which in neither case would originally have emerged from Scripture.[208] Larger, religious-historical connections appear to link Philo and Hebrews, without leading them to a relation of direct dependence upon each other. *In Philo and Hebrews it is possible to observe an underlying tradition of doctrines of redemption, and from two different aspects.* Philo, as well as the κατάπαυσις speculation in Hebrews, indicates that further clarification of this tradition must be awaited from Hellenism. From this series of conclusions, at first set up in merely analytic fashion, we could grasp the juxtaposition and opposition between Philo and Hebrews. The same basic motif conditions the

---

[208]If this is true of Philo in any case, the κατάπαυσις speculation proves that it is also true of Hebrews.

extensive parallelism in both views. But in both instances
the basic motif and individual views are set in a differently oriented frame. If metaphysics and psychology deter-
mine Philo's point of view, Hebrews inquires into the eschatological redemption of the people of God who bear
the promise. Though Philo may refer to a mystery of cosmic redemption in his background, and though on the
other hand Hebrews may at times make use of metaphysical ideas to clarify its concerns, the tendency of each is
away from the other.

This reconstruction, however, is not sufficiently secure, and requires further evidence. It may be we shall
obtain such evidence from that doctrine of redemption in
which the motif of the journey to heaven again plays a decisive role, that is, from the Gnostic myth of the redeemed Redeemer and the soul's journey to heaven.

3. The Heavenly Journey in Gnosticism

At this point, we assume acquaintance with the essential characteristics of the Gnostic myth of the redeemed
Redeemer, so often dealt with in the last decades. *In it,*
the motif of the wandering people of God appears in its
most conceivably pronounced form. Since the *Urmensch*
about to be redeemed embraces all the heavenly parts of
souls scattered about the earth, his redemption includes
that of his "seed," "race," or "relationship." Cosmic and
collective in the sharpest sense, this redemption is realized when the *Urmensch* and his parts are reminded of
their divine origin and are induced to detach from the
material world as well as to return to their heavenly
homeland.

[53]   Now we must ask: Could there be a connection between this Gnostic sphere of thought and Hebrews, or
has the motif of the wandering people of God in Hebrews and in the myth emerged independently at some
point and been developed? Consequently, possible
points of contact must first be explored from the standpoint of the myth. It would be a long-drawn-out and
needless procedure, were we to hunt through the entire
body of Gnostic literature for this purpose. First of all,
we are not concerned with positive proof of Gnostic influence on Hebrews in every instance, but only with a
parallelism of lines that sketch out the basic conception.
But these lines are deliberately traced from a sphere of literature in which the myth, though later in time yet in respect of content is described in a particularly detailed and
complete way, that is, from the Mandaean literature.[209]
Should a direct relation of dependence between the myth
and Hebrews then be likely, the question of priority
must in any case be decided by individual exegesis.

In Mandaean Gnosticism the existence of the Gnostic
continually appears as *existence on a way.* So the soul
asks, "How far is my way?"[210] What is meant is "the way
of life"[211] or of "those who are perfect"[212]—a name for
the faithful: "I inquired of you, Yahya, on the way which
the men of proven piety walk without hindrance."[213]

---

[209]On pp. 135ff. of his *Religionsgeschichtliche Untersuchungen,* Schlier comes
to speak of the way of the martyr, the scheme of which is also adopted from
that of the Gnostic heavenly journey, and as a result is to be compared here.
[210]*Das Johannes-Buch der Mandäer,* ed. M. Lidzbarski (1915), p. 59, 4ff.
[211]*Ginza,* ed. M. Lidzbarski (1925), pp. 26, 3 and 473, 25.
[212]*Johannes-Buch,* p. 236, 1.
[213]*Ibid.,* p. 119, 9ff.

And, of course, this way is decribed as ἄναδος,[214] thus
contrasted with the "path of the trunk."[215] This aspect of
ascent includes redemptive liberation from earth and the
material world: "Free yourselves from the Tibil and the
worthless abode,"[216] summons the call of redemption.
And Adam says to the Great Life: "I was apart from
you...then I was redeemed and ascended upwards."[217] As
a result, "to ascend" and "to conquer"[218] are identical,
just as the conquerors[219] dwell in the heights.

Earth is "the house without solidity,"[220] thus as in He-   [54]
brews it is unstable and transitory. Since for Gnostic doctrine without exception the world belongs to the demons, souls linger in it as in an "alien existence."[221] The
obverse side of this thought is that the believer's heavenly
goal and also "the place from which he was created"[222] is
viewed as his native place[223] or home.[224] Other names are
"the great, first house of the Father,"[225] the Place of Life,[226]
the House of Life,[227] or the House of Perfection.[228] As in
Hebrews so in Gnosticism, the heavenly city is the object

---

[214]Most clearly in the *Hermetica*, ed. W. Scott (1924), I, 24ff.
[215]*Ginza*, p. 455, 1.
[216]*Johannes-Buch*, p. 92, 5.
[217]*Ginza*, p. 489, 37ff.
[218]*Ibid.*, p. 444, 25f., passim.
[219]"Life stands fast in its Skina, Life is victorious," *Ginza*, p. 429, 29ff., passim.
[220]*Johannes-Buch*, p. 126, 8.
[221]The idea is expressed in a particularly beautiful way in the "Hymn of the
Pearl" in the *Acts of Thomas* 109 (Bonnet II, 220; H.-S., p. 499).
[222]*Ginza*, p. 457, 12.
[223]*Ibid.*, p. 455, 37.
[224]*Ibid.*, p. 459, 4.
[225]*Ibid.*, p. 426, 15.
[226]*Johannes-Buch*, p. 220, 7ff.
[227]*Ibid.*, p. 62, 3 and 64, 4ff.
[228]*Ginza*, p. 565, 9 and 222, 13.

of κληρονομία. In *Pistis Sophia*[229] we read: "For God will
save their souls from all matter, and a city will be prepared in the light; and all souls which will be saved will
dwell in that city, and they will inherit it." In Gnosticism
also the goal is variously described as a city or country.
The *Odes of Solomon* refer to the latter: "Blessed are they
who are planted in your land and who have a place in
your paradise, who...have wandered from darkness to
light."[230] The νέφος μαρτύρων in Heb. 12:1 is most likely to be construed in purely figurative fashion, but we
may recall that Gnosticism also describes the goal as a
cloud of light identical to the heavenly οἰκοδομή.[231]

An indispensable condition for the soul's journey to
heaven is the forsaking of the body as a component of the
material world. Only in this way is alien existence in this
world brought to an end. The Mandaean Liturgies of the
Dead in particular express this idea: "Sitil, the son of
Adam said, 'Upon this road, path and ascent which I ascended, true, believing, glorious and perfect men shall
ascend and come, when they leave the body.' "[232] This at
once yields two further motifs which deserve special attention.

First of all, the ascent is described as the way of the
perfect,[233] and the goal thus as completion. Second, this

---

[229]Ed. C. Schmidt, Leiden (1978), p. 31, 35f.

[230]11:15f. Cf. the "Hymn of the Pearl" in the *Acts of Thomas* 111 (Bonnet II,
222; H.-S., p. 501): ἀποδυσάμενος τὸ ῥυπαρὸν ἔνδυμα ἐν τῇ αὐτῶν
κατέλειψα χώρᾳ, ηὔθυνον δὲ αὐτὸ καὶ τὴν ὁδὸν πρὸς τὸ φῶς τῆς κατὰ
ἀνατολὴν πατρίδος ["And their dirty and unclean garment I took off and
left in their land, and directed my way (that I might come) to the light of our
homeland, the East"].

[231]Cf. the details on this in H. Schlier, *Christus und die Kirche im
Epheserbrief* (1930), p. 50f.

[232]*Ginza*, p. 429, 17ff.

[233]*Ginza*, p. 95, 15; 271, 26 and 516, 2ff.; *Johannes-Buch*, p. 236, 1.

way is more precisely defined by the fact *that the* [55]
Urmensch-*Redeemer first walked it.* So it is said of
Adam's work that "rest and salvation prevail on the way
which Adam rightly built...the way taken by the soul."[234]
The Redeemer paves it anew for every generation.[235] For
this reason, then, the faithful praise him: "You showed
us the way by which you have come from the House of
Life. On it we will walk as truthful, believing men, that
our spirit and soul may dwell in the Skina of Life, where
the spirits of our fathers abide."[236]

The Redeemer is viewed as leader and helper: "He
freed me from the hand and works of the Seven. He
showed me the way at all times and made me a path to the
Light. He raised me up with him and did not leave me in
the worthless abode."[237] Thus sounds redemption's call:
"Rise up then from the earth, thou art become wholly
above it. See the light, for the Lord does not allow those
who love him to walk in darkness. Look upon the
συνοδοιπόρος of his servants."[238] And the Redeemer
is not only a companion on the way, but also δεσπότης
πάντων καὶ πατήρ· πατὴρ δὲ οὐ τῶν ἐν σώμασιν
οὐσῶν ψυχῶν ἀλλὰ τῶν ἐξελθουσῶν.[239] He himself says:
"My sons called me loudly, and I came to rouse this
world. Hail to the one who hears my words and proceeds
upon my path!"[240] In following him, one arrives at the
goal. In the *Odes of Solomon* 7:13f., just as God has

---

[234]*Ginza,* p. 513, 28f.
[235]Cf. for example "Hibil" in *Ginza,* p. 259, 24f.
[236]*Mandäische Liturgien,* ed. M. Lidzbarski (1920), p. 38, 4ff.
[237]*Ginza,* p. 500, 26ff.
[238]*Acts of Thomas* 119 (Bonnet II, 229; H.-S., p. 506).
[239]*Ibid.,* 30 (Bonnet II, 147; H.-S., p. 459): "Lord of all and Father—but Father not of the souls that are in bodies, but of those that are gone out."
[240]*Johannes-Buch,* p. 218, 13f.

paved and completed a way for knowledge by setting the traces of his light and his footprints upon it from beginning to end, so the Redeemer summons: "On my path shall the chosen come; in my steps shall the faithful go."[241] Or: "Hail to the one who listens to you and follows you on the path."[242] He also instructs his own about the dangers on the way: "The way which the souls must traverse is wide and without end."[243] But the demons have conspired: "We will seduce the Family of Life."[244] It is their goal to hinder souls and make them like themselves.[245]

By contrast, believers are reminded of the word of life: "Put on your garment that you may stand firm in your own splendor. Forget not what the Great (Life) commanded you."[246] And they are warned: "Woe to the [56]   masterbuilder who has built no building before himself; woe to the road builder who has leveled no road for himself. He does not ascend to behold the Place of Light."[247] Everything depends on ὑπομονή: "Whoever remains firm and steadfast will ascend on the path of Kuschta to the Place of Light."[248] *Here also patience is identical to* pistis: "Remain firm and steadfast in your faith";[249] "be faithful and steadfast, then you will ascend."[250]

---

[241]*Ginza,* p. 185, 3ff.
[242]*Ibid.,* p. 274, 28f.
[243]*Johannes-Buch,* p. 180, 22f.
[244]*Ginza,* p. 114, 30.
[245]*Ibid.,* p. 489, 11ff. Cf. in addition Schlier, *Christus und die Kirche,* p. 8ff.
[246]*Ginza,* p. 488, 12.
[247]*Johannes-Buch,* p. 171, 8ff.
[248]*Ibid.,* p. 210, 2f. There is also reference to the Path of Kuschta elsewhere, thus to the truth grasped by faith. Cf. *ibid.,* 107,3f., and Ginza 19, 25; 22,17, and 37,4.
[249]*Ginza,* p. 51, 33.
[250]*Ibid.,* p. 496, 23f. Faith is also a way in the *Odes of Solomon* 22:7; 34:6 and 39:5f.

Souls can overcome their distress by looking at their leader.[251] He watches over them, as when asked he himself explains: "Why do you stand there so (long), whose way do you guard? I guard the way of the one who must sit in the world."[252] The redeemed have his promise— "and his word is with us in all our way"[253]—and they know its content: "Of themselves they cannot leave you or bar you from your father's place of origin."[254] Thus they conquer as confessors: "My soul confessed the Place of Light;"[255] "my Father, the Great One, knows of me; the Powerful One knows of me."[256] As confessors they are strengthened from heaven: "What I said to him pleased the Great (Life). Daily he created and sent me voice, power and speech...and what the Great One sent me, awakened my heart so that I did not stumble. So long as he heard the call of Life he did not alter the task which the Powerful One gave him. I endured as long, I persevered as long as the Great One wished."[257]

We already pointed out that the myth cannot be charged with individualism, though the topic often seems merely to be the fate of the individual soul. But if the individual soul is always only a member and component of the *Urmensch*-Redeemer, its way of life consequently reflects a cosmic event. *Redemption refers primarily to the "Family of Souls."*[258] Thus, for example, it is said that "the man of tested piety was victorious and aided his entire

---

[251]For example, from Jokabar-Ziwa, *Johannes-Buch*, p. 220, 7ff.
[252]*Ginza*, p. 582, 23ff.
[253]*Odes of Solomon* 41:11.
[254]*Ginza*, p. 460, 11f.
[255]*Ibid.*, p. 509, 23.
[256]*Ginza*, p. 487, 1f.
[257]*Ibid.*, p. 485, 16ff.
[258]For example, *Ginza*, p. 140, 32; 187, 23 and 189, 26.

race to victory."[259] The Redeemer says, "I approached to
[57]   issue the call of life and to arouse the Family of Life,"[260]
or, "The Life has sent me; I approached to bring the race
victorious to the heights."[261] This is identical to the "Fellowship of Souls,"[262] also described as a "company,"[263] or
occasionally as a "people."[264] The soul says to its companions: "My good brothers, if it pleases you, lead me with
you in your company. I wish to be a fellowship to the
good, a companion to believers."[265] By common origin
from the world of life, this fellowship for individual souls
is described as a sharing: "You are a share of
brilliance...of the earth light."[266] To the demons it is said:
"The sharer with those who are perfect cannot be called
your sharer."[267] *This expresses the well-known Gnostic
doctrine of συγγένεια which describes the relation of the
family to the world of light as a sonship, and that of souls
to each other as a brotherhood.*

The following lines may serve to illustrate the idea of
sonship: "I want to do good to the sons of the sublime
fellowship,"[268] or, "my Father, the Great One, knows of
me."[269] The following illustrate the idea of brotherhood:
"Brothers in the flesh pass away, but brothers in the
Kuschta abide";[270] "I beheld the Great House of the Fa-

[259]*Johannes-Buch*, p. 161, 6ff.
[260]*Ibid.*, p. 220, 2f.
[261]*Ginza*, p. 336, 19f.
[262]Cf. for example, *ibid.*, p. 302, 16f; *Johannes-Buch*, p. 188, 11ff.
[263]*Ginza*, p. 361, 25f.
[264]*Odes of Solomon* 10:6.
[265]*Ginza*, p. 541, 9ff.
[266]*Ginza*, p. 458, 20ff.
[267]*Johannes-Buch*, p. 160, 14f.
[268]*Ibid.*, p. 186, 31f.
[269]*Ginza*, p. 487, 1f.
[270]*Ibid.*, p. 20, 14.

ther in which my brothers dwell,"[271] as well as the line from the *Hermetica:* φωτίσω τοὺς ἐν ἀγνοίᾳ τοῦ γένους, μοῦ ἀδελφοὺς, υἱοὺς δὲ σοῦ.[272] To the extent one attains the heavenly world only as member of the Redeemer, believers are also his sons, as can often be proved at will.[273] Finally, insofar as the Redeemer encounters souls as envoy, enlightens them concerning their way, and becomes their leader, he is more than all other heavenly creatures also their brother.[274] This entire relationship appears with especial clarity when Jorrabba swears[275] not to have sinned against the sons of Hibil-Ziwa, and when in the same verse the term "sons" is replaced by "disciples," since it is precisely the teaching that makes them sons. Before, however, it was said that Hibil-Ziwa goes "to his brothers."[276]

It is this Gnostic idea of the συγγένεια that leads us now to treat directly the first portion of Hebrews. There the relationship of believers to Christ is similarly described as sonship and brotherhood. As a result, in that portion the question of Gnostic influence on Hebrews can be quite concretely tested. In any case, our investigation to this point has yielded such strong parallelism between Hebrews and the myth in basic motif as well as in individual details *that the attempt as such to establish a tradition common to both seems justified.* The boundaries between myth and Hebrews lie clearly in the naturalism

[58]

---

[271]*Ibid.,* p. 577, 34f.

[272]*Hermetica* I, 32. ET: "I enlighten those in ignorance of the race, my brothers and your sons."

[273]For example, *Johannes-Buch,* p. 218, 3f.; *Mandäische Liturgien,* p. 183, 1ff.

[274]For example, *Johannes-Buch,* p. 132, 11f. and 133, 8f.; *Ginza,* p. 371, 4f.

[275]*Johannes-Buch,* p. 186, 25.

[276]*Johannes-Buch,* p. 184, 7f.

of the myth, a naturalism unacceptable to Christianity. Conversely, due to its purely soteriological scheme, the myth moves closer to Hebrews than does, for example, Philo with his cosmology and psychology, from which we first had to extract the redemptive mystery of the King's Highway.

CHAPTER 2

The Son and the Sons

When J. Kögel[1] gave to his treatise on Heb. 2:5ff. the title *Der Sohn und die Söhne,* he most appropriately seized upon a motif that claims decisive significance in Hebrews, and which is related to that other motif of the wandering people of God which we must now give greater precision. But he also touched on a theme that is as characteristic of the myth as that of the celestial journey, and which is suited to answer further the question of the impact of Gnosticism on Hebrews.

A. The Presentation of the Son in the Letter to the Hebrews

1. The "Son" Title as Predicate of the Exalted Christ

The Son—this is the theme of Hebrews 1. Christ was expressly invested with this title by God himself. Because

---

[1]Gütersloh, 1904.

of 1:3-4, we should no longer be able to dispute the datum of this investiture. Here the term "Son" appears as content of a κληρονομεῖν, and this concept in its pregnant use refers solely to the attaining of eschatological and heavenly blessings. Further, acquisition of the name in verse 4 refers to what was cited directly prior, to the ἐκάθισεν ἐν δεξιᾷ τῆς μεγαλωσύνης ἐν ὑψηλοῖς in verse 3. *Thus the ascension also gives to the Christ the rank of "Son."* This fact could only be called into question since in 1:2 and 5:7 the human person of Jesus already appears to bear the title "Son."[2] From this, one felt justified in having to distinguish between the title of Son and that of high priest, and conceived the first as conferred in a pretemporal act[3]—in the promulgation of the Old Testament prophecy in Ps. 2:7,[4] in the incarnation,[5] or even in the baptism of Jesus.[6] But according to 5:5f., installation to the office of high priest clearly corresponds to bestowal of the title "Son." The preterite λαλήσας in 5:5 denotes a concrete act of solemn naming. To this extent it corresponds to the κεκληρονόμηκεν in 1:5 and the προσαγορευθείς in 5:10, and thus may not be distinguished from the λέγει in 5:6[7] which refers to contemporary testimony by the Scripture. Bestowal of the title "Son" and of the rank of high priest thus coincide in the same action that in 5:9 is linked to Jesus' τελείωσις, and in consequence must occur in heaven.

[59]

---

[2]Cf. Riggenbach, p. 18; Strathmann, p. 65.
[3]As an hypothesis in Windisch, p. 14.
[4]Riggenbach, p. 16.
[5]Windisch, p. 14.
[6]Strathmann, p. 65.
[7]Strathmann, p. 65, refers the predication of Son to a "period before the assumption of his priestly service."

Accordingly, we note in 1:2 and 5:7 a proleptic application of the title "Son."

The perception *that the description in 1:5ff. repro-
duces an act of enthronement* has of late gained acceptance.[8] In that case, the λέγειν of 1:5ff., as well as the
λαλήσας of 5:5, and the parallel προσαγορευθείς of
5:10 denote a "solemn proclamation."[9] Though before
God the earthly Jesus may already have been in essence
the "Son," he was so only as hidden within the Godhead.
The history of his flesh as described in 5:7f. shows well
enough how little we may infer from it that the title of
Son is present throughout. But it is true that here, as well
as in Phil. 2:7f., Jesus' earthly history furnishes the basis
for the official and heavenly declaration of his sonship.
Here, as in Phil. 2:9, the official conferring of the ὄνομα
denotes a heightening of power in contrast to Jesus'
earthly history. What previously existed within the Godhead as capacity or essence undergoes eschatological dis-
closure in the heavenly act of enthronement, and only
from that point can be trajected back into the earthly history by the believing community.

He who learned obedience on earth while suffering
(5:8), and could not be recognized as Son, now, following his ascension and in close analogy with Phil. 2:9ff.
and Revelation 5,[10] assumes a sonship to match his divine   [60]
power[11] in the presence of an eschatological company,
and in so doing is solemnly confirmed by a heavenly
proclamation. So this accession to power is also linked to

---

[8]Cf. Windisch, p. 15; Jeremias, *Die Briefe an Timotheus und Titus* (1936), p.
17 (on 1 Tim. 3:16); Michel, p. 26.
[9]Windisch, p. 14.
[10]Cf. Lohmeyer, *Die Offenbarung des Johannes*, pp. 48ff.
[11]It is not by accident that the concept of δοξάζειν is used in 5:5.

an εἰσάγειν. The πάλιν εἰσαγάγῃ in 1:6 refers to a first "bringing in" which did not occur with the incarnation[12]—an event not at all accented in Chapter one—but rather with an entry to heaven. Further, just as in 1:6, "to bring in" has a technical sense and denotes presentation of the Son before the angels as part of the act of enthronement.[13]

Only in this way does *the contrast between Christ and the angels in 1:4—2:5* take on meaning. All talk[14] of "deliberate disparagement of the angels"[15] is out of the question. They are, of course, distinguished and set off from Christ. But this does not occur because the debate with Judaism also requires mention of the Son's relation to the angels,[16] to say nothing of the existence of a heresy concerning angels. The exegesis of Hebrews should finally be freed from the effects of Tübingen tendency criticism. Where Jesus' heavenly glory requires comparison so as to give it greater emphasis, the first to come to mind are naturally not the dwellers on earth, but rather the angels who comprise the divine court. In the presence of these witnesses, the Christ event reaches its culmination in the enthronement and presentation of the Son following his ascension.[17] In their presence the veils of the mystery of the Son within the Godhead are first torn aside and, since not even the angels are hailed as sons, in such fashion that these witnesses as first in rank are also made subject to the sphere of the Son's lordship.

---

[12]And the incarnation can by no means be described as an εἰσάγειν.
[13]Cf. Windisch, p. 15.
[14]As again in Riggenbach, p. 15.
[15]Windisch, p. 17.
[16]Contra Michel, p. 31; Strathmann, p. 67.
[17]Cf. Revelation 5.

One final act of the Christ drama is of course still to come. The πάλιν εἰσαγάγῃ refers to it. Here the firstborn is no longer presented merely to angels or his companions, but to the entire οἰκουμένη, thus clearly at the parousia.[18] This indicates that Hebrews 1 exhibits a fixed Christological scheme in which the revelation of the Son describes ever widening circles and embraces different acts. This scheme deserves to be subjected to closer examination. [61]

2. The Son as Anthropos in Terms of the Gnostic Myth

At several points, a striking analogy—seen by Lohmeyer[19] with special clarity—has emerged between Heb. 1:5ff. or 5:5ff., and the Christ hymn in Phil. 2:5ff. *Now we must maintain that Hebrews 1 and Phil. 2:5ff. are oriented to the same Christological scheme.* But since there is no doubt that the Philippians passage has taken its essential stamp from the Gnostic doctrine of the *Urmensch,* the question arises: *To what extent is Christ understood, and only to be understood, in Hebrews 1 as* Anthropos *in terms of the Gnostic myth?*

Of importance here are the very first verses of Chapter 1 dealing with Christ's preexistence. According to 1:2, Christ is creator and heir of the world, a motif especially well known to us from Col. 1:15ff. Further, it cannot be disputed that in its spatial sense[20] as well as elsewhere in the New Testament, αἰῶνες denotes the superimposed layers of the world structure. Otherwise,

---

[18]Cf. Riggenbach, p. 19f. Michel, p. 25, is of a different opinion, and links the πάλιν with λέγει, a connection already made impossible by the position of πάλιν in the sentence.

[19]Lohmeyer, *Kyrios Jesus* (1928), pp. 70ff.; cf. Michel, p. 135.

[20]Cf. Sasse, *TDNT* I, 204.

κληρονόμος πάντων and ἐποίησεν τοὺς αἰῶνας would not correspond as they clearly should. The existence of the creator and heir of the world is interpreted from the fact that he is the ἀπαύγασμα τῆς δόξης καὶ χαρακτὴρ τῆς ὑποστάσεως αὐτοῦ, and bears all things by his word of power (1:3). Kittel[21] has defined the concept ἀπαύγασμα in such a way that it can denote both "effulgence" as well as "reflection, image, or likeness." But when he gives preference to the former on the basis of unanimous patristic opinion,[22] we may counter that the concept takes its most precise definition from the parallel term, χαρακτήρ. This term, identical to σφραγίς,[23] indicates we should rather construe it as "image."

Yet perhaps we dare not distinguish so sharply. ἀπαύγασμα as well as χαρακτήρ clearly reflect that Hellenistic concept of the εἰκών[24] for which something is always only an image, so that it also appears as effulgence. When, for example, according to the *Odes of Solomon* 7:15f., the Light "shone forth in the Son, so that it pervades the All for the sake of its redemption, so that the Most High may be made known among His holy ones,"* this is not merely a remarkable parallel to our text. Here, rather, the Son is also viewed as the Highest's effulgence and image for his holy ones. The Hellenistic concept of

[62]

---

[21]Kittel, *TDNT* I, 508.
[22]Cf. also Riggenbach, p. 9, n. 14.
[23]Cf. Dölger, *Sphragis* (1911), p. 112f.
[24]So also Michel, p. 22.
*Translators' note: Käsemann's German translation of the Odes does not agree with the English translation of e.g., Charlesworth, which reads: "And he was pleased by the Son. And because of his salvation He will possess everything. And the Most High will be known by His holy ones"; cf. the *Odes of Solomon*, p. 36.

εἰκών is also not foreign to Hebrews, as 10:1-4 shows. Michel, of course, disputes this last remark. But his thesis can hardly be maintained, according to which εἰκών in the sense of "archetype" as appears in 10:1-4 derives from Jewish tradition, while Hellenism uses the term to denote image, the σκιά.[25] Again and again in Gnosticism it is precisely the Redeemer or heavenly "I" who is the εἰκών of earthly souls.[26] But it is difficult to give any clear definition to this concept. What is actually involved is a most intimate connection between two corresponding entities and a metaphysical arrangement and gradation extending to the earthly. If the Redeemer or the heavenly represents the image of the divine nature, this does not rule out its character as archetype for the redeemed or the earthly. Perhaps we may say that the rabbinic concept of εἰκών more strongly accents this latter aspect, dominant also in Heb. 10:10f. But there can be no doubt of the Hellenistic tone, at least in 1:3. The predicates ἀπαύγασμα and χαρακτήρ are no differently assigned to Christ than the title "seal of God"[27] given the Philonic Logos, or again in Philo,[28] the title μακαρίας φύσεως ἐκμαγεῖον ἢ ἀπόσπασμα ἢ ἀπαύγασμα given the spiritual one akin to the Logos. If in Philo the term ἀπαύγασμα is conferred on the human νοῦς which is merely derived from the divine Logos, then its original application is clear from two

---

[25]Michel, p. 130.

[26]Cf. E. Käsemann, *Leib und Leib Christi* (1933), pp. 81ff.

[27]Cf. Dölger, *Sphragis*, p. 67. Thus the Logos of *Allegorical Interpretation* III, 96, is also the σπιά and ἀπεικόνισμα of God. Parallel with this is the description of the spiritual world as ἀρχέτυπος σφραγίς and of the material world as μίμημα θείας εἰκόνος in *On the Creation* 25.

[28]*On the Creation* 146: "Having come into being as a copy or fragment or ray of that blessed nature."

additional parallels. In the *Acts of Thomas*[29] it is said of the "Daughter of Light": ἧ ἐνέστηκε καὶ ἔγκειται τὸ ἀπαύγασμα τῶν βασιλέων τὸ γαῦρον, and in the *Wis. of Sol.* 7:25f., Wisdom is addressed as the ἀπόρροια τῆς τοῦ παντοκράτορος δόξης εἰλικρινής and as ἀπαύγασμα...φωτὸς αἰδίου καὶ ἔσοπτρον ἀκηλίδωτον τῆς τοῦ θεοῦ ἐνεργείας καὶ εἰκὼν τῆς ἀγαθότητος αὐτοῦ.[30] Thus Sophia, whose myth also lies behind the "Daughter of Light" in the *Acts of Thomas*, is originally [63] the "likeness" of God. And of course she is such insofar as she is also creator of the world, just as the Logos of Philo or as Christ in Col. 1:15ff. and Heb. 1:2f.

Thus in regard to its terms and to the content of ideas, this passage in Hebrews is set within an already fixed religious-historical scheme.[31] The statement in 1:3, according to which Christ upholds the universe by his word of power, further suits this contention. For here as in 11:3, ῥῆμα is the creating Word and as such is able to uphold all things.[32] Windisch[33] correctly observes that "to uphold" means "to preserve from decay." We need merely add that φέρειν is used in a technical sense in the language of Hellenistic aeon theology.[34] This rounds out

---

[29]*Acts of Thomas* 6 (Bonnet II, 109; H.-S., p. 445): "Upon her stands and rests the majestic effulgence of kings."
[30]RSV: "A pure emanation of the glory of the Almighty...a reflection of eternal light, a spotless mirror of the working of God and an image of his goodness."
[31]This is also considered by F. Büchsel, *Die Christologie des Hebräerbriefes* (1922), p. 17f.
[32]Windisch, p. 12.
[33]*Ibid.*
[34]In the *Manichaica* the ἀνὴρ τέλειος bears the world as pillars of light; cf. Schlier, *Christus und die Kirche*, p. 29. On the *Shepherd of Hermas*, Sim. IX, 14, cf. Käsemann, *loc. cit.*, p. 85. For Jewish parallels cf. Lueken, *Michael*, p. 140 on *Enoch* 69:14ff., and Odeberg, p. 125f. on *3 Enoch* 40:1.

the picture: The doctrine of the εἰκών and the predicates of aeon theology combine to describe the Gnostic Redeemer[35] in exactly the same way as the εἰκών doctrine there coincides with the predicates of creator and heir of the world derived from the Sophia myth. This result can be further confirmed from Phil. 2:5ff. There, too, the preexistent Christ is the heavenly εἰκών, as is clear from the description ὅς ἐν μορφῇ θεοῦ ὑπάρχων. Lohmeyer has correctly emphasized this motif and linked it to that of the bestowal of the name.[36] But the connection with the Hellenistic εἰκών doctrine must be more sharply indicated than was the case with Lohmeyer: Only God's image and the archetype of the redeemed possesses the μορφὴ θεοῦ, as conversely the Pauline μορφωθῆναι of believers[37] denotes their being conformed to the image of God and is to be understood against the background of the Gnostic idea of the συνάρθρωσις τοῦ λόγου.[38] Thus Lohmeyer,[39] again with good reason, sets the Philippians passage within the framework of Paul's doctrine of the σὺν Χριστῷ, which in turn is most closely linked to the εἰκών idea.[40] It is no longer surprising, then, that in Phil. 2:10f., just as in Col. 1:15ff. and Heb. 1:3, Christ appears as heir of the world. Only to him does every knee [64] bow, and in every level of the world. But again, only the creator of the world is heir of the world, thus the form of the divine εἰκών, whoever may represent it in the individual instance. Heb. 1:3, together with Col. 1:15ff. and

---

[35]Käsemann, *op. cit.*, pp. 85ff.
[36]Lohmeyer, *Kyrios Jesus*, p. 51f.
[37]Cf. Rom. 8:29; 12:2; Gal. 4:19; and Phil. 3:10,21.
[38]Cf. Käsemann, *op. cit.*, pp. 74ff. and 166f.
[39]Lohmeyer, "σὺν Χριστῷ"(1927), pp. 221ff.
[40]Cf. Käsemann, *op. cit.*, p. 167f.

Phil. 2:5ff., clearly advances the same religious-historical scheme that we meet in the Hellenistic εἰκών doctrine and in the Sophia myth linked to it.

Now it is maintained of the divine ἀπαύγασμα that it became flesh. Heb. 1:3 abruptly passes over the thought and points only to the outcome of this incarnation in the "purification of sins." In 5:5f. this stage of the way of Christ is dealt with more fully, and in striking analogy with Phil. 2:7f. In both instances, the incarnation is viewed as a humiliation. *The concrete description in Heb. 5:7 plainly appears as illustrative material for Phil. 2:8.* But in either case, the humiliation is seen especially as proof of Christ's obedience which derives from the divine saving will and serves the divine saving plan to realize obedience also in the world.[41] The καθαρισμὸς τῶν ἁμαρτιῶν or "restoration of the cosmos ruined by sin" has no other purpose than to establish obedience toward God in the world.[42] This is effected by the exemplary obedience of Christ extending even to his death, Christ who himself ἔμαθεν ἀφ' ὧν ἔπαθεν τὴν ὑπακοήν (5:8).

Heb. 10:5ff. bases this obedience of Jesus on a heavenly dialog between Christ and his Father before the incarnation. The extant parallels[43] indicate that this motif is likewise drawn from the framework of a traditional scheme. According to 10:5ff., the coming of the Son to do God's will is not only predicted in the Bible, but the

---

[41]Though in Heb. 5:9 the obedience of the redeemed results from Christ's obedience, whereas in Phil. 2:10 it is that of the entire cosmos.

[42]Windisch, p. 12.

[43]So *Barnabas* 14:6ff. presupposes the same dialog, likewise reconstructed from the Old Testament. In addition, Windisch in his commentary, supplement to Lietzmann's *Handbuch*, p. 380, refers to parallels in the *Ascension of Isaiah* 10:7ff. (H.-S., p. 659), and in the Naassene Psalm contained in Hippolytus' *The Refutation of All Heresies* 5:10 (H.-S., p. 807f.).

God who rejects gifts and sacrifices has to this end also prepared a σῶμα offered to him by Christ as a better and more perfect sacrifice. If the Son's consent to this activity of the Father illustrates the word in Phil. 2:6, that he "thought it not robbery to be like God" (KJV), then the motif of the offering of Christ's body, which also effects the redeemed's obedience to God, is further linked to the ἀποκατήλλαξεν ἐν τῷ σώματι τῆς σαρκὸς αὐτοῦ διὰ [65] τοῦ θανάτου[44] in Col. 1:22. Though we would not assume Hebrews' acquaintance with Phil. 2:5ff. or Col. 1:15ff., the same scheme is nevertheless apparent in all three passages. But this scheme can be so far described that it allows the divine εἰκών to be humbled, to become man, to learn obedience in suffering even unto death, and by this means to redeem the cosmos. In other words, *in each of the passages dealt with, the doctrine of the εἰκών that creates the world has its continuation in the scheme of the God-man who humbles himself, and thus in the scheme of the Gnostic* Anthropos marked by the two foci of incarnation and death. In Hebrews as in Philippians, these foci are held together by the motif of the obedience of the heavenly *Anthropos*, and in both instances effect the obedience of the redeemed or of the cosmos, a theme which Colossians for its part also expresses by means of the ἀποκαταλλάξαι. Philippians and Hebrews differ merely by the fact that in the one instance the effects of Christ's obedience are construed as cosmic, whereas in the other they are related to the community, and in the

---

[44]In addition, cf. the *Odes of Solomon* 41:11f.: "The Savior who gives life and does not reject ourselves. The Man who humbled himself, but was exalted because of his own righteousness. The Son of the Most High appeared in the perfection of His Father." Here too, then, appears that synthesis of Son, *Anthropos*, and Redeemer!

latter case construed in cultic fashion as a "purification of sins."

Finally, Col. 1:15 indicates how both variations are possible within the framework of the *Anthropos* doctrine. On the one hand, the whole *Pleroma* dwells in Christ bodily, and, on the other, he is head of the body, that is, the Church. In Heb. 1:2ff., Windisch finds a "synopsis of two natures," first, "of the heavenly Son of God, who as hypostasized divine Wisdom…and as possessor of the divine Word…was mediator of creation and rules the created order through all time," and second, "of a man who (such as Hercules) has performed a work on earth and in return has been exalted above the angels."[45] This observation is not altogether unjustified due to the fact that the εἰκών doctrine and the *Anthropos* scheme are combined. But we miss the actual state of affairs totally when we cite, say, Hercules as example or refer to an adoptionist Christology. The combination just noted was long since achieved in the New Testament as well as in Gnosticism, and it now marks the various stages of the way of Christ. And since the *Anthropos* is not just any sort of man, but the God-man, there are no material hindrances to this combination into a unified whole. Quite the contrary, precisely in this way the unity within the stages of Christ's way are clearest to Hellenistic readers of the epistle.

[66]

In addition, Hebrews carries through the scheme of the *Anthropos* myth by allowing Christ's exaltation to follow directly upon his humiliation, without regard for the resurrection, or better, by including it in the ascen-

---

[45]Windisch, p. 12f.

sion,[46] which also corresponds to the parallels in Phil. 2:5ff. and Col. 1:15.[47]

What was stated earlier concerning Christ's enthronement and the proclamation of his sonship before the heavenly powers now takes on coloration. *The enthronement is an integral part of the* Anthropos *doctrine*, as it appears in the New Testament not only in Philippians 2 but also in 1 Tim. 3:16. The ὤφθη ἀγγέλοις in the latter little hymn can only be understood as the presentation before the angels denoted by the εἰσάγειν in Hebrews 1.[48] And just as in Hebrews 1, a proclamation is attached to it: ἐκηρύχθη ἐν ἔθνεσιν. If its content is not given in more detail here, we learn of it from Philo and Hebrews, since both refer to the conferring of a title which Christ receives from God.

In antiquity, the name denotes a person's status and nature, for which reason a change of name involves the attainment of a new status. This also applies to the exalted Christ. *The title conferred on him confirms the conclusion of his humiliation and his new heavenly position of authority.* Hence it is not accidental that in Phil. 2:9, it is preceded by a ὑπερύψωσεν and in Heb. 5:4 by a τελειωθείς.[49] Where God himself proclaims Jesus' new name within the heavenly throne assembly, there

---

[46]On the basis of 13:20, Michel, p. 232, disputes the suppression of the doctrine of resurrection in Hebrews. But the ἀνάγειν ἐκ νεκρῶν simply indicates that the redemption in the ascension is viewed as following immediately upon Jesus' death, that the resurrection is thus almost absorbed by the ascension.

[47]What was just said of Heb. 13:20 applies to the πρωτότοκος ἐκ νεκρῶν in Col. 1:18.

[48]Revelation 5 also contains features of the divine enthronement and the proclamation of Christ's sonship before the angels.

[49]Lohmeyer, *Kyrios Jesus*, p. 78, n. 1, sees the concept of Jesus' heavenly *doxa* in the δοξάζειν of Heb. 5:5.

τελείωσις or δόξα has won a place which the earthly
[67] *Anthropos* did not yet share. And only by way of humiliation could Christ share in the newly won perfection and
doxa,[50] as the διό in Phil. 2:9 and the ἐγένετο αἴτιος
σωτηρίας of Heb. 5:9 suggest. Of course, to what extent
this perfecting of Christ implies a position of power sur-
passing his preexistent status can only be fully recognized
from a more precise treatment of the new name. To begin
with, we must be content to state that the name proclaimed by God himself in the midst of the heavenly
throne assembly represents a mystery, which is not at all
immediately intelligible to the entire world.[51] Only the
one who in some fashion shares in that heavenly world
can understand the name of the exalted One in its entire-
ty. When he is revealed to the angels, then it takes place in
the presence of the μέτοχοι of Christ (1:9). When, according to Phil. 2:11, every tongue will confess the name
"Kyrios," then this is not on any day in history, but on
that eschatological date of the parousia as the universal
and public manifestation of the world ruler. But if in Philippians, as in Hebrews, this name is already given to the
Christian community today, then with that name the
community is given a divine revelation and, so to speak,
caught up into the heavenly proclamation. Thus Christians, like the angels, are called the μέτοχοι of Jesus

---

[50]Windisch, p. 15, gives a moral twist to this set of circumstances when he
calls Jesus' apotheosis the "reward for Christ's rectitude during his earthly
sojourn."

[51]The idea is beautifully explained in the *Acts of Thomas* (Bonnet II, 276;
H.-S., p. 528), where in answer to his question concerning Jesus' name,
Misdaios is told that in this time he cannot yet bear Jesus' true name, but
only the name given him now and for this time: Jesus Christ. According to
the *Extracts of Theodotus* 26:1, the ἀόρατον of Jesus is the name of "the
only begotten Son."

(3:14). Whoever knows and confesses Christ's heavenly name is a member of his body, is in the Holy Spirit,[52] and is a candidate for the new heavenly name.[53]

Conversely, it is already part of Christ's exalted fulness of power that his heavenly name is not only known to angelic powers but also to the redeemed earthly community. Lohmeyer[54] has correctly pointed to the correspondence between this new name and the form of the appearance of the preexistent one. But he obscures the actual state of affairs with the categories of modern philosophy. "Thus," he writes, "the name takes on a dual function: It is the totally universal, the innermost heart of a form. It is such as its word and spirit, and at the same [68] time it embraces what is external and particular in this reality, through which it alone exists." But it is actually still the case that Christ's nature as εἰκών is hidden within the Godhead, and that it was unknown even to the angelic powers. On the other hand, through the heavenly bestowal of the name his nature appears in the clarity of an eschatological revelation. If this bestowal is first of all declared only to angels and the redeemed community, one day it will be disclosed to the whole world at the parousia. But since it already began to be manifest, Christ is already operative in the cosmos today as an eschatological reality and power.

Nor has this fact emerged with sufficient clarity for Windisch, when he speaks of an "insoluble tension be-

---

[52] 1 Cor. 12:3
[53] Cf. Rev. 2:17.
[54] Lohmeyer, *Kyrios Jesus*, p. 52.

tween preexistence and exaltation Christology."[55] Not only is the preexistent one as εἰκών directed toward his enthronement—as conversely the enthronement establishes the preexistent one as the true εἰκών of God—but since Jesus' enthronement represents the public declaration of his eternal significance, it also actualizes the true glory of the Christ, whose significance would remain a mystery purely on the basis of his character as εἰκών. Thus we further obstruct access to the inner drama of the way of Christ when we begin by subsuming Jesus' preexistence, earthly appearance, and postexistence under the generic term of sonship. In that case, the τελείωσις given with the exaltation must also be reinterpreted in moral terms. That such procedure is inadmissible is clear from the fact that the way of Christ envisions yet a final stage which is not at all ethically based, but rather completes the eschatology already begun.

At the parousia, the Son's presentation before the angels or the redeemed community must and will be followed by his presentation before the entire cosmos. This presentation holds in prospect the πάλιν εἰσάγειν τὸν πρωτότοκον εἰς τὴν οἰκουμένην of Heb. 1:6. It is perplexing, of course, that its significance is seen in the *proskynēsis* (1:6) of all the angels of God. For as early as at his exaltation Christ is introduced to the angels. So we will have to put the stress on the angels' *proskynēsis*, not on their new giving of the name. But this *proskynēsis* will be performed by the angels as the supreme representatives of the entire creation.[56] In this sense the motif clearly belongs to the scheme of the *Anthropos* doctrine,

---

[55]Windisch, p. 12.

[56]In addition cf. the parallels in Rev. 5:8ff., while Rev. 14:6f., similar to Phil. 2:11, awaits the *proskynēsis* of the entire world.

and in fact as its crowning conclusion.[57] A. Seeberg has al-   [69]
ready pointed to the striking parallel in the *Ascension of
Isaiah* 11:23, which of course applies to the Redeemer
rising victoriously to heaven: "...and all the angels of the
firmament and the Satan saw him, and they worshipped
him."[58] According to Lohmeyer's interpretation,[59] the
ἐπιστεύθη ἐν κόσμῳ in 1 Tim. 3:16 comes even closer to
the situation in Heb. 1:6, insofar as in this passage the
same event is obviously linked to the datum of the
parousia. Finally, it is absolutely clear in Phil. 2:11 that
*the universal and cosmic homage concludes the Christ
drama based on the* Anthropos *doctrine.* At the same
time, the inference to be drawn from the term
καταχθονίων, as well as from the passage cited by
Seeberg, is that in the original scheme special stress was
laid on the subjection of the demonic powers. This is also
documented in the *Odes of Solomon* 23:17ff.: "...and
hence all regions were gathered together. And there was
seen at its head, the head which was revealed, even the
Son of Truth from the Most High Father. And He inher-
ited and possessed everything, and then the scheme of the
many ceased. Then all the seducers became headstrong
and fled. And the persecutors became extinct and were
blotted out." It may still be possible to see in Heb. 1:13 a

---

[57]Unfortunately, it is this very aspect which J. Horst in his volume
Proskynein (1932), p. 250, has not set forth with sufficient clarity. But what
he hints at is important, that is, that the invocation of the deity forms a component part of the angels' homage; cf. p. 193. May we infer from this that
Heb. 1:8-13 is the epiclesis that concludes the act of enthronement?
[58]Cf. Seeberg, p. 15 (H.-S., p. 662). If in this passage homage is already paid
the one ascending, then it is because in Gnosticism the Redeemer's ascension
is in part already construed as concluding the redemptive drama; cf. the parallels in Schlier, *Religionsgeschichtliche Untersuchungen*, pp. 17ff.
[59]Lohmeyer, *Kyrios Jesus*, p. 63, n. 1.

reminiscence of this situation,[60] more frequently attested to in Gnosticism[61] where God's enemies shall be made a footstool for Christ's feet. In any event, this final *proskynēsis* actually denotes the public assumption of that world dominion already awarded to Christ at his exaltation in the presence of the heavenly throne assembly, an exaltation comparable to apotheosis. Apotheosis and world dominion in any case correspond in Hellenistic thought. But in addition, the series of quotations cited in Heb. 1:8ff. expressly sets Christ forth as king of the worlds.[62]

[70]   *In Hebrews 1, therefore, a way of Christ has been disclosed which advances by degrees*: What Jesus as the divine εἰκών possessed as claimant, and as though in hiddenness within the Godhead, he has legitimately acquired on earth through humiliation in his obedient suffering unto death. Following his ascension in the presence of the angels about the throne and the redeemed community, it has been solemnly awarded him by God's proclamation and, as touching his lordship over the heavenly powers and the redeemed community, has already been realized. At the parousia it will become visible to every eye and will find its conclusion and unlimited recognition in a universal and cosmic *proskynēsis*. With this portrayal of the way of Christ, Hebrews 1 falls within the

---

[60]This motif, transferred from the Redeemer to the one redeemed identical to him, appears in the *Odes of Solomon* 29:8. The one redeemed receives "the scepter of His power" that "I might subdue the devices of the Gentiles, and humble the power of the mighty."

[61]Thus also Michel, p. 29.

[62]But we will hardly dare concede the question put by Schlier, *TDNT* II, 472, whether perhaps the inference to be drawn from the use of Psalm 45, a wedding psalm, in 1:9 is that here, just as in Rev. 19:7 and 21:9f., the Son's exaltation introduces the Messiah's marriage to the heavenly community.

context of a broadly pervasive scheme, also expressed in Phil. 2:5ff., Col. 1:15ff., and 1 Tim. 3:16, and which in respect of its content is to be described as the scheme of the Gnostic *anthropos* doctrine. In any event, as the New Testament parallels indicate, Hebrews is not the creator of this tradition. But since all the New Testament passages complement each other and are fully intelligible only from Gnostic analogies, the Gnostic myth is to be regarded as source for the *anthropos* scheme in Hebrews 1, as is already the case with Phil. 2:5ff., Col. 1:15ff., and 1 Tim. 3:16.

Finally, *comparison with the portrayal of the Metatron figure in Third Enoch* should make clear that this tracing of the Christology of Hebrews 1 to the tradition of the Gnostic myth can also be justified chronologically. If in a number of passages[63] Metatron is identified with the "prince of the world" already present at creation, the *Urmensch* idea also occasionally appears in connection with Enoch.[64] The abundance of detail with which the act of Enoch-Metatron's heavenly enthronement is told following his ascent to the divine throne room is of decisive importance within the framework of the whole. Just as in Hebrews 1, all the angels are assembled to receive the divine proclamation recited by a herald. God himself builds Metatron a throne surpassed only by that of his majesty.[65] A metamorphosis invests the ascended one with a heavenly *doxa* that overshadows [71] even the angels.[66] In Odeberg's translation, the proclamation reads: "This is Metatron, my servant. I have made

---

[63]Cf. 3:1; 9:1; 14:1; 38:3; and Odeberg on these passages.
[64]Cf. 9:1; 48C, 1:5, and Odeberg, I, pp. 83, 122, and II, p. 25f.
[65]Chapter 10:1; 48C, 1f.
[66]Chapter 8:2; 9:ff.; 48C, 1f.

him into a prince and a ruler over all the princes of my kingdoms and over all the children of heaven except the eight great princes."[67] Like the angels, world dominions are also subject to him, dominions into whose mysteries he is initiated.[68] He receives the key to heaven[69] and, especially significant, he receives a new heavenly name which sets him in closest proximity to God and in the highest position of honor conceivable, that of "the little Yahweh."[70] The act of enthronement closes with the *proskynēsis* of all the angelic powers before Metatron portrayed as king of the world, with special mention being given the homage of the angels who represent the elemental powers.[71] From now on, Metatron utters all those words and commands of God by which the world is governed.[72] The parallelism of this scheme with that of Hebrews is unmistakable. What renders this fact so remarkable is, first of all, the dating of the central portions in Chapters 9-13 and 48:3,5,7-9 within the first century after Christ—a dating clearly established by Odeberg[73]—and, secondly, the origin of these portions in orthodox Judaism, albeit concerned with esoteric doctrines. Both facts set this tradition in immediate proximity to Hebrews. They indicate the possibility of Gnostic influence on Hebrews, both with regard to chronology and place of origin, thus coinciding with our examination of its

---

[67]Chapter 10:3f.
[68]Chapter 10:4; 48C, 7.
[69]Chapter 48C, 3. This function reaches over into the concept of the ἀρχηγός to be dealt with later.
[70]Chapter 12:5, 48C, 2.
[71]Chapter 14.
[72]Chapter 48C, 9. Thus Metatron is described as the revelation of God, as his name also makes clear.
[73]Cf. Odeberg I, pp. 79, 188.

content, which had achieved the same result. At any rate, in view of the Christology of Hebrews 1, we will no longer dare assert that "the myth of the Son of Man is scarcely of influence in Hebrews."[74]

3. The "Son" Title and its Significance

In Hebrews, Christ's present and future significance is linked to the title of "Son." The modification of this ὄνομα over against Phil. 2:11 is striking. But a relationship between "Son" and "Kyrios" cannot be denied insofar as at the parousia the Son will be worshiped as King of the worlds. Thus, while Philippians 2 appears more interested in the datum of the parousia and its cosmic revelation, Hebrews 1 gives greater attention to Christ's presence and his relation to the redeemed community.   [72]

In this connection it should be noted that according to Chapter 2, the community receives the name υἱοί (cf. 2:10ff.). This means that *as Christ is the Son, he is such principally in relationship to the sons.* In other words, he is Son as πρωτότοκος (cf. 1:6). Col. 1:18 further clarifies this situation: ὅς ἐστιν ἀρχή, πρωτότοκος ἐκ τῶν νεκρῶν, ἵνα γένηται ἐν πᾶσιν αὐτὸς πρωτεύων· A passage from Philo belongs within the same framework. There it is stated first of all that "they who live in the knowledge of the One are rightly called sons of God." It is further stated that "if there be any as yet unfit to be called a son of God, let him press...κοσμεῖσθαι κατὰ τὸν πρωτόγονον αὐτοῦ λόγον, τὸν ἀγγέλων πρεσβύτατον, ὡς ἄν ἀρχάγγελον, πολυώνυμον ὑπάρχοντα· καὶ γὰρ ἀρχὴ καὶ ὄνομα θεοῦ καὶ λόγος καὶ ὁ κατ᾽ εἰκόνα ἄνθρωπος

---

[74]Windisch, p. 13.

καὶ ὁ ὁρῶν, Ἰσραήλ, προσαγορεύεται."[75] This passage is significant not only because of the tradition transmitted in it, a tradition according to which the figure of Sophia,[76] the *Urmensch* εἰκών, the Redeemer-Logos, the ὄνομα θεοῦ, and thus quite obviously the υἱός,[77] conjoin and consequently furnish the most beautiful analogy from the pre-Christian period to the scheme in Col. 1:15 and Hebrews 1. Far more, this passage demonstrates that the "Son" title in fact belongs only to the Redeemer-Logos who, for this reason, is called πρωτόγονος, and also that the Gnostics as the redeemed share in it in merely derived fashion. Due to this latter circumstance, the Logos here is called the ἀρχή—just as Christ in Col. 1:18—and in fact the πρωτόγονος, corresponding to the πρωτότοκος in Col. 1:18. Accordingly, the ἐκ τῶν νεκρῶν in the Colossians passage is a Christian interpretation of the original Gnostic title of the "firstborn."[78] So even the ἵνα γένηται ἐν πᾶσιν αὐτὸς πρωτεύων, which appears without modifier in Col. 1:18, establishes "the first" as an independent title. The title "firstborn" in Heb. 1:6,

---

[75]*On the Confusion of Tongues* 145f.: "...To take his place under God's Firstborn, the Word, who holds the eldership among the angels, their ruler as it were. And many names are his, for he is called, 'the Beginning' and the Name of God, and His Word, and the Man after His image and 'he that sees,' that is, Israel."

[76]Schlier, *Christus und die Kirche*, p. 62, connects the πολυποίκιλος of Eph. 3:10 with πολύμορφος, and by so doing gives evidence of a typical epithet for God's Aeon and the Sophia identical to it. The examples given there allow us to identify these attributes with the term πολυώνυμος that appears here in Philo.

[77]It should be noted that in this context the divine name simply means "Son."

[78]A "mystical" note is no doubt perceptible in the ἐκ τῶν νεκρῶν. The "dead" are those who have really died, but they are also all souls to the extent they are still imprisoned in the material world. Bodily death is the final coming to a crisis of the "spiritual." Christ brings both to an end as risen and ascending Redeemer.

identical to υἱός, is likewise to be understood from this perspective.

Christid is "firstborn" as Lord and ἀρχηγός (cf. 2:10) of [73] *the redeemed community.* And this should be understood from the context of the Gnostic myth that determines Hebrews 1 throughout and interprets Jesus' title here and elsewhere: In him the event of redemption is conceived as *anagennēsis.* The ἐγὼ σήμερον γεγέννηκά σε quoted in Heb. 1:5 from Ps. 2:7 gives weight to this conception: Christ's exaltation as the τελείωσις of Jesus represents the first begetting from God, to be followed by others with the perfecting of the redeemed. As he, the εἰκών, was marked for this goal of sonship and thus is proleptically named "Son" prior to his exaltation, so they, the redeemed, likewise in view of their certain perfection, are already "sons." The ἀρχή led the way; those who were once νεκροί on earth (cf. 2:14f.) follow the "firstborn."

Thus the title υἱός, which the exalted Christ receives in heaven, does not only characterize his relationship to the Father or the angels. He is also "Son" as firstborn and head of his redeemed community.[79] This point is so important to Hebrews that it opens the treatment of its theme of the wandering people of God with it. Only on the basis of this datum will Hebrews be able to prove that salvation is certain and the attainment of the goal guaranteed to God's wandering people, provided they do not allow themselves to be overcome by weariness. Hebrews 1 is the key passage from which an ever new παράκλησις or παρρησία enters the earthly tedium of the communi-

---

[79]Likewise Büchsel, *Die Christologie des Hebräerbriefes,* p. 5.

ty. All further exposition till 10:8 will merely unfold the topic of Christ as firstborn Son and its significance for the sons already redeemed but not yet perfected.

First of all, the proclamation of Jesus' sonship denotes the beginning of his lordship over the "sons." This harmonizes perfectly with the idea that beyond this stage still lies the parousia, at which the Lord of the redeemed will then be revealed as King of the worlds. Again, the Gnostic myth has helped to clarify a decisive, in fact the final, point that awaits interpretation. *Permit us to cite a few examples from the abundance of Gnostic testimony to* [74] *the Redeemer's title as "Son."*[80] In so doing, we omit from the outset the use of this title which has often paled to a formula and become stereotyped under Christian influence. Of importance here are only such passages that also assume a heavenly conferring of the title and in addition allow us to see the original characteristic of the Son as "firstborn."[81]

Thus it is stated in the *Extracts of Theodotus* 33:1: υἱόθετος μέντοι γέγονεν ὁ Χριστός ὡς πρὸς τὰ πληρώματα ἐκλεκτὸς γενόμενος καὶ πρωτότοκος τῶν ἐνθάδε πραγμάτων.[82] If the reference here is to an appointment to sonship in view of Christ's heavenly elec-

---

[80]Cf. especially the *Odes of Solomon* or the *Ginza* 91,7ff., and the *Johannes-Buch* 168,6ff. The correspondence between the Son and the sons in the *Shepherd of Hermas*, Sim. IX, 12-16, is especially pronounced. There the believer is continually described as one who bears the name son of God. Further, the Son of God is also the *eikon* who created and preserved the world.

[81]Norden, *Die Geburt des Kindes* (1924), p. 128, already drew attention to the fact that Horus is greeted in the heavenly throne assembly as "Son of Isis and heir of Osiris."

[82]ET: "Indeed, Christ was made an adopted Son, since he was elect with regard to the perfected beings, and firstborn of the creatures there."

tion, it also embraces a relationship to all the heavenly "family." The doxology in the *Acts of John* expresses this more clearly:[83] δοξάζομέν σου τὸ λεχθὲν ὑπὸ τοῦ πατρὸς ὄνομα. δοξάζομέν σου τὸ λεχθὲν διὰ υἱοῦ ὄνομα. δοξάζομέν σου τὴν εἴσοδον τῆς θύρας. This assumes the divine announcement of the Christ title, describes this name as "Son," and in that sonship also gives to the redeemed entry through the heavenly gate. If Jacob is addressed as "my firstborn" in 3 Enoch 44:10, then this title matches that of Abraham as "my beloved" or of Isaac as "my elect one" in the very same passage and has its explanation in the fact that the patriarchs are viewed here as heads of their generation.[84] Finally, in the *Odes of Solomon* 36:2ff., we meet with transference of the motif to the redeemed: "...where I continued glorifying (Him) by the composition of His Odes. (The Spirit) brought me forth before the Lord's face and because I was the Son of Man, I was named the Light, the Son of God; because I was the most glorified among the glorious ones, and the greatest among the great ones." Accordingly, attainment to the rank of Son takes place as a birth in the assembly of the glorious ones, the angels.[85] But since the title of Son or firstborn describes his relation to the divine world, it directly raises the question of the relation between the Redeemer and the redeemed, now further pursued in Heb. 2:5ff.

---

[83]*Acts of John* 109 (Bonnet I, 207; H.-S., p. 255.): "We glorify thy name that was spoken by the Father; we glorify thy name that was spoken through the Son. We glorify thine entering of the Door."

[84]Cf. *3 Enoch* 45:3.

[85]We venture the observation that by this time a series of parallels clearly fixes the role of the angels in Hebrews 1. In every instance they function as the heavenly court and only as such.

[75] B. The Relation of the Son to the Sons in Hebrews 2:5—3:6

Hebrews 2:5ff. deals thematically with the problem of the relation of the Son to the sons already signaled in Chapter 1. The term ἄνθρωπος or υἱὸς ἀνθρώπου which appears in the quotation from Psalm 8 furnishes the starting point for this treatment. The decisive question concerning this term is: *Does it from the outset and in the fullest sense denote the messianic Son of Man* or does it in the first instance denote simply "man," just as in the Hebrew text?

1. Kögel's Interpretation

In the essay already cited, J. Kögel pursued this question in a manner that was especially thorough and is still instructive today. He concludes that "we are to think of man as such, but at the same time are not to ignore the further connection with the Son of Man κατ᾽ ἐξοχήν.... The Son and the sons belong together and are dependent on each other."[86] Kögel does not merely support this view—according to which we are at once led from earthly man first denoted by the term to the Messiah as the "preeminent type of the human race"—from the original Old Testament text of the quotation.[87] Where a purely messianic interpretation is concerned, he also requires a sharper distinction between the humiliation in verse 7a and the exaltation in verse 7b, since in this passage two

---

[86]Kögel, *Der Sohn*, p. 22. Similarly Riggenbach, p. 37f.; Seeberg, p. 18f., and Loew, *Der Glaubensweg des Neues Bundes* (1931), p. 24.
[87]Kögel, *ibid.*, p. 22f.

temporarily successive stages are marked off from each other. This is not necessary where *Anthropos* would first of all be construed as "man" in general, for, just as in the Old Testament Psalm, this term may also be examined for its varying position toward the material or transcendental world.[88] On the basis of this exegesis, Kögel thinks he sees verse 8b as a proper and harmonious transition to Christology. In his opinion, however, the advocate of an interpretation which is from the outset Christologically oriented must regard this phrase as an abrupt objection raised by the author on behalf of the readers themselves, but which does damage to the unity of the argument.[89] "The heavy accent on the name of Jesus (in v. 9), singled out by its position in the sentence, proves there can have been no previous reference to him. Otherwise, it would amount to a plerophoric, solemn repetition."[90] On the other hand, for Kögel there is no hiatus between the anthropology expressed to this point [76] and the Christology just beginning to emerge, insofar as it is precisely in Christ that the glory promised to humankind achieves fulfillment. Though this fulfillment may first be realized in a merely figurative sense, that is, in and for Jesus, it is nonetheless realized in fact, since, following his humiliation, Jesus is the representative of the human race.[91] As "the humiliated One" he now becomes "the exalted One,"[92] which raises not only the problem of the context but also of the entire letter.[93] At this point it

---

[88]*Ibid.*, p. 29.
[89]*Ibid.*, p. 32.
[90]*Ibid.*, p. 33.
[91]*Ibid.*, p. 34.
[92]*Ibid.*, p. 38.
[93]*Ibid.*, p. 39.

must still be proved "that it was the very humility and sufferings of death that opened to Jesus his glory."[94]

The consistency of this exegesis is as much to be admired as is its keen grasp of the formulation of the question that governs the text. Actually, the entire Christology of the section rests on the statement that Christ as the humiliated one is at the same time the exalted one. Kögel interprets and establishes this key motif in pertinent and thoroughly appropriate fashion. *And yet the route to this result is inadmissible, as more precise criticism shows.*

The meaning of the Old Testament Psalm does not suffice as proof. Even according to Kögel's exegesis, Hebrews radically disregards it. It simply cannot be proved from the Old Testament Psalm that the humiliated one is the exalted one. This paradox emerges only from that Son of Man speculation which Kögel for that reason immediately inserts into his investigation. But he still does not take note of its full significance, and he cannot because he is unaware of its religious-historical connection with the *Urmensch* doctrine. In this doctrine the basis is laid for all those assertions that the humiliated one is identical to the exalted one, that the one in need of redemption is identical to the Redeemer.[95]

Once we are aware of this, however, it is needless to draw a sharper contrast in the wording of verse 7 as fixed by the quotation. We cannot even speak of a real contradiction within the myth, because in it the humiliation and the exaltation of the *Urmensch* are only stages on his way. Further, Kögel wrongly assumes an antithesis in

---

[94]*Ibid.*, p. 41.
[95]Cf. in addition Käsemann, *Leib und Leib Christi*, pp. 66ff.

verse 8b. While he notes only the alleged contrast between humiliation and exaltation, in the public taking
possession of all things and the universal *proskynēsis*
linked to it, Chapter 1 has already indicated a further
stage on the Redeemer's way. Now, if verse 8b should
turn on this further stage, then of course the Son of Man's   [77]
exaltation may already have taken place. But just as in
Chapter 1 the subjection of all things occurs only in the
eschatological future, so at the present time the fulfillment of the Psalm quotation on this point is yet to come.
Hebrew 2:5 indicates that verse 8b really does turn on
this further stage. To a degree, the angels share the state
of Christ's exaltation; they are nevertheless subordinate
to the future heir of the world already declared as such in
his announcement as Son.

The thought of the text is thus clear and consistent:
*The humiliated is now the exalted one, but the exalted
one shall be ruler of the world. His world dominion, however, cannot yet be seen, but only its presupposition, that
is, Jesus' exaltation.* Thus verse 9 does not represent a
plerophoric repetition of earlier utterances, and the reason for emphasizing the name of Jesus likewise becomes
clear. It is not the future ruler of the world who can be
seen, but the "man" Jesus who in the historical past of his
life was for a time made lower than the angelic powers,
yet who is crowned with glory and honor in the present
because of his suffering death.

Kögel's refutation of a purely Christologically
oriented exegesis of 2:5 collapses with the assumption—
established on the basis of Chapter 1—that Hebrews is
aware of the myth of the *Urmensch. Even beyond this
point it can be shown to be fragile and untenable.* It can be
maintained only on the basis of that totally inadmissible

view of Jesus as the "preeminent type of the human race." Nowhere in the New Testament is Jesus set on the same level with us in such fashion. Hence, nowhere is the result of his life and death transferred to us because he is a type of our race. And the Son of Man is not at all a representative of our world, but of the divine. Humankind may be included in the saving work of the Son of Man only where, in wake of the myth, we understand the *Urmensch* as representative of those heavenly particles which have fallen and are in need of redemption. But Kögel is still not aware of this myth and takes a leap εἰς ἄλλο γένος, seduced by a reminiscence of the Son of Man title in the term "man." But if we cannot juggle the term ἄνθρωπος or υἱὸς ἀνθρώπου and apply it now to the earthly person, now to the Messiah, then the basis for Kögel's exegesis is removed. We must then decide for [78] one or the other, and can decide only for an exclusively Christological interpretation.[96] An insurmountable gap would otherwise yawn between the Old Testament citation and its Christological framework, and there would be no bridge from the *Anthropos* of the Psalm to the Christological scheme, the need for which Kögel had already conceded at the outset. This argument can be further supported by the fact that the promise of the subjected οἰκουμένη μέλλουσα (2:5), totally without meaning when applied to humankind, concerns only the *Urmensch*.

At this point we may insert the comment that *a messianic use of Psalm 8* is verified not only by Heb. 2:5ff., but

---

[96]Thus also Michel, p. 32; Strathmann, p. 70, and Lohmeyer, *Kyrios Jesus*, pp. 70ff. Incidentally, we reject the latter's thesis of a prehistoric temptation of Jesus as referred to in Heb. 12:2 and Phil. 2:5ff.

also by *3 Enoch* 5:10. In that passage, the ministering angels accuse humankind before God and in so doing cite Ps. 8:5, which according to Odeberg's translation is interpreted as follows: "Mah Adam is not written here, but 'Mah Enosh,' for he (Enosh) is the head of the idol worshippers." Thus, on the basis of the Hebrew wording, "man" or *enosh* is identified here with Enosh, an incarnation of the *Urmensch* well known in Gnosticism. But while Enosh is polemicized against in 3 Enoch 5:10, no damage is done the messianic interpretation of Psalm 8.[97] Rather, Enosh remains bearer of the *Urmensch* idea (though distorted into the demonic), clearly read into Psalm 8 by certain Jewish circles.

Finally, the total context of Heb. 2:5ff. is rendered intelligible on the basis of this *Urmensch* doctrine. It was already shown what good sense verses 8-9 make from that perspective. Further, it is only on the basis of the myth that light is shed on the relationship of the Son to the sons.[98] For emphasizing this aspect Kögel deserves special thanks: "The Son and the sons belong together";[99] "put paradoxically, just as humankind depends on Jesus, so he is dependent upon it, since his entire significance derives from the fact that as Redeemer he has the redeemed behind him."[100] This statement is appropriately based on the title of the Son in 2:10 as ἀρχηγὸς τῆς σωτηρίας. In addition, Jesus' perfecting is related to his [79]

---

[97]In fact, it may be just this polemic that proves that here *3 Enoch* is attempting to divert to the *Urmensch* an interpretation of Psalm 8 already in circulation, and to refute it by opposing Adam, the first *Urmensch*, to Enosh as head of idol worshipers, and thus as a false Messiah.

[98]As the following investigation will show in detail, Windisch incorrectly denies that this phrase marks the central theme of our chapter; cf. p. 21.

[99]Kögel, p. 44.

[100]*Ibid*.

status as ἀρχηγός:[101] " By the fact that the ἀρχηγός was advanced and attained his goal, the sons, dependent upon him as his own, were in turn led toward their destiny."[102] But here, too, Kögel cannot establish his legitimate observations and conclusions on a historically appropriate understanding of the text. For he is not able to show on the basis of what quality humankind shares the saving work of Christ. It is certainly not on the basis of its sheer humanity, since not all acknowledge Christ as ἀρχηγός. Conversely, Loew[103] quite rightly accents the terms "everyone and everything" that are continually repeated in verses 8-10, and which thrust the saving work out from isolation into world significance. Here too, then, faith is not referred to as the presupposition for the relation of the Son to the sons, no matter how obvious it is from the entire message of the New Testament that only faith establishes this relationship.

The detailed analysis will solve these difficulties and in particular set forth the extent to which "Christ cannot remain for himself alone, but moves out from himself and turns toward those who as υἱοί also have the divine seal imprinted on their forehead."[104]

2. Christ as ἀρχηγός

Kögel already recognized the significance of the phrase ἀρχηγὸς τῆς σωτηρίας in 2:10 for our section. In fact, this phrase is an essential aid to the understanding of its immediate context as well as of Hebrews as a whole.

---

[101]*Ibid.*, p. 54.
[102]*Ibid.*, p. 55.
[103]Loew, *op. cit.*, p. 25.
[104]Kögel, p. 118.

Scholars undertook the interpretation of this phrase on the basis of the parallel form αἴτιος τῆς σωτηρίας[105] —altogether possible from the perspective of Hellenistic usage. In such usage, ἀρχηγός describes the hero and guardian of a city, or the originator and leader of a fellowship.[106] Without question, the αἴτιος of 5:9 is most intimately connected with the ἀρχηγός of 2:10. And yet it is advisable to ignore this connection at first, because under his αἴτιος-title Christ performs priestly functions which are not immediately identical with his saving work in Chapter 2. Likewise, we must certainly pay attention to *the formulation in 12:2*, according to which Christ appears as τῆς πίστεως ἀρχηγὸς καὶ τελειωτής. But it is totally misleading when Delling chooses to refer this first of all to the moral consequences of faith. He writes that [80] Christ, of course, is also ἀρχηγός since "as the first man, He gave an example of faith in God, that by His death He 'fulfilled' this faith in God's unconditional love and its overcoming of the barrier of sin, and that He thereby gave this love concrete and once-for-all actualisation in the history of salvation."[107]

In essence, this statement repeats Kögel's thesis, and Christ is interpreted as representative of humankind, which necessitates altering the text's soteriological utterances to ethical statements. But it is a huge misunderstanding to interpret Heb. 12:1ff. in ethical fashion. To the extent this passage refers to an ἀγών, it has far more to do with a historical than an ethical argument. So faith in Hebrews is not at all linked to the love of God that forgives sins, but rather to the attainment of the heavenly

---

[105]Riggenbach, p. 49, and Delling, *TDNT* I, 487f.
[106]Delling, *TDNT* I, 487.
[107]*Ibid.*, 488.

world and an attitude that transcends all ethics and overcomes the cosmos as such. Michel correctly stresses this
historical aspect when he compares the correspondence
of ἀρχηγός to τελειωτής with that of ἀρχή to τέλος,[108]
alluded to in Col. 1:18 and contained in the union of A
and Ω in Rev. 1:18.

If our discussion of the title of Jesus as "firstborn"
pointed to the connection between the Colossians
passage and Hebrews' use of the ἀρχηγός-title for
Christ, this fact now gives to the term τελειωτής intelligibility: In Christ the entire *plērōma* is so encompassed
that it comes to rest in him. In him the redemption and
completion of fallen creation is accomplished. Insofar as
the fallen creation must be redeemed and completed by
him, he is the "completer of faith." But his completing
action is not to be separated from his activity as ἀρχηγός;
it rather assumes it.[109] In no other way does Christ bring
redemption and completion than that he himself becomes
the πρωτεύων[110] who first sets out on the path from the
world of fall and death toward the sphere of completion
or the *plērōma*. There is no reason why the term
ἀρχηγός in 12:2, taken in this sense, should be understood differently from that in 2:10,[111] since the designation of Jesus as πρόδρομος in 6:20 expressly confirms this
sense.

[81]   This discussion has brought us again to the Gnostic
myth, just as it underlay Col. 1:15ff. Gyllenberg[112] al-

---

[108]Michel, p. 35.
[109]Cf. Schlatter, *Der Glaube im Neuen Testament*, p. 532, and Büchsel, *Die Christologie des Hebräerbriefes*, p. 64.
[110]Cf. Col. 1:18.
[111]So Riggenbach, p. 389.
[112]Gyllenberg, p. 671.

ready acknowledged this in fact when he construed the content of the ἀρχηγός-title according to Philo's formula of the ἀρχηγέτης νέας ἀνθρώπων σπορᾶς,[113] though he was inclined to find in it a mere description of the relation of the ancestor to his posterity. This formula of Philo no doubt is rooted in the context of the *Urmensch* myth, as further Gnostic parallels now confirm.

Thus the Adam identified with Hermes in the Naassene Psalm[114] is called ψυχαγωγὸς καὶ ψυχοπομπὸς καὶ ψυχῶν αἴτιος, paralleling the Christology of Hebrews, not only in the first, but also in the last title. Just as in the Mandaean literature the title of leader is conferred on the Redeemer,[115] so also in the *Odes of Solomon* 14:4, the believer entreats: "Stretch out to me, my Lord, at all times, thy right hand, to me a guide till the end...." Frequently, the name "conductor" or "companion of the way" appears in place of "Leader" without assuming another sense. The Redeemer knows the way only because he first took it; he alone knows this way, so that he himself is invoked as ὁδός and εἴσοδος τῆς θύρας.[116] Thus in the *Hermetica* the redeeming mystagogue is the καθοδηγός of those in need of redemption.[117] And in the *Acts of Thomas* the latter call upon the Redeemer as the συνοδοιπόρος in the land of error,[118] as the

---

[113]*On Abraham* 46: "Founder of a new race of men."
[114]Naassene Psalm 12, cited from Reitzenstein-Schaeder, *Studien zum antiken Synkretismus* (1926), pp. 161-173 [ET: "Leader and conductor and cause of souls"].
[115]Cf. Jokabar-Ziwa as guide in the *Johannes-Buch*, p. 220, 7ff.; cf. in addition the parallels on 90 ff. above.
[116]Cf. *Acts of John* 109 (Bonnet I, 207f.; H.-S., p. 255).
[117]*Hermetica* I, 29.
[118]*Acts of Thomas* 37 (Bonnet II, 155; H.-S., p. 464).

ὁδηγῶν καὶ εὐθύνων τοὺς εἰς αὐτὸν πιστεύοντας,[119] or in the *Acts of John* as the one "who hast saved from the illusion of the present and guided me into that (life) which endureth for ever."[120] This motif emerges even more clearly in the invocation: "A refuge and lodging of the weary who pass through (regions of darkness)...and thou didst ascend with great glory, and gathering all those who took refuge in thee thou didst prepare a way, and in thy footsteps they all journeyed whom thou didst redeem."[121] The following passage shows that the topic of the ἀγών may also be combined with this motif: ὁ ἐπαμύντωρ καὶ βοηθὸς ἐν ἀγῶνι τῶν ἰδίων δούλων... who in many battles dost fight for us and make us conquer in them all; ὁ ἀληθὴς ἀθλητὴς ἡμῶν καὶ ἀήττητος· ὁ στρατηλάτης ἡμῶν ὁ ἅγιος καὶ νικήφορος.[122]

Only where this mythical framework is recognized and may be assumed does the view of the Redeemer as leader of the redeemed (a view underlying Col. 1:18 as [82] well as the passage in Philo first cited) clearly appear, and the title ἀρχηγός in Hebrews now take on full color. Though Hellenistic sacral language may have coined the title,[123] it does not derive its sense in Hebrews 2 primarily from that language, but just as in *II Clement* 20:5,[124] from

---

[119]*Ibid.*, chapter 10 (Bonnet II, 114; H.-S., p. 447): "Who doth guide and direct those who believe in him."

[120]*Acts of John* 113 (Bonnet I, 213; H.-S., p. 257).

[121]*Acts of Thomas* 156 (Bonnet II, 265; H.-S., p. 524f.).

[122]*Ibid.*, chapter 39 (Bonnet II, 157; H.-S., p. 465): "The defender and helper of thine own servants in the fight...our true and invincible champion, our holy and victorious commander."

[123]In this sense it appears in Acts 3:15 and 5:31.

[124]σωτὴρ καὶ ἀρχηγὸς τῆς ἀφθαρσίας ["Saviour and prince of immortality"].

Gnostic tradition. *Hence we must not construe* ἀρχηγός *after the terminology of the Hellenistic hero cults as "author," but simply as "leader,"*[125] *corresponding to the term* πρόδρομος *in 6:20.*

Now there is clear agreement between 2:10 and 12:2. If in the latter passage Christ's leadership is linked to faith, then this Christian modification derives from the connection with Chapter 11. This makes altogether good sense, since in that very chapter faith is described as a wandering. But as was indicated, the addition of the τελειωτής removes every last doubt as to the mythical origin of the formula. Finally, from this point a bridge is spanned to the αἴτιος τῆς σωτηρίας in 5:5. If Hellenistic sacral language paves the way for such a connection, then it is taken up again in Gnosticism, as the illustration from the Naassene Psalm indicates. Christ is αἴτιος insofar as he who is the beginning and the end of his community cares for it by reigning from heaven as high priest, and with the result that his community is drawn after him. It is characteristic of all these terms and titles for Jesus that we may not isolate the one from the other; one overlaps the other and all are encompassed and coordinated in the nature of the heavenly *Anthropos.*

3. *The Meaning of* τελειοῦν

We obtain further support for our conclusion from an investigation of the terms for completion in Hebrews. If the importance of this word group derives solely from its frequent use in the letter,[126] then the understanding of it to

---

[125]So also Schlatter, *Der Glaube im Neuen Testament,* p. 532.
[126]In the New Testament τελειοῦν occurs 23 times; in Hebrews 9 times. Apart from Luke 1:45 and Col. 3:14, τελείωσις, τελειότης, τελειωτής occur only here.

date has not at all been fixed through exegetical unanimity. In a separate treatise, *Der Begriff τελειοῦν im Hebräerbrief,*[127] J. Kögel set forth what follows as the central problem: "What is certainly most remarkable regarding the use of this concept is that it is connected with what applies to Jesus, and that something similar may be said of him. In this the Letter to the Hebrews is unique."[128] In other words, *how is it possible to assert that Jesus is not only "completer" but is himself "the completed one"* (cf. 2:10; 5:9; 7:28)? Kögel solves the problem by labelling the word group as ethically neutral, and treats the completing of the community and of Jesus as a mere matter of external development[129] which consists in the conferring of *doxa* as "fellowship with the Father."[130] For Kögel, however, Jesus' completion does not apply to him personally, but only to his "attribute as mediator of salvation": "Inherent in the idea of a leader is that he possesses those ahead of whom he marches."[131] Since the sons attained to *doxa*, Jesus himself arrived at his goal according to his "calling as leader."[132] And by the term ἁγιάζειν,[133] parallel with τελειοῦν in Hebrews, the intention is not to incarnate a moral but a religious idea: "To sanctify means to take up into the sphere of God's salvation, and being sanctified means nothing else and nothing more than to become God's possession."[134]

[83]

---

[127]Leipzig, 1905.
[128]*Ibid.*, p. 38.
[129]*Ibid.*, p. 62.
[130]*Ibid.*, p. 56.
[131]*Ibid.*, p. 61.
[132]*Ibid.*, p. 62.
[133]Cf. 2:11 and 10:14; the term is used in cultic fashion in 9:13; 10:10,29, and 13:12; ἁγιασμός appears in 12:14.
[134]Kögel, *op. cit.*, p. 58.

Michel takes another position: "The concept... describes neither a moral nor religious development, nor does it assume a Stoic-Philonic development, but it is the doctrine of justification cast in Old Testament cultic form. The presupposition and root of our group of ideas lie in the Old Testament Septuagint; their connections move over into Greek thought."[135] Michel writes that the possibility of a cultic nuancing of these terms is of course attested in the Old Testament as in Gnosticism, but miscarries in Hebrews at precisely the most signal passages such as 5:9 and 7:28. τέλειος rather denotes what is perfect in the Old Testament sense, "the right relationship of humankind to God," in which God's commandment is acknowledged and obedience performed.[136] If in the Old Testament the one who is perfect is contrasted with the μανθάνων, and thus in Heb. 5:11f. the perfect one is referred to as teacher in contrast to the νήπιοι, then in his earthly existence Jesus was a learner in the Old Testament sense and subsequently completed by God in regard to his person as well as his work.[137]

With this statement Michel also rejects the thesis of Windisch, who proceeds from a general definition of τελειοῦν as "bringing to a close or to maturity" as appears, for example, in 7:9; 9:9; 10:1,14 and 11:40, and from that point, particularly in 5:9 and 7:28, finds the idea of a "moral-religious development begun by God." But perhaps, writes Windisch, τελειοῦν may also be a term used in the mysteries for initiation, which may be [84] argued especially for the cultic passages in 9:9; 10:1,14

---

[135]Michel, p. 81.
[136]*Ibid.*, p. 139.
[137]*Ibid.*, p. 140.

and perhaps in 2:10, though not for 5:9 and 7:28: "The author then slides over from the one meaning to the other."[138]

The problem has thus been taken up from the most varied perspectives. No satisfactory solution has resulted. Michel to the contrary, *the antithesis of τέλειοι and νήπιοι in 5:14* already makes this clear. We do not solve the problem with the rabbinic contrast between student and teacher. The concept of teacher as the perfect one involves a fundamentally positive evaluation of the μανθάνων as on the way to perfection. But this positive evaluation is just as fundamentally ruled out by the context of 5:14. If, for example, this passage reprimanded merely tardy progress on the way of teaching, the danger of apostasy, indeed, the ἀνασταυροῦν and παραδειγματίζεσθαι (6:6) of Christ could never be so sharply accented. Though there may be a way toward perfection to be traversed, in light of this passage the community would already have to be at its goal. And yet it possesses the character of the φωτισθέντες who have tasted the heavenly gift and become partakers of the Holy Spirit (6:4). But this does not disclose a gradual progress within the this-worldly relation of student to teacher, *but the all but metaphysical contrast between a heavenly and an earthly type*, between the "enlightened" and the "ignorant." So also Christ advances from learner to one made perfect only by his entry into heaven (5:9; 7:28). Michel does not observe this metaphysical contrast sharply enough, and for this reason arrives at the contradictory assertion that Jesus remains a μανθάνων on earth while Christians may pass the stage of apprenticeship al-

---

[138]Windisch, p. 45.

ready in this life. But Michel's thesis regarding the influence on Hebrews of the Old Testament-rabbinic doctrine of perfection shatters on this contradiction. Rather,
in Hebrews, that one is perfect who attains to heaven or
shares in the heavenly gift while still on earth. If not, then
guilt and the danger of apostasy are at hand. Such a one
must then be asked whether the enlightenment has become ineffectual or even been frivolously abandoned.

We meet the same situation in the Gnostic idea of
τέλειος, likewise contrasted with the νήπιος or
ψυχικός who has not yet attained to solid food.[139] In
Gnosticism, of course, just as in Heb. 5:11f., this diasta-   [85]
sis is metaphysically conditioned, and the perfecting is
based on an "enlightenment," which leaves behind the
learning of elementary doctrines as a childhood stage.
Just as in Heb. 6:4 the perfected one is described as par-
taker of the Holy Spirit, so in Gnosticism such a one is
the pneumatic absolutely.

If Michel's interpretation of Jesus as μανθάνων in the
rabbinic sense collapses on the basis of 5:14, the inevita-
ble result of 7:28 is that we have as little leave to speak of
Jesus' moral development.[140] There is no moral gradation
between earthly priests surrounded by weakness and the
completed and eternal Son. Both are representatives of
different worlds, and at best are related to each as prototype to shadow. There is thus a metaphysical contrast
here also.   ˙

This contrast is not eliminated by the fact that over
against their master, who was completed only at his ascension, Jesus' disciples somehow share in the

---

[139]Cf. Preuschen-Bauer, col. 1295, and Schlier, *TDNT* I, 646.
[140]Contra Büchsel, *Die Christologie des Hebräerbriefes*, pp. 44, 56ff.

τελείωσις while still on earth. Not without reason,
Michel distinguishes perfection and completion.[141] If the
former is accessible to the disciples in this life, then it is
not in bodily fashion but only with respect to the gnosis
and enlightenment given them from heaven; bodily and
eternal completion await them only in heaven.

As the Mandaean literature already indicated,[142] *the
Gnostic myth offers precisely the same train of thought* in
bewildering variety. Among the Valentinians, the gathering of the parts of the *Urmensch* as the divine seed is
called τελειωθῆναι.[143] If according to Heb. 2:7 the completed Christ is crowned with *doxa* as the attribute of the
heavenly sphere, then, according to the *Odes of Solomon*
36:2, perfection and heavenly *doxa* unite when the Holy
Spirit sets the redeemed "on my feet in the Lord's high
place, before His perfection and glory." It is instructive
that according to 36:6 the Redeemer has anointed the redeemed "with His perfection; and I became one of those
who are near him." The τελειότης thus only enables access to the heavenly Man. It is further clear from this
[86]   passage that the myth not only speaks of a future completion,[144] but views the Gnostic as endowed with heavenly
power already in this life, thus as τέλειος. Just as in
Heb. 5:11f. and 6:4, so also in the *Odes of Solomon* 35:6,
the imparting of heavenly power occurs as it were
through a divine food: "I grew strong in His favor, and

---

[141]Cf. Michel's essay "Die Lehre von der christlichen Vollkommenheit nach
der Anschauung des Hebräerbriefes," *Theologische Studien und Kritiken*,
1934-1935, p. 350.
[142]Cf. pp. 90ff.; heaven is the "house of completion" toward which the soul
as "sharer of those made perfect" moves, and whose way he goes.
[143]Cf. Irenaeus, *Against Heresies* I, 7:1, and *passim*.
[144]On this feature, cf. in addition the *Odes of Solomon* 9:4: "And His purpose
is eternal life, and your perfection is incorruptible."

rested in His perfection." Put literally, this refers, as in Heb. 6:6, to enlightenment through the message of the mysteries: ὅσοι μὲν οὖν συνῆκαν τοῦ κηρύγματος καὶ ἐβαπτίσαντο τοῦ νοός, οὗτοι μετέσχον τῆς γνώσεως καὶ τέλειοι ἐγένοντο ἄνθρωποι.[145]

It was not our intention to sift through or refer to the entire mass of Gnostic materials. The purpose behind the few examples was merely to point out their connection with the use of terms previously identified in Hebrews. *And in this case we can no more speak of a moral development leading to completion than in the case of Heb. 7:28.* But the same is true even of Heb. 5:7ff., to which Windisch makes special appeal. The parallel in Phil. 2:7f. expresses it clearly: The heavenly *Anthropos* descends to earth as a sphere in which every knee does not yet bow to him in *proskynēsis*. It is not yet true that there is nothing ἀνυπότακτος to him (cf. Heb. 2:8); rather, he must himself bow in suffering here. This expresses the qualitative difference from his heavenly nature: Instead of lordship he must now practice obedience; he is set within earthly suffering instead of within the divine *doxa. Jesus' obedience is thus an attribute of his earthly nature.* It is not the enduring of a moral test, but a recognition of the plan of salvation and the mark of his humiliation that sets him on a level with the earthly community. While we may speak of a moral development or the enduring of a test only in a purely this-worldly sense, Jesus' obedience marks a stage of that way which leads from heaven to earth and back again, that is, his deepest humiliation. Conversely, the

---

[145]*Hermetica* 4:4 [ET: "As many then as understood the preaching and were baptized in the Mind, these became partakers in the Gnosis, and were made perfect men"].

τελειωθείς represents a renewed, qualitative alteration of existence in which the sphere of humiliation is left behind. That one is made complete who is returned to heaven, just as he comes from heaven. Obedience and completion are not two poles of an earthly development but two contrasting,[146] superimposed stages on the way of the [87] heavenly Man, as such called the ἀνὴρ τέλειος in Gnosticism.[147] This way no more ends with Jesus' ascension than it began with his obedience. The less a moral development was possible for the one who once was the likeness of the divine glory, the less it would explain the advance by which the one made complete becomes future king of the worlds.

Kögel thus properly and completely fractured the ethical interpretation of the concept of τελειοῦν. But since he was not yet aware of the myth of the ἀνὴρ τέλειος, he had to derive the concept from the secular use of the term τέλος and construe it "neutrally" as "leading to the goal." And yet he could maintain his thesis of a "universal concept without specific content"[148] only by subtly altering and shattering it. Counter to his own thesis, that is to say, under restraint of the text, he gave content to the alleged "universal concept" by tacitly and as though matter-of-factly substituting for the neutral "leading to the goal" the no longer neutral "leading to the heavenly goal." With this alteration Michel's concern "that the

---

[146]Use of the passive τελειωθείς already shatters the idea of moral development, just as the οὐχ ἑαυτὸν ἐδόξασεν of 5:5 excludes any autonomous behavior on the part of Jesus.

[147]In connection with 2:10; 5:9; and 7:28, Windisch, p. 45, already hypothesized on the Gnostic ἀνὴρ τέλειος; Lohmeyer, *Kyrios Jesus*, p. 78, carried through this hypothesis in consistent fashion.

[148]Kögel, *Der Begriff* τελειοῦν, p. 34. Similarly Riggenbach, p. 48, n. 21

biblical concepts always contain a concrete reference and for the most part are in contrast to Greek abstraction and Hellenistic formalism"[149] is in practice preserved. But for Gnosticism at least, the label "Hellenistic formalism" does not hold, precisely because its use of τελειοῦν, contrary to secular Greek usage, is marked by furnishing such concrete content.

Into the framework just drawn by our interpretation of the most disputed passages, 9:11; 11:40; and 12:23 may be directly inserted. In contrast to the earthly, the τελειοτέρα σκηνή is portrayed as a heavenly sanctuary.[150] Completion of the righteous, as well as of the Old Testament witnesses of faith, occurs through entry into heaven or through membership in the divine festal gathering. *Perfection and completion are thus allotted only to the heavenly creature.* For this reason, in 7:11 and 18 the possibility of creating τελείωσις must then be denied the Levitical priesthood of the Old Testament *nomos.* Yet the latter passages still deserve special attention because [88] they give notice of a new element for the investigation of our concept, which is then more clearly marked in 9:9; 10:1; and 14. *The cultic act of Christ's self-sacrifice effects the completion of his people* which the cultus of the first testament was unable to do. Cultus and perfection are thus connected here.[151]

This gives rise to a problem: If on the one hand Christ's completion and that of the "righteous ones" and Old Testament witnesses of faith is linked to their entry

---

[149]Michel, *Die Lehre von der christlichen Vollkommenheit*, p. 335.
[150]*Ibid.*, p. 354.
[151]Riggenbach, p. 350.

into heaven, on the other hand, through Jesus' self-sacrifice Christians are in some sense already made complete, despite their continuing sojourn on earth. It is clear from 10:4 that these two aspects are not antithetical. As *ἁγιαζόμενοι, but only as such, Christians are already made complete here and now*. What is meant by this term (cf. 2:11; 9:13; 10:10,14,19; and 13:12)? No doubt, in Hebrews it is used in exclusively cultic fashion. The sanctification of Christians is based upon Jesus' προσφορά (10:14) and his blood offered here (10:29 and 13:12). The meaning of the term ἁγιάζειν ought not be exhausted in the forgiveness of sins,[152] which of course is the first definition to be cited. As 2:11 shows with special clarity, the term is almost always used without modifier or further explanation, though the additional connotation of καθαρίζειν cannot be ignored. In any event, an ethical nuance may not be imposed on the term, since it does not describe a human attitude but the result of a cultic event. *So we will do best to render ἁγιάζειν "to consecrate."*[153] In this sense the concept is quite well known within the Hellenistic environment of Hebrews.[154] But in Hellenism every "consecration" aims at participation in the heavenly sphere of perfection, and in a real sense gives the right to it by introducing a change in human nature. Through consecration one becomes a member of the heavenly sphere even while still on earth.[155] But this always assumes

[89]

---

[152]"To sanctify" and "to purify" are parallel in 9:13f.; but according to 9:22f. and 10:2, "to purify" clearly keeps uppermost the act of cleansing from sins.
[153]Cf. Preuschen-Bauer, col. 12f.
[154]Cf. *ibid.*, and Reitzenstein, *Hellenistic Mystery Religions* (1978), p. 41. To undergo consecration makes one ὅσιος or ἅγιος. This use of the concept appears most clearly in 1 Cor. 6:11; 7:14; Eph. 5:26; and John 17:19.
[155]In *Hermetica* I, 32, all the quality of God-likeness inherent in the aeon title is in fact connected with this consecration: ὁ σὸς ἄνθρωπος συναγιάζειν

a final and comprehensive completion still to come, toward which one is in fact consecrated.

The use of certain terms in Hebrews is also to be understood from this perspective. *As leader, Christ is at the same time the completer of his community*: He leads the community toward the heavenly completion as their common goal. But since his own completion, this goal is no longer hidden from his own in distant and transcendent fashion. In the sacrifice of his body and blood he has obtained for them, while still on earth, some measure of participation in his completion, and has stood the test as perfecter. Thus 10:14 reads τετελείωκεν, and in 5:14 his own are addressed as τέλειοι. To be sure, Christians are recipients of the heavenly gift, partakers of the Holy Spirit (6:4), and share in perfection only through expectation of the entire and abiding possession of these blessings. They are thus ἁγιαζόμενοι, but only in a provisional way. *In other words, at the moment, their perfection consists solely of their connection with the ἁγιάζων*, that is, with the heavenly *Anthropos* (2:11). And this connection was effected through the sacrifice of his body and blood. It is thus founded upon a cultic act and, in the first instance, has nothing to do with moral perfection.

Now the exegesis of Hebrews 2 can be carried a step further. As guide, the heavenly Man in his earthly humiliation has begun to lead[156] many sons to the heavenly

---

σοὶ βούλεται καθὼς παρέδωκας αὐτῷ τὴν πᾶσαν ἐξουσίαν [ET: "Your Man would be holy as you are holy, even as you gave him your full authority"].

[156]Kögel, *Der Sohn*, p. 56; Riggenbach, p. 48; Windisch, p. 21 and Michel, p. 34, incorrectly refer the ἀγαγόντα to God. This might even be difficult from a purely grammatical point of view. We ought not fear a tautology with ἀρχηγόν since the participle is ingressive. Cf. Delling, *TDNT* I, 488, n. 1.

doxa.[157] Since he is thus the ἀρχηγός of his own toward their completion, he is also himself the object of God's τελειῶσαι. Thus, in Kögel's words, this completion actually affects him in his "character as mediator of salvation," and consequently corresponds to the completion of his own through him. What this completion consists of is clear from the entire context and especially from the εἰς δόξαν ἄγειν of the redeemed—it is, as in 5:9 and 7:28, the heavenly exaltation. But, as mediator of salvation, Christ could achieve completion only by way of suffering, for only in this way did he become the ἁγιάζων of his own, and only in this way did the ἁγιαζόμενοι receive a share in his completion. That Christ becomes ἁγιάζων is already part of his completion and corresponds to the divine decree which summoned him to lead. As the one who completes, he is consequently himself completed, and in fact he is both in his character as leader on the way to heaven. Kögel has correctly seen this fact without being able to anchor it in the text or its terminology in a sufficiently exegetical manner. *Both aspects can be fully explained only when we are aware of the myth of the* Urmensch, *in which the Redeemer, as guide to heaven and home of souls, himself returns home and is thus the "redeemed Redeemer,"* τελειωτής *and* τελειωθέις *alike.*

[90]

4. Brother and Children

B. Weiss is not in error when he sees in the contrast between the ἁγιάζων and ἁγιαζόμενοι "the specific dif-

---

[157]Thus, according to this passage, the completion is described as a way into the heavenly world of light, just as according to 2:7 the completed Christ was crowned with the splendor of heavenly light.

ference" between Jesus and his own.[158] Yet this sentence must be supplemented to read that, within that same contrast, the specific connection between the two is just as greatly accented. The context clearly emphasizes this latter aspect. Jesus, like his own, must be completed. In 2:10 many sons are set alongside the Son, and according to 2:11 he, like them, ultimately originates ἐξ ἑνός. It is quite misleading to construe this εἷς of Adam[159] or Abraham,[160] who are not mentioned at all. Since v. 11a intends to establish the fellowship between the Son and the sons, their lineage can only, without qualification, be derived from God[161] because only he is the Father of Jesus. There is good reason for resisting this conclusion, since the view that emerges here is in fact most unusual. It is far too bland and does the text no justice at all when we paraphrase it to read that the Redeemer and the redeemed had "their final determinate source and point of union," "the ultimate root of their inner as well as outer life," in God,[162] and that "in origin and plan of salvation" they derived from him.[163] Rather, this passage clearly states what the New Testament anxiously guards against elsewhere, and what Gyllenberg actually anticipates in Hebrews without being able to document it directly,[164] that "not only the goal, but also the original home of the redeemed is with God."

---

[158]Weiss, p. 79.
[159]Thus Riggenbach, p. 52; Seeberg, p. 20, and Proksch, *TDNT* I, 112.
[160]Weiss, p. 86.
[161]Cf. Kögel, *Der Sohn*, p. 59; Windisch, p. 22; Loew, *Der Glaubensweg*, p. 25, and Michel, p. 35.
[162]Kögel, *ibid.*, p. 59.
[163]Michel, p. 35.
[164]Gyllenberg, p. 668.

[91]   We cannot interpret this concept simply from the perspective of creation.[165] The creation does not establish the rank of "firstborn" who is himself the Creator. Only one possibility remains: In this passage, Gnostic mythology is breaking through, which derives the redemptive event metaphysically from the common heavenly preexistence of Redeemer and redeemed. No doubt, 2:11 reflects extreme reserve over against the myth and its broad portraiture of precisely this aspect. One might almost speak of vagueness. In particular, the divine origin of the Redeemer and the redeemed is not at all described as linking them in a natural way, as is self-evident and fundamental in the myth. On the contrary, the Christian author will totally reject such an interpretation of his words. But it is still characteristic of our passage that it takes its historical explanation only from the Gnostic myth and carries on its tradition in a way inoffensive to Christian faith.

The interest that induced the author to take up this tradition is obvious. *Just as he had distinguished the ἀγιάζων from the ἀγιαζόμενοι, so conversely, he was concerned to exhibit the Son and the sons in their closest connection.* For this reason he describes them also as "brothers." But just as his entire argumentation in this chapter leans heavily on the myth's train of thought, so also the myth offered the possibility of making this interest concrete, and it does so by its doctrine of the συγγένεια of Redeemer and redeemed, which the Mandaean literature already brought to our attention.[166] In that literature, Re-

---

[165]Contra Windisch, p. 21, and Büchsel, *Die Christologie des Hebräerbriefes*, p. 6, who refers to a divine sonship of humankind as such.
[166]Cf. p. 94.

deemer and redeemed are plainly identified as members of the same heavenly world of light.[167] And just as both are conceived in totally materialistic fashion (i.e., according to their substance) as deriving "from one," so also a brotherhood exists between them on the basis of the same heavenly *physis* which embraces them.

This is especially clear when, for example, in the *Acts of Thomas*,[168] the nickname "twin" is referred to Thomas' relationship to Christ: ὁ δίδυμος τοῦ Χριστοῦ, ὁ ἀπόστολος τοῦ ὑψίστου καὶ συμμύστης τοῦ λόγου τοῦ Χριστοῦ τοῦ ἀποκρύφου. But this term is also unhesitatingly applied to the relation among the re-   [92] deemed. Thus Mariamne addresses Nicanora in the *Acts of Philip*: "You are my sister, one mother bore us as twins."[169] A further characteristic of this notion is that Redeemer and redeemed can no longer be distinguished. Thus the predicates of the Redeemer are transferred to his messengers, or, conversely, the Redeemer appears in the form of his messenger. For example, Christ appears in the shape of Philip[170] or in the ἀπεικασία of Thomas.[171]

But now in the Mandaean sect,[172] just as in all of Gnosticism, this relationship is complicated by the fact that the Redeemer is never denied a certain priority among his

---

[167]Käsemann, *Leib und Leib Christi*, p. 66f.
[168]*Acts of Thomas* 39 (Bonnet II, 156; H.-S., p. 464): "Twin brother of Christ, apostle of the Most High and fellow initiate into the hidden word of Christ." Cf. Chapter 31 (Bonnet II, 148; H.-S., p. 459).
[169]*Acts of Philip* 115 (Bonnet II, 46).
[170]*Ibid.*, 148 (Bonnet II, 89).
[171]*Acts of Thomas* 11 (Bonnet II, 116; H.-S., p. 448). It is particularly instructive for the identity established with the Gnostic brotherhood that Christ observes that he is not Thomas but his ἀδελφός. Here brother and εἰκών are precisely the same.
[172]Cf. above, p. 94.

brothers which belongs to him precisely on the basis of
his redemptive function. If, as members of the heavenly
homeland, they are also his brothers, and like him are
also sons of God, [173] then conversely he is still πρωτότοκος
πολλῶν ἀδελφῶν. [174] For this reason one becomes a
"son" [175] only in that union with him that establishes the
link with the heavenly world anew. And to the extent the
redemption is considered an *anagenēsis*, [176] *the redeemed
become sons of God only because they first become sons* [177]
or children [178] *of the Redeemer.* Heb. 2:10ff. is to be under-

---

[173] Cf. the prayer of the Mystes before his deification in the *Hermetica* I, 32:
"Fill me with this grace that I might give light to those ἐν ἀγνοίᾳ τοῦ
γένους, my brothers and your sons!" In the *Acts of Philip* 109 (Bonnet II,
42), the redeemed are addressed: "Our brothers, sons of the heavenly Father, you are τὸ πλοῦτος τὸ καλὸν καί ἡ ὕπαρξις τῆς ἄνω πόλεως [ET: "the
rich, the good, and the citizen of the city above"].

[174] *Acts of Thomas* 48 (Bonnet II, 164; H.-S., 469).

[175] Cf. the *Odes of Solomon* 3:7f.: "Because I love Him that is the Son, I shall
become a son. Indeed he who is joined to Him who is immortal, truly shall
be immortal."

[176] Cf. the quotation of the *Odes of Solomon* 36:2f. on p. 121.

[177] Cf. *Pistis Sophia*, ed. by C. Schmidt (1978), p. 561: "O Saviour...because
thou didst take away our souls and they strove to come forth from us toward
thee, for they are from thee." Cf. also the *Odes of Solomon* 31:4f.: "And
[He] offered to Him those that had become sons through Him." In the
Martyrdom of Peter 15 (Lipsius, p. 19), Christ is called *pater et amicus* [ET:
"father and friend"]. Cf. the Greek of Chapter 10 (Lipsius, p. 98): σύ μοι
πατήρ, σύ μοι μήτηρ, σύ μοι ἀδελφός, σὺ φίλος, σὺ δοῦλος, σὺ
οἰκονόμος [ET: "You are my father and my mother; you are my brother.
You are friend, servant, and steward"], and the *Acts of Thomas* 30 (Bonnet
II, 147; H.-S., p. 459): "Thou Lord of all and Father—but Father not of the
souls that are in bodies, but those that are gone out." The same title is
transferred to the apostle as the εἰκών of Christ, as in the *Martyrdom of Andrew* I. 9 (Bonnet I, 52), or it is transferred to the mystagogue of the mystery
cults; cf. Bousset, *Kyrios Christos*, p. 360, n. 30; Reitzenstein, *The Hellenistic Mystery Religions*, p. 40f.; Pascher, op. cit., p. 154, and R. Knopf in the
supplement to Lietzmann's *Handbuch, Apostolischen Väter* I, p. 13, on the
Didache 3:1.

[178] There is no difference between υἱοί, τέκνα, and παιδία. So the *Hermetica*
XIII, 14 reads: ἀγνοεῖς ὅτι θεὸς πέφυκας καὶ τοῦ ἑνὸς παῖς [ET: "Do

stood from this mythical background of the Gnostic doc- [93]
trine of συγγένεια.

It is striking indeed how in that passage the names for
the redeemed vary. If it suits the relationship of brotherhood[179] described in verses 11ff. and 17 to explain the
υἱοί of verse 10 as sons of God, then the παιδία of verse
13f. can certainly be interpreted only as children of
Christ. When Kögel speaks here of children of God, because the entire section concerns only sonship with
God,[180] or when Riggenbach actually translates παιδία as
"human children,"[181] they are in conflict with the clear
statement of the text, according to which in verse 13 the
children expressly appear as given to the Redeemer by
God. Only the myth explains this striking variation in
names in a historically satisfactory manner, as was just
shown. From a backward look, then, this observation
again yields justification for the interpretation given the
ἐξ ἑνός of verse 11, according to which we found in it an
allusion to the doctrine of the preexistence of souls in the
Gnostic myth.

The interest of the myth in this aspect is clear: The
preexistence of souls establishes the humiliation of the
Redeemer in which he cares for his brothers as ἀρχηγός.
We can understand how this possibility of establishing

---

you not know that you have been born a god and son of the One?"]. In the
Acts of Thomas 66 (Bonnet II, 182; H.-S., p. 479), the apostle calls his faithful ones τέκνα καὶ ἀδελφοί. The *Extracts of Theodotus* 41:1 reports that the
διαφέροντα σπέρματα did not go forth ὡς κτίσις but ὡς τέκνα. The *Odes
of Solomon* 41:1f. reads: "Let all the Lord's babes praise him...and His children shall be acknowledged by him."

[179] According to the quotation in 2:13, which is somewhat difficult to understand, this brotherhood is proved in Jesus' reliance on God's plan together
with his brothers.

[180] Kögel, *Der Sohn*, p. 70 n. 1.

[181] Riggenbach, p. 54.

Christ's relationship to his own had to attract the author of Hebrews, once he had described Jesus as ἀρχηγός. In verse 10 he also referred to a divine ἔπρεπεν, which of course first applies only to Christ's way toward his own completion, and yet which inseparably yokes his status as leader to this way. So this ἔπρεπεν is then resumed and explained by the γάρ and the ἐξ ἑνός of verse 11, and is heard again in verse 13 when, according to the quotation from Isa. 8:17, Jesus is described as the one who relies on God's plan together with his brothers. Just as the myth, so the Christian author is also concerned to establish the need for redemption in the history of revelation and to make clear why Jesus appears as ἀρχηγός. Like the [94] myth, he also points to the divine origin of the redeemed and for that reason can likewise portray them as brothers of the Redeemer. But since he also describes them as children of Jesus and as ἁγιαζόμενοι, finally, like the myth, he too is on guard lest the specific difference between Christ and his own be ignored in favor of their specific connection.

To conclude, once we have duly accented the identity of concern and the parallelism in individual expressions, we must take note that at one decisive point in Hebrews the author corrects and breaks through the tradition of the myth from his Christian perspective. *As certain as it is that Chapter 2 can be historically illumined only by evaluating the Gnostic tradition in question, it is just as certain that the naturalism of the myth has not been adopted.* A typically Christian restriction may already appear in the fact that verse 10 refers only to "many sons," and verse 13 only to "the children God has given me," while in Gnosticism all souls are embraced by redemption and only dead matter is abandoned on earth.

Christian proclamation is aware that salvation and guidance through Christ are attained solely in the decision of faith which separates sons from lost children. At this point it must thus draw back from the myth, however much it may make use of its terms. And thus, in addition, the ἐξ ἑνός in verse 11, which can be historically interpreted only from the mythical speculation of the preexistence of souls, is modified in a Christian sense by the ἔπρεπεν in verse 10. This mythical speculation is wholly intolerable to Christian proclamation linked to revelation. Here, the union of Christ with his own as well as the entire process of redemption can be grasped in no other way than from God's saving will. Here, in contrast to the arbitrariness of mythical thought, recourse to an alleged state of preexistence in order to explain the fact of redemption as such is out of the question. So, then, it is also no accident that in the Old Testament quotation of verse 12, the term ἐκκλησία absorbs the other terms of sons and brothers originating in Gnostic tradition. The history of the ἐκκλησία simply does not begin with a metaphysical state or mythical idea, but rather historically, with the fact of purification for sins (cf. 1:3).

The message of Christ in Hebrews makes use of [95] mythical tradition to portray the redemptive event, but does not submit to it totally and without reservation. It appropriates elements of it only to the extent they can make clear the way of Christ to a Hellenistic environment, but also sees to it that this way is truly the way of Christ and not of mythical fantasy. For this reason it breaks resolutely with Gnostic naturalism and with speculation on the preexistence of souls. Of course verse 11, the Christian modification of which cannot fully conceal the sense of the original tradition, indicates how keenly the boundary of that speculation is touched in the given instance.

5. *The Apostle and His House*

The first chapters of Hebrews are distinguished by a peculiar accumulation of names assigned to Jesus. While it was necessary to ascertain the historical origin of these names, the present investigation encountered the tradition of the Gnostic myth with ever greater intensity. Apart from the title ἀρχιερεύς, which requires more detailed and separate treatment, what may be the most enigmatic description of Jesus in Hebrews has till now still been ignored—the name ἀπόστολος in 3:1.

The results obtained in the course of the analysis of Chapters 1–2 allow us from the outset to ask whether even this title may perhaps be understood from Gnostic contexts. The possibility is certainly given with the myth's preference for this title. Rengstorf disputes the correctness of this hypothesis, and has Jewish traditions in mind, where the idea of the one sent by God is at times applied to ordinary priests.[182] He finds support for this contention in the intimate connection between ἀπόστολος and ἀρχιερεύς in 3:1, made especially clear by the omission of the article before the latter title. In the link between the two names he finds Jesus' absolute authorization for his word and work set forth. He states that Hebrews has no connection with the Gnostic sphere of ideas regarding the one who is sent, as is reflected, for example, in John's gospel.[183] Further, the two titles for Jesus

---

[182]Rengstorf, *TDNT* I, 423.
[183]Cf. the examples in *ibid.*, I, 443f.

that appear so closely associated in 3:1 would have to be pulled apart. The correctness or incorrectness of this latter assertion must be determined later. But the former is clearly refuted by our investigation to this point. And if Rengstorf's observation proves true, that is, that the concept under discussion summarizes everything said earlier of Jesus,[184] then, on the basis of our analysis, its Gnostic character is beyond question.[185] Then we must in fact assume that in ἀπόστολος Jesus "as the one uniquely sent by God, is contrasted with Moses, the greatest bearer of revelation in the OT,"and in ἀρχιερεύς "with Aaron, the leading representative of the priesthood under the Law."[186]

[96]

To be "one who is sent" is an attribute of the Urmensch,[187] to which Hebrews 2 also referred. So then it is no accident that 3:3 again takes up the keywords δόξα and τιμή, which already appeared in 2:7 and give the status of the exalted one, and that 3:5 directs us back to the starting point of the entire exposition, to the dominant υἱός title. It is not just any notion of the nature of ordinary priesthood which is applied to Jesus here, and

---

[184]*Ibid.*, 423.

[185]Thus also Windisch, p. 29.

[186]Riggenbach, p. 67, quoted by Rengstorf in *TWNT* (cf. TDNT I, 424).

[187]Cf. examples from the Mandaean writings, e.g., from the *Johannes-Buch* 57:3ff., and 61:10f.: "The God-sent-one of Life," or "The sent one who has come from the Most High." On the Sent One as Redeemer, cf. e.g., the *Johannes-Buch* 61:96; *Ginza* 14:26; 16:5; 26:1; 57:33; 58:11, and many other passages. Cf. also the examples in the *Acts of Thomas* 10 (Bonnet II, 115; H.-S., p. 525): ὁ πρεσβευτὴς ὁ ἀπὸ τοῦ ὕψους ἀποσταλείς ["ambassador sent from the height"] or, in intimate connection with the title "Son," cf. *ibid.*, Chapter 156 (Bonnet II, 265; H.-S., p. 525): υἱὸς σπλάγχνων, ὁ κατὰ φιλανθρωπίαν ἀποσταλεὶς ἡμῖν υἱὸς ἀπὸ τῆς ἄνω πατρίδος τῆς τελείας ["Son of compassion, the son sent to us out of love for me from the perfect fatherland above"].

which occasionally may have played a certain role. Rather, Jesus' significance in relation to his own is conclusively described.[188] But this description can occur with the predicate ἀπόστολος only where there is a tradition in which this predicate is centrally anchored. The brevity with which Hebrews throws out this concept without preparation is in inverse relation to its importance and excludes its original invention on the part of our author. Finally, the less we can demonstrate the centrality of that motif of the one sent by God within the framework of ideas regarding Jewish priesthood, the more indisputably we can do so on the basis of the mythical tradition of Gnosticism.

In addition, *Gnostic influence appears discernible elsewhere in 3:1-6.* This is especially true of the concept οἶκος in this section. It is, of course, introduced by way of an Old Testament quotation. But its paraphrase in the κλήσεως ἐπουρανίου μέτοχοι (3:1) makes clear that it is not used in merely figurative fashion. The heavenly [97] κλῆσις is concretely the city of God, the angels of which were likewise described as μέτοχοι in 1:9,. and whose companionship according to 6:4 is granted by the Holy Spirit. So also μέτοχοι plainly assumes the Gnostic doctrine of συγγένεια[189] which, rooted in the idea of the

---

[188]It is obvious that in 3:1 the title of apostle is firmly fixed, and is not an idea occurring now and then.

[189]If on p. 32, Windisch already called to mind the *Epistula Apostolorum* 19 (H.-S. I, p. 202: "You will be my brothers and companions"), his note is supplemented by the Mandaean parallels cited on pp. 93 ff. Cf. further the address in the *Acts of John* 16 (Bonnet I, 203f.; H.-S., p. 254): ἀδελφοὶ καὶ σύνδουλοι καὶ συγκληρονόμοι καὶ συμμέτοχοι τῆς τοῦ κυρίου βασιλείας ["My brethren and fellow servants, joint heirs and partners with me in the Kingdom of God"]; and according to the *Passion of St. Paul the Apostle* 10 (Lipsius, p. 34) it is said of Christ: *faciet illum verum adoratorem*

physical-metaphysical connection of all heavenly parts, aims at membership in the heavenly *Anthropos* and his body.[190] In Hebrews, however, the reference is not to the body of the *Anthropos* but to his house, which in Gnosticism is identical[191] to it. Thus the myth describes the redemptive event as οἰκοδομή, and thus the *Anthropos* is also the οἰκονόμος.[192] The multitude of the redeemed is then his "house" in the heavenly home, or in proleptic fashion while on earth.

In this connection we may perhaps include the expression σπέρμα Ἀβραάμ of *2:16*, which describes[193] the New Testament community of the saved. Its appearance is not established in the text through any sort of external association. It takes on meaning when we assume that Christian Gnosticism used this term because it believed it saw reflected in it the familiar Gnostic doctrine of the σπέρμα. This interpretation is altogether possible when, for example, we call to mind the *Odes of Solomon* 31:12f.: "And I bore their bitterness because of humility; that I might redeem my nation and instruct it. And that I might not nullify the promises to the patriarchs, to whom I was promised for the salvation of their offspring."

In any case, Heb. 3:1-6 marks the conclusion of the epistle's first chapters which treated the relation between the Son and the sons. Just as the title ἀπόστολος sums up

---

atque cultorem suum consortem et socium angelorum suorum [ET: "Truly he made him adored and the worship of him a sharing and a fellowship with his angels"].

[190]The intention is thus to pursue the suggestion of Hanse, *TDNT* II, 832, that in the term μέτοχοι there is "an echo of participation in God."

[191]On this subject, cf. Schlier, *Christus und die Kirche*, pp. 49ff.

[192]Cf. the *Martyrdom of Peter* (Greek) 10 (Lipsius, p. 98).

[193]Contra Riggenbach, p. 58, who sees a reference here to the physical-earthly relationship with Jewish Christianity.

all the names of the *Anthropos* Jesus who humbles him-
[98] self, so the community of the redeemed as οἶκος of the
Son is the fruit of his activity as apostle and the sum of believers called to the heavenly city, by means of which
both concepts derive from the tradition governing Chapters 1-2.

6. *The Meaning of Jesus' Death for His Own*

To this point, our interpretation of Hebrews 2 has
omitted mention of Jesus' death. The reason is that our
investigation must culminate in the death, as does the argument in Hebrews 2. When now we take up this question in a thematic way, we are at first glance struck by the
fact that, in contrast to Paul, for example, this chapter
does not describe Jesus' death as an independent soteriological center that relegates all other aspects of soteriology to the periphery. Rather, in Hebrews 2 just as in Phil.
2:5ff.—a piece already handed down to Paul—*Jesus'
death is regarded as an extension and conclusion of the incarnation* which allows this end to be awaited as though it
were a logical consequence. This is the sense when in
verse 14 Jesus' death is described as a παραπλησίως
μετέχειν, or in verse 17 as a κατὰ πάντα ὁμοιωθῆναι:
Here the intention of the incarnation finds total fulfillment. And of course, as the parallelism of μετέχειν and
ὁμοιωθῆναι shows, what is at issue is not, for example,
merely the assertion of an external likeness between
Christ and his children. "It expresses the identity of nature," concretely, of human nature, "which has death as
its consequence."[194] This μετέχειν of Jesus thus corresponds to the existence of Christians as μέτοχοι, or

---

[194]Kögel, *Der Sohn*, pp. 74ff.; cf. Windisch, p. 24, and Michel, p. 38.

more correctly, because he shared our nature we may be sharers and comrades of the exalted one.

We meet the same set of circumstances in the *Odes of Solomon* 7:3ff.: "He has generously shown Himself to me in His simplicity, because His kindness has diminished His dreadfulness. He became like me, that I might receive Him. In form He was considered like me, that I might put Him on. And I trembled not when I saw Him, because He was gracious to me. Like my nature He became, that I might understand Him. And like my form, that I might not turn away from Him." *Once again, it is the context of the Gnostic doctrine of the* συγγένεια *and* κοινωνία *that yields the religious-historical background for the entire chapter.* This doctrine is concerned to set over against the relationship among all earthly matter another, heavenly relationship which is not inferior to the first in corporeal intensity.[195] In fact, this heavenly relationship is concretely the unity of all the redeemed as γένος or φύσις of the Redeemer.[196]   [99]

For the sake of his brothers, the divine *Anthropos* is humbled as man beneath the angelic powers (2:7). Since to be human here means to belong to the sphere of flesh and blood,[197] *Christ thus comes under the ban of flesh and blood.* "Flesh and blood" describes a sphere of power. *Human existence within this sphere is under the* φόβος

---

[195]Cf., for example, the *Acts of Thomas* 61 (Bonnet II, 178; H.-S., p. 476f.).
[196]Cf. the *Acts of Thomas* 48 (Bonnet II, 164; H.-S., p. 469); 39 (Bonnet II, 121; H.-S., p. 464); Chapter 15 is particularly clear (Bonnet II, 121; H.-S., p. 450): ὁ σεαυτὸν κατευτελίσας ἕως ἐμοῦ καὶ τῆς ἐμῆς σμικρότητος, ἵνα ἐμὲ τῇ μεγαλωσύνῃ παραστήσας ἑνώσῃς σεαυτῷ ["who didst humble thyself to me and my smallness, that setting me beside thy greatness thou mightest unite me with thyself"].
[197]The κεκοινώνηκεν of Heb. 2:14 specifically appropriates Gnostic terminology.

θανάτου *and in this fear of death knows itself to be* ἔνοχος δουλείας. Yet the fear of death not only creates bondage; it reveals that bondage as existing διὰ παντὸς τοῦ ζῆν (cf. 2:15). A correlation thus obtains between fear of death and bondage, in which both are originally united and mutually illumined. In terms of ancient philosphy, certainly, redemption could otherwise be effected by stripping away the fear of death from humankind, while here, as Gyllenberg[198] rightly observes, redemption occurs from without by an inner necessity. Unfortunately, Gyllenberg notes merely the antithesis of the Christian attitude, which does not deny the fear of death, to the attitude assumed by ancient philosophy. In so doing, he obscures the recognition that Christian and Gnostic proclamation agree on this point. Gnosticism, no less than Hebrews, is aware of the fear of death rooted in human existence, and which for that reason can be set aside only by redemption from outside humanity.[199] For Gnosticism, souls are captive to the material world and are set free only by the Redeemer sent from beyond it. This deliverance commonly occurs within the framework of an earthly journey on the part of the heavenly *Anthropos.* But while it can also be mythically described as occurring through a descent into hell, it is clear that the material imprisonment of souls climaxes at death, and that it is actually death that is held to be the goal and efficient power of the material world.

[100]   *Human captivity is without escape in the world because it is rooted in the demonic.* Death and hell belong

---

[198]Gyllenberg, p. 683.
[199]In general, the situation is the same in the mystery religions; cf. Bousset, *Kyrios Christos,* p. 360, n. 30.

together,[200] as is especially clear from the *Odes of Solomon*. Thus, for example, 29:4 reads: "He caused me to ascend from the depths of Sheol, and from the mouth of death He drew me," or 15:9: "Death has been destroyed before my face, and Sheol has been vanquished by my word," and 42:11: "Sheol saw me and was shattered, and Death ejected me and many with me." The union of matter and perdition is described in 17:3: "I have been freed from vanities, and am not condemned. My chains were cut off by His hands." The devil, with his demonic host, is regarded as the ultimate ruler of the kingdom of the dead. For this reason the call to redemption in the *Acts of Philip* reads: φυγοῦσα τὸν ἐχθρόν, ὅτι αὐτός ἐστιν τὸ κατοικητήριον τοῦ θανάτου,[201] or, "God wants to have mercy on you and save you ἀπὸ τῆς πονηρᾶς παγίδος τοῦ ἐχθροῦ.[202] The *Odes of Solomon* 33:1 has the same set of circumstances in mind: "But again grace was swift and dismissed the Corruptor, and descended upon him to renounce him. And he caused utter destruction before him, and corrupted all his construction."[203] The naive appearance of the διάβολος in Heb. 2:14 as the one with the κράτος τοῦ θανάτου is to be understood from this perspective.

Christian reflection may secondarily add that the devil became such only by reason of human sin. But what marks our passage is that such reflection is not expressly anchored in it: "On the contrary, it appears as though the

---

[200]Cf. Rev. 1:18.

[201]*Acts of Philip* 115 (Bonnet II, 46). ET: "Flee the enemy because it is the dwelling place of death."

[202]*Ibid.*, 112 (Bonnet II, 44). ET: "...from the evil scourge of the enemy."

[203]There are many additional illustrations in the Mandaean liturgy of the dead.

devil were given absolute mastery here over those who have succumbed to death."[204] *In fact, the author has appropriated a mythical idea without reservation.* Thus even the context of 2:14ff. gives way to Gnostic influence. Christ, just as the Redeemer of the myth, came under the spell of human δουλεία[205] when he became like his children. And to the extent this bondage is demonic, we may state with Gyllenberg that "if we intend to judge the matter fairly, the devil has a legitimate claim also to him."[206] Now it is just this entry into the sphere of the demonic power of death which allows the Gnostic redeemer to deliver his own: ὁ δι' ἡμᾶς κρινόμενος καὶ φυλακιζόμενος ἐν δεσμωτηρίῳ καὶ λύων πάντας τοὺς ἐν δέσμῳ ὄντας, ὁ καλούμενος πλάνος καὶ τοὺς ἰδίους [101] λυτρούμενος ἀπὸ τῆς πλάνης.[207] The same is true of Christ, as indicated by the διὰ τοῦ θανάτου in 2:14.

How this is possible is, of course, not set forth here. Windisch interpolates when he allows the devil to be robbed of his basis for power by the expiation of sins, or supposes that the devil was guilty of overstepping his authority by the death of God's Son.[208] *It is characteristic of our passage that the removal of sins does not appear in the foreground, that rather Christ's act of redemption is directly aimed at the destruction of the power of death.*

---

[204]Gyllenberg, p. 685; cf. Michaelis, *TDNT* III, 907.
[205]Cf. the phrase δουλικὸν ὑπεισῆλθες ζυγόν in the "Hymn of the Pearl" of the *Acts of Thomas* 110 (Bonnet II, 221; H.-S., p. 500).
[206]Gyllenberg, p. 685.
[207]The *Acts of Thomas* 48 (Bonnet II, 164; H.-S., p. 469): "Who for our sakes wast judged and shut up in prison, and dost set free all that are in bonds; who wast called a deceiver, and dost deliver thine own from deception."
[208]Windisch, p. 23.

When we reflect on the origin of this (to the Christian) alien element, only one answer can truly make it clear: The
myth knows no pregnant concept of sin, since void and
destructive matter is the actual evil, and individual vices
are viewed merely as its attributes and effects. The transitory as such is evil; if death is conquered, the other attributes of matter immediately perish with it. Here, then,
everything aims primarily at redemption from the fate of
death, which alone is celebrated as the Redeemer's decisive act.[209]

Actually, the myth explains the redemptive event in
more detail, to the effect that the Redeemer breached the
material world[210] construed as a wall separating earth from
the heavenly world.[211] He does so at his ascent by again
putting off the matter of his own body assumed at his incarnation. This is expressed clearly in Odes of Solomon
17:9ff., where, precisely in view of its force which en-
slaves even him, the materiality of the Redeemer's body
is spoken of as an iron: "And I opened the doors which
were closed. And I shattered the bars of iron. For my
own iron(s) had grown hot and melted before me. And
nothing appeared closed to me, because I had become the

---

[209] A few examples may be cited in support. In the Acts of John 113 (Bonnet I,
213; H.-S., p. 257), the Redeemer is called the one "who hast saved me from
the illusion of the present and guided me into that (life) which endureth
forever"—ὁ τοῦ πικροῦ θανάτου στερήσας με ["who has snatched me
from a bitter death"]; in the Acts of Philip 117 (Bonnet II, 42), he is called the
one "who freed us through baptism from the bondage of death." The Odes
of Solomon 22:8f. says to him: "And it [you] chose them from the graves,
and separated them from the dead ones. It [you] took dead bones and cov-
ered them with flesh."
[210] For more detail on this aspect, cf. Schlier, Christus und die Kirche, pp.
18ff.
[211] Cf. the παγίς in the quotation from the Acts of Philip 112, on p. 159; in the
Odes of Solomon 39:9, this wall is replaced by the waters of death.

[102]   opening of everything. And I went to all my bondsmen in order to loose them, that I might not leave anything bound or binding."

Christian Gnosticism has transferred to Christ's death this act of stripping away the material. For it, the significance of Christ's death lies precisely in loosing the soul from the body. In fact, the mythical Redeemer can automatically thrust matter from him because at his incarnation he assumed it merely as a mask over his true, heavenly nature. But if he accomplishes this for himself, by that act the constraint of matter repressing every soul is broken at one point, and a breach made through which other souls may also escape. So then, in Christian Gnosticism, Jesus' death is an introduction to the ascension for him and his own.[212] Through the breach made, both Redeemer and redeemed may now escape the compulsion of matter.[213]

This scheme, as it appears in the Deutero-Paulines,[214] *seems also to underly the statements in Hebrews 2.* Only on that assumption can we explain the fact that in both instances Jesus' death and resurrection are so closely situated, and that in Hebrews 2 neither Christ's resurrection nor his overcoming of sins is entered into in more detail

---

[212]While the *Anthropos* of pagan Gnosticism puts off his body voluntarily at his ascension, Christian Gnosticism was compelled by the historical fact of Jesus' death to give to that event relatively independent significance and to construe it as a prelude to the ascension.

[213]Thus we read in Ignatius, *Trallians* 9:4 [sic]: ἀνῆλθεν δὲ μετὰ πλῆθους, and in the "Acts of Thaddaeus" in Eusebius' *The Ecclesiastical History* I, 13:20: ἀνέβη δὲ μετὰ πολλοῦ ὄχλου. Cf. Schlier, *Christus und die Kirche*, p. 19. We may also refer here to the broad description in the *Odes of Solomon* 42:14-20, where the story is told of the formation of the "Community of the Living Ones" among the dead.

[214]Cf. Käsemann, *Leib und Leib Christi*, pp. 139ff.

or referred to at all. Only then does a fixed tradition explain to what extent Jesus' death is given redemptive character and distinguished from an ordinary human death. It is characteristic indeed that Hebrews 2 does not deal with this question at all. But on the basis of the Gnostic tradition we have described, this formulation of the question is superfluous. Here, the Redeemer's death is precisely the stripping away of his material body and thus the liberation of the heavenly nature hidden behind the earthly mask. Only in this fashion can Jesus' death finally be the culmination of his incarnation and at the same time the καταργεῖν[215] of the demonic power of death; an end to imprisonment for his own; their redemption from the fear of death; and lastly the basis for the completion of Redeemer and redeemed.   [103]

From this perspective *the involved sentence in 2:9* also makes sense, according to which Christ, for a little while made lower than the angels, now, because of the suffering of death, is crowned with δόξα and τιμή, ὅπως χάριτι θεοῦ[216] ὑπὲρ παντὸς γεύσηται θανάτου. Strathmann in particular has taken offense at this passage. He denies that the "crowning with glory and honor" should be referred to Jesus' exaltation, since otherwise the final clause loses its meaning. Jesus already tasted death before his exaltation, and it would be differently stated if, for example, this death had taken on universal saving worth through his exaltation. Rather, Strathmann continues, "glory and honor" denote that high priestly status already belonging to the humiliated one, and with

---

[215]καταργεῖν is a technical term for the eschatological destruction.
[216]We prefer this textual variant to the χωρὶς θεοῦ, since the entire context is under the divine ἔπρεπεν, made concrete in the χάρις.

which he is endowed "for the sake of his suffering death, that is, that he might taste death for everyone."[217] The less we can assent to this interpretation when forced to adhere to the idea of exaltation,[218] the more it reveals the difficulty in the text. Without a knowledge of the tradition that lies behind it, or merely by the aid of logic, we cannot solve it. Windisch already alluded to the tradition in question by referring to John 12:23f. and 32,[219] according to which Jesus' exaltation results in that of his people, just as in the myth. If Jesus' death as a laying aside of the material sphere of flesh and blood is prelude to his exaltation, then, conversely, this exaltation reveals that Jesus' death has another character than that of all other persons. The grace that exalts and crowns the Christ makes clear that Jesus has suffered and should suffer death[220] ὑπὲρ παντός.[221] This grace appointed him as leader and could make him complete only through suffering as such, just as he was able to break the ban of the material world and clear a way only through his suffering death.

If, then, the significance of Jesus' death is clear only on the basis of Gnostic tradition, now we must again give evidence of *the demarcation of Christian proclamation* [104] *from this tradition* at decisive points. We already indicated that in Hebrews the redemptive event is not, as in the myth, speculatively based by recourse to the metaphysical preexistence of souls and thus does not enjoy the cosmic universality of the myth. Rather, in purely historical

---

[217]Strathmann, p. 71f.
[218]Cf. p. 124.
[219]Windisch, p. 20. This tradition is also taken up in Heb. 10:5ff., 19f.
[220]Cf. Behm, *TDNT* I, 677.
[221]Riggenbach, p. 46, correctly translates "on behalf of," thus not "instead of everyone."

fashion, Hebrews sets God's saving decree at the very beginning and, in so doing, guarantees the possibility of a decision of faith. So then, the Gnostic doctrine of the συγγένεια of Redeemer and redeemed cannot simply be appropriated on the basis of their common heavenly origin. It is not the identity of divine nature, but the mercy of God's ἔπρεπεν that unites the two in such fashion that they appear ἐξ ἑνός. Thus, from a Christian perspective, the κοινωνία of the two is realized only through Jesus' humiliation.

The result is that Hebrews assigns this humiliation a quite different weight than does the myth. It is taken seriously as an actual entry into the sphere of flesh and blood and is no longer interpreted as the putting on of a mask, as in Gnosticism. This is so much the case that it must be expressly emphasized that Christ became like his brethren χωρὶς ἁμαρτίας (4:15). For the myth, on the other hand, the identity of Redeemer and redeemed is anchored metaphysically, for which reason the question of the Redeemer's historical liability to temptation and sin does not at all emerge as problem. Only where the *Anthropos* truly and totally humbles himself, where he thus assumes not merely the seed of angels but of Abraham,[222] can the question arise whether by doing so he also fell into sin.

Conversely, the phrase "without sin" makes clear that the identity of Christ with his own is not conceived naturalistically as in Gnosticism. It is not a physical-metaphysical state that unites them, but the historical act

---

[222]Heb. 2:16. The seed of Abraham is the purely earthly race, in contrast to the angels, and by nature has no claim to heaven.

of Jesus' entry into flesh and blood. This does not exclude a difference in the historical attitude of the two toward sin. *But since both hold differing attitudes toward sin, for Hebrews Jesus' breach of the earthly sphere of death cannot yet, as in the myth, automatically guarantee completion of his brethren.* Even after exposing the breach—to put it in Gnostic terms—one is aware from the Christian point of view that the power of sin naturally does not hinder the sinless Christ from exploiting this breach, though it does indeed continually hinder the earthly people from doing so. In Hebrews, the way to heaven is truly open only where the power of sin also loses its power over the community. God must be reconciled even where the curse of death belonging to flesh and blood was broken.

[105]

So then, it is not accidental that a new train of thought begins with 2:17, which has for its content Christ's high priestly activity commencing with Jesus' death. Characteristically enough, it appears as a postscript in Hebrews 2—against the background of the myth it was not needed before. But authentic Christian teaching cannot make do without it. It must penetrate the naivete of mythical speculation on redemption. For Christian teaching, it is not merely the relation to the sphere of the transitory that is a vexation or problem, as is the case with the myth, for which the relation to the heavenly world seems from the outset automatically to be solved in reflection on the immortality of the soul. Christian teaching encounters the vexation and problem of transitoriness only in the sense that it knows it is totally subjected to it and at the same time is aware that it is cut off from God by sin. *The earthly curse of death is for it an indication of the bondage of sin.* Though the sinless Christ may have broken through the curse, so long as the bondage still exists, "access to God" is still closed to it. Thus Hebrews can speak of redemption only when it can show that in Christ there is surety for the destruction of sin's power and the reconciliation of God. Because it did not do so immediately in Chapter 2, Hebrews reveals its dependence on alien tradition. On the other hand, because this becomes its central concern in ever increasing measure from 2:17 onward, Hebrews reveals that it uses alien traditions in purely critical fashion, and is resolved to protect the boundaries of its legitimate Christian message. In other words, the myth is drawn upon to make clear the Christ kerygma in a Hellenistic environment, but only within strict limits, without its being allowed to define or overrun this proclamation.

C. The Ὁμολογία as Call to Discipleship

A. Seeberg did us the service of putting the question regarding the concept of ὁμολογία in Hebrews (cf. 3:1; 4:14; 10:23) in a way that we cannot ignore. He did so by construing ὁμολογία as *a confession of the community which was firmly fixed and tied to the letter.*[223] Though [106] Windisch[224] and Michel[225] agree, Strathmann[226] on 3:1 asserts that "there never was a Christian confessional formula that spoke of Jesus as high priest." Rengstorf also construes this concept as a subjective confession, when he regards 3:1 as summarizing what was stated earlier

---

[223]Cf., for example, Seeberg, p. 32.
[224]Windisch, p. 29.
[225]Michel, p. 41.
[226]Strathmann, p. 76.

"from the viewpoint of the readers' decision."[227] Finally, Gyllenberg chooses not to construe the concept as a subjective confession, but rather "Christianity as an objective entity and thus as synonymous with πίστις."[228]

If exegesis till now is so thoroughly at variance on this point, it is in any case striking how pointedly and without comment Hebrews refers to ὁμολογία, without once detaching the noun in a relative clause.[229] The passage in 3:1 is at the center of our consideration. Curious here also is the sudden appearance of the title *apostle*. Though its meaning may be explained against the background of the myth, it still lacks any concrete preparation or anchoring in the text, just as it never again appears in Hebrews. In fact, it would be easiest to understand if 3:1 were an allusion to a fixed confession of the community in which the title of *apostle,* linked to that of high priest, had assumed a place.

Now there is no doubt that Hebrews is aware of school traditions already given shape, aware even of catechetical fragments, as A. Seeberg states, and that it utilizes them. From this standpoint, recourse to an existing community confession would thus be entirely possible.[230] *But it is less probable that precisely such school traditions or catechetical fragments should be labeled ὁμολογία.* Nonetheless, ὁμολογεῖν used in the pregnant sense has a certain proclamatory character.[231] And, of course, it is clear from

---

[227]Rengstorf, *TDNT* I, 423.
[228]Gyllenberg, p. 673.
[229]To begin with, the ὁμολογεῖν of 11:13 and 13:15 may be left out of consideration because it has no Christological orientation there.
[230]The reference in 4:14 to a κρατεῖν, in 10:23 to a κατέχειν of the confession is quite objective. One may hold fast only what is handed down.
[231]Thus in antiquity, as well as in the New Testament, ὁμολογεῖν is a term readily used in legal circles; cf. Preuschen-Bauer, col. 900f. Now, from the

Heb. 13:15 to what sphere this use of ὁμολογεῖν is assigned. Quite obviously, the praise of God intended here is of a cultic sort. If the quotation which derives from an Old Testament cultic Psalm already supports this theory, [107] then the ἀναφέρειν as a term for offering the sacrifice dispels all doubt. The ὁμολογεῖν τῷ ὀνόματι αὐτοῦ intends nothing other than the cultic homology of the Kyrios,[232] as is most clearly represented in the κύριος Ἰησοῦς of 1 Cor. 12:3. *Should then the ὁμολογία of 3:1; 4:14; 10:23 also have its setting in worship celebration and denote the liturgy used there?* The cultus is of course the only place where the community as such actually confesses and "speaks together," just as the credal formulas of the Christian community which were first given shape did not accidentally derive from the liturgy. Conversely, such liturgical tradition is not yet fixed in dogma or unalterable. Here, too, the difference between objective and subjective confession would not get at the real heart of the matter, since in this instance the individual subjectively appropriates the objective tradition of the community. This would explain how, on the one hand, "holding fast" the confession may be spoken of in quite objective fashion, while on the other hand statements concerning the ὁμολογία in 3:1 and 4:14 are more subjectively paraphrased by παρρησία καὶ τὸ καύχημα τῆς ἐλπίδος, or by the ἀρχὴ τῆς ὑποστάσεως in 3:6 and 14.

It is obvious that within such a framework *the title of high priest* as applied to Jesus occupies a significant place.

---

fact that legal and cultic language are in general closely connected, results that transition to patently cultic usage, which we will discuss directly.
[232]Cf. Rom. 10:9; 1 John 2:23; 4:2f.,15; and 2 John 7. According to 1 Tim. 6:12f., this cultic homology is also a juridically obligatory and binding act in which an eschatologically valid and public decision is made.

It actually originates from the liturgy, as R. Knopf has convincingly shown in his commentary on *I Clement*.[233] In *I Clement* 36:1; 61:3 and 64,[234] the high priestly title clearly appears in a liturgical context. Naturally, *I Clement* is already aware of Hebrews. But the formulas in *I Clement* which are uninfluenced by Hebrews and are obviously original (ἀρχιερεὺς τῶν προσφορῶν ἡμῶν— "high priest of our offerings," and ἀρχιερεὺς καὶ προστάτης τῶν ψυχῶν ὑμῶν—"high priest and guardian of our souls"), prove that there is no direct dependence on Hebrews here, as conversely the connection in Hebrews between Jesus' death and the idea of the high priest is missing in *I Clement*. Thus Knopf, who relies here on the investigations of P. Drews[235] (which we will soon take up), *correctly derives the concept of high priest in Hebrews and in* I Clement *from the liturgy of the community available to both*.[236] In that case, we have no reason for construing differently the few other early Christian examples of Jesus' high priestly title,[237] since they all appear just as abruptly and surprisingly in their contexts.

[108]

---

[233]R. Knopf in the supplement to Lietzmann's *Handbuch, Apostolischen Väter* I, p. 106f.

[234]R. Knopf, *op. cit.*, p. 107, correctly describes *I Clement* 36 as extraordinarily distinct from the usual moralism of the letter. And it is not unimportant to note that 36:2 is dominated by the εἰκών speculation.

[235]P. Drews, *Untersuchungen über die sogenannte klementinische Liturgie* (1906).

[236]The parallelism in terminology and subject matter between Heb. 1:3ff. and *I Clement* 36:2ff. could actually lead to the question whether Hebrews 1 and *I Clement* 36 interpret and reproduce in summary fashion the same liturgical tradition. The title, βοηθὸς τῆς ἀσθενείας ἡμῶν ["helper of our weakness"] documented in *I Clement* 36:1 also belongs in this context. Cf. Heb. 4:15f.; 2:18, and I Clement 59:3.

[237]Cf. Ignatius, *To the Philadelphians* 9:1; Polycarp, *To the Philippians* 12:2, and *The Martyrdom of Polycarp* 14:3.

Further, it is from a liturgical perspective that we best grasp the concept of ἀπόστολος in 3:1 which is so peculiar in the New Testament, and which together with the title of high priest is obviously part of the same tradition. All liturgy relies on an already fixed store of ideas, and in doing so prefers especially peculiar ideas, though arisen on strange soil. Gnosticism, with its wealth of hymnic pieces, had to attract the formation of primitive Christian worship. That it actually did so, is proved not only by the odes of Revelation, but above all by Phil. 2:5ff., and 1 Tim. 3:16, and perhaps also by the prologue of John's gospel.[238] At least the middle sections of these passages, which unmistakably reflect Gnostic influence, doubtless represent the liturgical material of the earliest church. But what gives this assertion added significance in our context is the fact that precisely Phil. 2:5ff. and 1 Tim. 3:16 are most closely related to the Christological scheme of Hebrews and are rooted in the same religious-historical tradition.

Thus a high degree of probability attaches to our assumption that the ὁμολογία of Hebrews not only denotes the primitive Christian liturgy of the community, *but that in addition the Christology of Hebrews represents a detailed exposition and interpretation of the community's liturgical ὁμολογία.* In fact, we could simply regard Phil. 2:5ff.; 1 Tim. 3:16; and *I Clement* 36 as fragments of the liturgical tradition on which the Christology of Hebrews is based.[239]

---

[238]Cf. Bultmann, *The Gospel of John*, p. 14. A hymn is no doubt present here; whether it was employed in the worship is doubtful.

[239]Naturally, this thesis intends merely to refer to an actually existing liturgical tradition, uniformly constructed in its basic features. But perhaps it could be further traced as the catechism of primitive Christianity, which

[109]   This hypothesis can be further reinforced by a few additional observations. Should it find ample support in the eminently cultic interest of Hebrews, then it could offer a suitable framework for the antithesis of Christ and the angels in Chapter 1. The less this antithesis can be construed polemically, the more it takes on concrete intelligibility from liturgical contexts in which it plays a role to this very day. A similar explanation for the antithesis of Christ to Moses in 3:2-5 would not be out of the question. Even in *I Clement* 43:1 we encounter the formula: ὁ μακάριος πιστὸς θεράπων ἐν ὅλῳ τῷ οἴκῳ Μωυσῆς ("the blessed Moses, a faithful servant in all his house"). Of course, its appropriation from Hebrews cannot be flatly denied. Yet we should note that P. Drews[240] finds the term πιστὸς θεράπων in the *Apostolic Constitutions*, and interprets it as liturgical material. Is the οἶκος of 3:3ff. perhaps concretely the community assembled for worship,[241] and as such attached to Christ the apostle and high priest? Should Hebrews in fact have originally been a homily,[242] then this entire conceptuality would be altogether intelligible as a continuous allusion to the community's liturgy. *Then also the numerous Old Testament quotations in Hebrews, especially in its first chapters, would take on a more fertile background.* Strikingly enough, these quotations are at times key words for individual sections and are thus not haphazardly juxtaposed, but derive from fixed contexts. Psalm 95 facilitates the unfolding of the motif of the wandering people of God; Psalms 2, 8, and 110

occupied A. Seeberg. In any case, the pieces named are only fragments extracted from a greater whole, to which the odes of Revelation also refer.
[240]Drews, *op. cit.*, p. 49f.
[241]With reference to 1 Tim. 3:15, Seeberg, p. 31, speaks of a saving community in which God has his dwelling place.
[242]Cf. Windisch, p. 122, and Michel, p. 6f.

furnish the basis for a presentation of the way of Christ. Are portions of the Psalter that were used in worship deliberately linked so as to secure and establish the continuity of the community's confession of Christ with the Holy Scripture of the Old Testament?

For the present, of course, we will not venture to regard these questions as settled. First of all, only this much appears to be certain, that the ὁμολογία of Hebrews is related to the liturgy of the community. To what extent this can actually be proved in the individual instance only a separate investigation could make clear. *In any case, this hypothesis sheds real light on the entire understanding of the letter.* This is true first of all from a historical point of view. As already indicated, liturgy is most easily open to foreign influences, so that from this [110] standpoint the emergence and considerable appropriation of the Gnostic myth in Hebrews would make sense. For the shaping of its worship, the community readily uses fixed traditions, as Gnosticism could supply them to Hellenistic Christianity, in rich abundance. The liturgy of the church in every period is evidence of this. Hebrews interprets these traditions already present in the community's liturgy and links them with the theme of the wandering people of God.

In so doing, Hebrews is also able to advance its material concern by one step. If the epistle's concern is with the need for persistent endurance on the wandering assigned the people of God, this need is explained in the first portion of the letter by way of Christ's example. The sons, weary of their journey, are reminded that they walk the way of the Son and thus in abandoning their own path would abandon his as well. If the inspired Scripture of the canon and the ὁμολογία of the worship prove the necessity of the Son's earthly sojourn, then his example by implication proves the need of the sons' persistence on their earthly sojourn.

Thus the cultic ὁμολογία summons the people of God to the discipleship of Christ as ἀρχηγὸς τῆς πίστεως. Only in such discipleship does it preserve its original ὑπόστασις. At the same time, the cultic ὁμολογία guarantees to the Christian community that such discipleship will bring it to its goal, since the perfecter of faith has already achieved it. By referring to the ὁμολογία in the worship, the first part of the letter thus takes up its entire theme in Christological fashion and anchors it Christologically.

D. Gnostic Myth and Christian History

The Letter to the Hebrews demonstrates that primitive Christian preaching was not chary of using mythical formulas and ideas for its own purposes. On the basis of the preceding investigation we may even assert that *both the drafting of the entire theme and the Christology of the letter in particular were possible only on soil made ready by Gnosticism.* We cannot lessen this fact by choosing to allow Hebrews' dependence on Gnostic concepts, formulas, and sphere of ideas to be restricted to the "formal." We ought not do so even if the elements appropriated would be less important than they really are. Form [111] and content are simply not to be lightly separated. Each conceptual form is an expression of a specific understanding of self and the world; as such and at any given time it gives to the content it embraces the stamp of the

understanding of self and the world from which it originally derives and the historical development of which it
reflects. We cannot simply pour any given content into
any given form and render caprice the artificer of historical life or shaper of spiritual developments.

*Accordingly, the primitive Christian message must
have been able to use the myth and its forms of expression
in a certain way.* To what extent could it do so? We must
note first that with its penetration of the Hellenistic
world it left the influence of Palestinian soil and inner-
Jewish history. It was thus compelled to think through
and form its content in a new way, so as to make the gospel accessible to new hearers originating in other contexts. And it could do so only by becoming contemporary with these hearers and speaking to their concrete situation. Today it is clearer than ever that the concrete
situation of the Hellenistic world into which Christianity
made its way was in essence characterized by the Gnostic
myth of the redeemed Redeemer and faith in this myth.
And this, of course, holds true in a more universal and in-
tensive sense than can be maintained for the classical, ancient or even Stoic philosophy. *If there ever were specific
centuries determined by the myth, then the first post-
Christian centuries certainly take priority.* This fact,
then, first raises the question of the relation of myth to
gospel in a historical way. The response of Christianity
to this question was not simply negative, as Paul, the
deutero-Paulines, John, the Apocalypse, and Hebrews
indicate. From the perspective of the gospel, the myth is
allowed to stand as question. Further, its position is actually given some recognition.

This decision has had incalculable consequences till
the present day, and deserves to be reckoned among the

greatest turning points in the history of the church and of
human thought. It paves the way for the Hellenization of
Christianity which does not begin with emerging catholi-
cism, but is merely continued there on the broadest scale,
and in part unchecked. It forms the basis for the fact that
in the history of the church a synthesis of gospel and
mysticism has continually resulted. *Wherever in history*
the message of Christ and the myth meet or clash, it occurs
by repetition and on the basis of that first meeting when
the gospel, disengaging itself from Palestinian soil, en-
countered the Gnostic myth in the Hellenistic world. If we
close our eyes to this fact, then we will never be able
clearly to carry on the discussion needed here. In particular, we will be deprived of insight into the attitude taken
by primitive Christianity, which should be of greatest
significance for us just now.

[112]

On the one hand, the Letter to the Hebrews
proves—and indeed from out of the core of its
proclamation—that primitive Christianity did not reject
the myth outright. On the other hand—emerging just as
centrally from that core—there is the fact *that here the*
myth has not absorbed the gospel, as for example in the
apocryphal acts of the apostles. Rather, the gospel in Hebrews makes use of the myth's fixed concept of the world
to explain to the Hellenist what lies at the heart of its concern. This is evidenced in the fact that it appropriates
mythical material only in a critically discerning way.
Thus, for example, the naturalism that supports the Hellenistic worldview is unacceptable to the Christian proclamation of Hebrews. Consequently, all speculation
about the preexistence of souls or of the individual persons, thus the entire foundation of Gnostic myth, falls
away. Only 2:11 contains a reminiscence of it, but with-

out being more than a meager fragment of a sphere of
ideas widely disseminated in Gnosticism, a fragment
now also supplied with another sense. From the Christian perspective it is simply not possible to infer the soul's
immortality, be it ever so hidden, from its sphere of activity. Likewise, Hebrews necessarily lacks that dualism
of spirit and matter that dominates the myth, the resul-
tant cosmology, and its teleology. For Christian theology, it is impossible to appropriate the motif of the metaphysical identity of Redeemer and redeemed. Of course,
this Gnostic motif enables Hebrews to explain the relationship between Christ and his brothers and sisters, but
no longer as the expression of a metaphysical condition.
Rather, the coordination of the Son and the sons is based
on Jesus' historical activity in his humiliation, thus on his
incarnation. But in Gnosticism the Redeemer's incarnation represents a recollection of kinship deriving from a
common heavenly origin, though not actually its cause.
Finally, it is characteristic of the myth that it feels fet-   [113]
tered only by the power of matter and oppressed only by
the distress of being fated for death. Thus that person
may regard himself as already redeemed where recollection of the heavenly home is wakened in such fashion that
the Redeemer reveals the soul's immortality to his brothers. By contrast, Hebrews is aware that penetration of
the material would not in itself suffice for redemption,
since it would not yet remove the power of sin which en-
snares in death and separates from God. Thus only Jesus'
sacrificial death and the high priestly activity of the exalted Lord commencing with it guarantee the reality of redemption. This roughly sketches the wall of separation
between myth and gospel as Hebrews exhibits it. We
may briefly characterize it by stating that *the Christian*

message refuses to become a metaphysic, that it rejects that pseudo-theology that bases the reception of revelation and the possibility of redemption on an innate human capacity, on the universal and innate nobility of an immortal, divine soul.

But while we take this fact into account, we must emphasize just as strongly that *in their soteriology—but only here—myth and gospel, according to Hebrews, may accompany each other part of the way.* This is true, first of all, of the portrayal of the Redeemer himself. Early Christianity of the Hellenistic world simply could not convey the significance of Jesus if it ignored the store of ideas about the one sent from heaven, the Son of God and the *Anthropos*, already in existence in that world and universally known. It is clear that by this means the tradition of the historical Jesus had to retreat more and more into the background. It is therefore correct when Windisch states that "the Christ faith of Hebrews is thus borne by cultic-dogmatic speculation."[243] This is true, of course, not only of Hebrews, but of New Testament Christology in general, insofar as not even the Gospels are concerned with a historical portrait of Jesus,[244] but also describe the Lord of the community as faith comes to know him. But the appropriation of the Gnostic *Anthropos* doctrine had to suggest itself to Hebrews as to other New Testament writings particularly because it offered the unique possibility of illumining the relation between Redeemer and redeemed from out of a universally religious [114] preunderstanding of Hellenism. *What Christ is, is not read off from an isolated observation of his historical per-*

---

[243]Windisch, p. 27.
[244]Thus also Büchsel, *Die Christologie des Hebräerbriefes*, p. 27f.

son. What he is, he is always and alone only to faith and as Redeemer of his community. The mythical doctrine of the *Anthropos* accentuates this aspect in precisely such fashion that its Redeemer figures are nothing in isolation, but are everything only in relation to their redeemed. For this reason they are called leader, father, brother, completer, the one sent by God, the *Anthropos.* But while from a Christian perspective they remain hypostases of pious speculation, that is, of persons who know their need of redemption, Christ appears to them as the fulfillment of all human longing, himself not a new myth, but the revelation and reality of divine grace.

Here, then, Christ is the τέλος of the myth as he may elsewhere be described as τέλος of the law. Because he is Redeemer for all—Jews and Hellenists—he gives to all the answer to their question, not only to the Jews concerning their law, but also to the Hellenists concerning their myth. *But in each case, he does so by at once shattering law and myth.* He shatters the Jewish law by giving himself to all the world, not merely to the chosen people. He shatters the myth by destroying human hubris, which in the world of matter appeals to its own most divine nature and is aware of its immortality as a self-evident presupposition of its earthly existence. He does not remind humankind of its indestructible, heavenly nobility, but only gives it candidacy for the kingdom of God. This makes crystal clear the fact that humankind does not possess this expectation of itself, either by nature or by virtue of its spirit. Only the humiliated and crucified one gives it, historically acting on it and binding it exclusively and permanently to himself.

Only after this dismemberment is the myth of use to Christian proclamation. It is such to the extent that

Christ can be portrayed entirely in terms of the myth as the one descending from and ascending to heaven, as leader and completer of his people. Now, too, Gnosticism's motif of the wandering people of God, which from a Christian perspective merely states humankind's need and longing for redemption, takes on new meaning: The one ascending to heaven snatches his children and [115]   brothers with him from the earth. *Here, then, the Gnostic motif of discipleship of the Redeemer—a particular characteristic of Hebrews—finally makes its way into the Christian message.* In general, the New Testament anxiously guards against describing faith as discipleship, because it believes it threatens the qualitative difference between the heavenly Son of Man and earthly humanity. When the motif of discipleship is sounded in the synoptic Gospels, it derives from the Jewish-rabbinic sphere of ideas concerning the relation between teacher and pupil,[245] and at exactly that point preserves the difference between the two.

It is otherwise in Hebrews. Here the motif of discipleship signifies that the disciples go the way of Jesus, receive a share in his sonship and thus in a certain measure become like him. Actually, the verb does not occur with reference to Jesus, which of course derives from an aversion to any final definition in terms of the Gnostic notion of identity. Yet Gyllenberg[246] correctly maintains that "the discipleship motif resonates throughout the letter from beginning to end." The expression πρόδρομος in 6:20 is already evidence of this: A forerunner is there for the disciples. But beyond that, the entire first portion of

---

[245]Cf. Kittel, *TDNT* I, 213ff.
[246]Gyllenberg, p. 686.

the letter is concerned to call the wearied people of God to renewed wandering by way of Jesus' example. For this reason it is reminded of its ὁμολογία at the center of which appears the concept of the ἀρχηγός.

This makes clear that the motif of discipleship in Hebrews is organically linked to the *Anthropos* Christology and along with it originates in the context of the *Anthropos* myth.[247] If the word of Philo has any application, then it is to the sphere of the mysteries and the myth: πρώτη δὲ τῶν εἰσαγομένων ἀρετὴ τὸ διδάσκαλον ὡς ἔνεστι τέλειον ἀτελεῖς μιμεῖσθαι γλίχεσθαι.[248] Hence it is no accident that in Phil. 2:5 as well, the discipleship motif emerges in connection with the Gnostic *Anthropos* doctrine. The myth has meaning only for disciples of the Redeemer, and it is precisely such that he intends to call.

When Hebrews adopts this motif, it does not do so because the nature of faith finds in it its most adequate expression. *Rather, Hebrews employs this motif with paraenetic intent*, in order by it to spur on the wearied community. On the whole, then, the Christology of the [116] first portion of the letter serves paraenetic purposes. Genuinely doctrinal statements may perhaps be sought only in 7:1—10:18. The scattered paraeneses as well as the otherwise unintelligible Chapters 3:5—4:13 in particular demonstrate that the first portion of the letter does not intend to offer doctrinal statements. In these chap-

---

[247]Thus, for example, in the apocryphal acts of the apostles the motif of discipleship clearly emerges as a constituent element of the myth, as Schlier's *Religionsgeschichtliche Untersuchungen zu den Ignatius-Briefen* amply indicates.

[248]*On the Sacrifices of Cain and Abel* 65: " Now the first virtue of beginners is to desire that their imperfection may imitate as far as possible the perfection of the teacher."

ters, paraenesis is offered on the basis of the Christ ὁμολογία, and of course in view of the general theme of the wandering people of God, to which then the paraenesis of the discipleship motif is imaginatively adapted.

The fact that only paraenesis is at issue here lessens to some extent the threat of this motif to Christian proclamation, a threat known to us from the church's history. The first part of the letter involves a preliminary stage about to be surmounted in Chapters 7ff.

At the same time, it is clear once more from this perspective that Hebrews' train of thought is fixed by the Gnostic myth, but it is also clear that signal concerns of its own theme induce Hebrews to employ this myth. The gospel in our epistle is thus not unrestrainedly surrendered to the Hellenistic environment. The appropriation of the mythical tradition does not occur naively, but critically. The gospel makes use of it only insofar as it retains mastery of the myth, construes it as a question put to Christ by the one in need of redemption, and interprets Christ as the answer to this question.

CHAPTER 3

The High Priest of His People

The concept of high priest in Hebrews towers up in our investigation to this point like an unmoveable mass totally unsuited to its surroundings. Its interpretation from Gnostic contexts appears at first to be excluded. But if this is actually true, then the result of our present treatment is not satisfactory, because it does not achieve a unified picture of the letter as a whole. Obviously, the idea of high priest in Hebrews is so deeply anchored in the texts already dealt with that it cannot be detached from the Christ ὁμολογία which underlies it or from the basic motif of the wandering people of God. Actually, the religious-historical derivation of the idea of high priest in Hebrews is the most difficult problem of the letter as such. Here all exegesis which sees itself forced at this point to fall back on exclusively Old Testament roots becomes conflicting and unclear, while elsewhere it cannot deny Hellenistic influence on Hebrews.

[117]   Before taking up this problem, we do well to put the prior question concerning the meaning of 5:11—6:12, since within the body of the letter this section definitely requires special examination.

A. Hebrews 5:11—6:12 as Preparation for a Λόγος Τέλειος

It was not only A. Seeberg who advocated *that Hebrews reworked common traditional materials belonging to primitive Christianity*, having chiefly in mind traditions of a catechetical sort.[1] Bousset took up and expanded this hypothesis from another perspective by locating in 5:10; 7:1—10:18, but also in Chapters 1–2 and 11 larger or smaller doctrinal discourses, which he believed originally existed independently.[2] Should Seeberg's contention be confirmed at least by 6:1ff., but also by the Christ ὁμολογία of the first chapters, Bousset's thesis proves even more useful for recognizing the character and structure of the letter.

It is widely acknowledged that *Hebrews 11* contains a type of school tradition traceable neither to the author of Hebrews nor to any Christian sphere of tradition.[3] We may leave open the question whether the composition of

---

[1]Cf. the summary in Seeberg, p. 5, where in addition to the catechetical portion in 6:1ff., he deals with the imitation in 12:14f. and 13:1-7 of the doctrine of the "two ways," and with the Christological formula in 3:1; 4:14; and 10:23.

[2]Bousset, *Jüdisch-christlicher Schulbetrieb in Alexandrien und Rom* (1915), p. 312.

[3]Cf. Seeberg, p. 121; Bousset, *Eine jüdische Gebetssammlung im siebenten Buch der apostolischen Konstitutionen* (1916), p. 473; Windisch, p. 98, and Schrenk, *TDNT* I, 759f.

this chapter corresponds to a general literary form in antiquity, and in particular is given a more rhetorical than directly literary shape, a more Hellenistic than Jewish cast.[4] In any case, we cannot imagine that a Christian or Christian community would write a history of the faith concluding with the Maccabean period. Mention of the pioneer and perfecter of the faith in 12:2f. is not even firmly anchored throughout, nor is it the clear goal of the listing. It is only added in and is nowhere prepared for except in the subordinate clause in 11:26. The statement in 11:3, that by faith we understand that the world was created by the Word of God, has nothing to do with the listing of the cloud of witnesses. It is best explained by a ready-made and firmly fixed exemplar which the author of Hebrews faithfully assumed, without giving particular attention to the other aspect in 11:3.[5] Of course, 11:39f. [118] establishes connection with the letter as a whole. But how can the author to this point devote such energy to portraying the witnesses' victory and distress, in order then to conclude that they did not receive what was promised but had to stand, as it were, before the open door? It appears as if the earlier tradition was forcibly twisted and made to serve another purpose. And if we ventured to link the spirits of the just men made perfect in 12:23 with the witnesses in Chapter 11, then Hebrews itself would prove that 11:39f. is merely a substitute for an

---

[4]Thus Michel, p. 157f.

[5]Seeberg, pp. 121 and 130, takes a similar position. Perhaps the contention of P. Drews in his *Untersuchungen über die sogennante clementinische Liturgie*, pp. 23ff. would take us a step further, according to which Hebrews 11 follows a liturgical scheme that is present also in *I Clement* 9-12, in Justin's *Dialogues*, 19:111,131,138, and in the eighth book of the *Apostolic Constitutions*; cf. pp. 23ff. In any case, this would explain 11:3, and admirably suit the framework of our discussion of ὁμολογία.

original conclusion that contained an account of the perfecting of the Old Testament people of faith. And, as to the underlying exemplar, it may be purely a matter of a Hellenistic synagogal tradition.

The latter is all the more probable, since *the κατάπαυσις speculation of 3:7ff.* points in the same direction and makes clear that the section in 3:7—4:10 also does not rest on the author's original allegory of Scripture, but is likewise part of a traditional scripture gnosis adopted by Hebrews. The important section in 12:18ff. bears the same stamp of scripture gnosis combined with curious secret traditions. Common to all these texts throughout is that the particulars of Old Testament salvation history appear as transparencies of a transcendental hope and take their light from it. But this is a trait of Hellenistic scripture gnosis extending from Judaism to Christianity, as was practiced especially in Alexandria and was in constant use in the schools.[6]

On the basis of such fixed contexts of tradition, the possibility again arises of interpreting Chapters 1–2 as an explication of the community's liturgical ὁμολογία. A gnosis of Scripture and cultus is most closely adjoined, since Scripture and cultus are the two pillars about which the postapostolic church is more and more stoutly grouped.

[119]   Finally, the great *middle section in 7:1—10:18* is set within this frame. Here again scripture gnosis contrasts the earthly data of Old Testament salvation history with their heavenly counterparts. And again at issue are the

---

[6]This should furnish some explanation of the problem of the origin of Hebrews, which will not be treated in detail here. At all events, from the standpoint of content, we seem compelled to look to Alexandria rather than to Rome.

author's interlocking traditions, reflected especially in the shape of the Melchizedek speculation that goes beyond the Old Testament.

Now it is striking that the context of the concept of high priest which begins at 4:14 is broken by the long paraenetic section in 5:11—6:20. And in fact this paraenesis is different from those in 2:1-4; 10:19ff.; and 12:1ff., not only by its length but chiefly by the fact that it cannot be construed as a mere transition to a new theme. This new theme already began at 4:14, and is clearly interrupted here.

We will grasp the real meaning of this interruption only when we realize *that Chapter 7 not only yields the "core of Hebrews but also the unveiling of secrets,"*[7] as the Melchizedek speculation most clearly indicates. For this reason, a λόγος πόλυς καὶ δυσερμήνευτος[8] is needed. Because secret teaching is presented, the recipients must be τέλεοι;[9] they are addressed as "enlightened," as "tasting the heavenly gift," and as partakers of the Holy Spirit (6:4). According to no doubt current Gnostic usage, they are no longer psychical (ψυχικοί) but pneumatic.

But since the adverb ἅπαξ appears with the participle φωτισθέντες[10] in 6:4, *this enlightenment is related to a concrete action that can only be Baptism.*[11] φωτίζεσθαι

---

[7]Michel, p. 73f.; in like manner Bousset, *Kyrios Christos*, p. 358, and Windisch, p. 46.

[8]5:11. Riggenbach, p. 140f., wrongly sees the difficulty in the readers' situation alone, and not in the material. The former is considered only for the sake of the latter, as Windisch, p. 123, clearly shows.

[9]5:14. With respect to its content, Michel, p. 63, correctly describes the τελειότης of 6:1 as a "Christ gnosis."

[10]This participle recurs in 10:32, where it unquestionably denotes the recipients' Christian status as evidenced shortly after their Baptism.

[11]In agreement with Michel, p. 64, and in contrast to Riggenbach, p. 155.

[120]

is a pregnant expression from the baptismal terminology of the early church.[12] This also explains the contrasting pairs, νήπιος—τέλειος and γάλα—στερεὰ τροφή, in 5:11ff. Both derive from a fixed topic of Gnostic origin. Milk is "a metaphor for basic elements of divine teaching, for elementary Christian instruction."[13] In other words, it is that very primitive Christian catechetical material which A. Seeberg in his exposition of this passage tried to give intelligible classification according to the teaching of the "two ways," "the doctrine of God," the distinction between water and Spirit Baptism, the laying on of hands, and eschatology.[14] But if the τελειότης of the Christian is linked to concrete enlightenment in Baptism, *then the στοιχεῖα τῆς ἀρχῆς (5:12) can only denote the content of primitive Christian baptismal instruction.* This is in contrast to the higher knowledge of the one who has become a pneumatic through Baptism, and described as solid food or the λόγος δικαιοσύνης (5:13). To paraphrase the latter term as a "word about proper behavior"[15] or "normal speech"[16] does not do justice to the noun. According to Riggenbach,[17] it also cannot be documented and finally does not suit the correlative τελειότης. The λόγος δικαιοσύνης is the teaching regarding the state of the baptized as δίκαιος, a role that it

---

[12]Just as in the *Hermetica* 13:19 σῷζε ζωή, φώτιζε φῶς, πνευμάτιζε θεέ [ET: "O Life preserve, O Light illumine, O God enspirit"], so also for Heb. 6:4 the enlightenment is construed as a being endowed with the Spirit. For 2 Cor. 1:22 also, the latter belongs with Baptism. On Baptism as the beginning of τελείωσις, cf. Schlier, *Christus und die Kirche*, p. 73.
[13]Cf. Schlier, *TDNT* I, p. 646, and Riggenbach, p. 142, n. 76.
[14]Seeberg, p. 62f.
[15]Thus Seeberg, p. 61.
[16]Thus Riggenbach, p. 144, and Strathmann, p. 89.
[17]Riggenbach, p. 144.

assumed in Christian Gnosticism.[18] This interpretation is warranted by the likewise anarthrous parallels in the *Epistle of Polycarp to the Philippians* 3:3 (ἐντολὴ δικαιοσύνης), and in the *Epistle of Barnabas* 5:4 (ἔχων ὁδοῦ δικαιοσύνης γνῶσιν). The link between *Barnabas* and the teaching of the "two ways," thus also with the primitive Christian catechetical and baptismal instruction,[19] is confirmed by *Barnabas*' accent on the contrast with the ὁδὸς σκότους.

Now *the statements in Heb. 6:4ff.* take on full clarity. If the letter's recipients are not yet ready for solid food, then the efficacy of their Baptism is in doubt, and they appear to have reverted to the period of their initial instruction prior to Baptism. But since they actually are baptized, this would assume an intervening apostasy from Christianity, thus an ἀνασταυροῦν or a παραδειγματίζειν of the Son of God, and would exclude an ἀνακαινίζειν εἰς μετάνοιαν (6:6). Because this inference is so absolutely compelling, the author who loves his readers can and may not share their assumption, and despite all apprehensions and the obvious signs of their weariness must treat them as τέλειοι and [121] leave the rudiments behind. But since he does so not by coming to terms with their supposed needs but rather with the unavoidable requirements of their Baptism, the δίο in 6:1, which at first appears strange, is explained. There is no summons to moral decision here.[20] Rather, the consequence is drawn from the existential decision already made at Baptism. Wrede thus correctly judges that

---

[18]Cf. the *Odes of Solomon* 25:10ff., and 29:5.
[19]In his supplement to Lietzmann's *Handbuch, Der Barnabasbrief* (1923), p. 308, Windisch explicitly refers to this in connection with Barnabas 5:4.
[20]Strathmann, p. 90.

it is not the readers' immaturity that requires the type of instruction which the author has chosen, but that their immaturity could deter them from such instruction.[21] We need merely add that the author does not choose to acknowledge this immaturity as actually existing, since he would otherwise have to concede the inefficacy of their Baptism and their apostasy from Christianity.

Now *the section in 6:9ff.* takes on meaning, in which the hope is maintained that, despite all, the community stands in σωτηρία. So the work of love and service practiced by the recipients takes on significance as an index of their Christian status. Then follows remembrance of the greatness of the divine promises and the admonition to hold true to them in ἐλπίς. Momentary weakness ought not allow the community to become totally νωθροί (6:12), though this danger exists relatively, that is, with respect to the ἀκοαί (5:11). The section concludes with reference to the certainty of the promise proclaimed under divine oath, and of the ἐλπίς become concrete, as it were, in Jesus the πρόδρομος and already existing in the present. The author has moved from harsh rebuke and persistent threat to a portrayal of the unavoidable consequences of eventual immaturity, to comforting encouragement on the basis of subjective signs and objective, divine deeds of salvation, and to the warning summons to be true to the end. If we attend to this outline, then it is at once clear that the primary intention here is not to give a reason for the detailed treatment of the Christ-Logos to follow,[22] but actually to explain its obscurity, hinted at in

---

[21]Wrede, p. 15.
[22]Contra E. Burggaller, "Das literarische Problem des Hebräerbriefes," *ZNTW* (1908), p. 117.

the δυσερμήνευτος λέγειν of 5:11. It is precisely for
this reason that the problem of the readers' maturity or
immaturity first arises. At the same time, we should be
able to detect from the rich and skilfully constructed
alternation of the motifs struck *that here in fact "some
rhetoric or attention to literary style is involved."*[23] This   [122]
does not yet militate against the basic, practical aim of the
letter, which is certainly present, but it by no means excludes the exposition of a particular doctrine.[24] On the
contrary, as in Chapters 1–2, so also in Chapters 7ff., this
practical aim actually involves presentation of a doctrinal
Christ Gnosticism. For the entire New Testament,
genuine παράκλησις flows from doctrine. Hence from
this standpoint Hebrews also seeks to overcome the community's weakness. The τελειότης of doctrine guarantees the perfecting of God's people won at Baptism, and
awakens them to new life in midst of threat and temptation.

Use of *the term τελειότης* for the Christ-Logos beginning in Chapter 7 finally rounds out the picture in
5:11—6:20. In this chapter, two things claim our attention. The first is that Chapter 7 takes us to the heart of the
epistle; the second is that it intends to reveal a mystery
accessible only to pneumatics and which actually
supercedes the community's Christ ὁμολογία earlier noted. But in this sense the term enjoys closest proximity to
analogies in the history of religions, now to be cited as
aids to its understanding.

In its sacred scriptures, Gnosticism occasionally describes the central, redeeming, and deifying revelation as

---

[23]Thus Wrede, p. 36, and Windisch, p. 59.
[24]Contra Seeberg, p. 5.

a λόγος ἱερός or τέλειος. *The pregnant expression τελειότης in Heb. 6:1 might indicate that our letter, along with its detailed expositions in Chapter 7 onward, intends to offer such a λόγος τέλειος.* Here, following the reference in Chapter 1 to the example of Jesus the ἀρχηγός, the basis for the wandering people of God's ultimate certainty of redemption is now disclosed in the activity of the heavenly high priest.

The *Epistle of Barnabas*[25] gives a striking parallel and support to this thesis. Here, too, a gnosis is imparted. Characteristically, however, it is multipled into a ὁδοῦ δικαιοσύνης γνῶσις[26] and a τελεία γνῶσις.[27] If the nature of the first gnosis is defined by baptismal instruction in the doctrine of the two ways, the second, which comprises the main section, takes its stamp from its revelation of mysteries accessible only to pneumatics. Naturally, this gnosis is clearly connected with the Old Testament. "It is the art of demonstrating and combining from the Pentateuch, prophecy, and Psalms the ethical and soteriological teachings of the Christian church, the requirements of true worship, the doctrine of Christ and his work, and our expectation of salvation."[28] "An exegetical method that discloses a deeper meaning in the Old Testament is the tool with which this gnosis operates. If one has the Old Testament, and if one has this 'key,' one also has gnosis."[29] What we have here, then, is an exact

[123]

---

[25]On what follows, cf. the excursus on *Barnabas* 1:5 in Windisch's *Der Barnabasbrief*, p. 307f.
[26]*Barnabas* 5:4
[27]*Barnabas* 1:5
[28]Windisch, *Der Barnabasbrief*, p. 308.
[29]*Ibid.*

correspondence with Hebrews 7ff., and, of course, both as touching the distinction between the content of baptismal instruction and a perfect gnosis, and as touching the latter's connection with a "mystical" exposition of the Old Testament.

If this thesis is conceded, then the other veils over the *section in 5:11ff.* are lifted. Proper to the usual form with which Gnosticism introduces such a λόγος τέλειος is that the initiates, thus the recipients of the Logos, are not only warned against divulging the secrets of initiation,[30] or tested for their worthiness[31] and summoned to self-examination.[32] They must also be continually confronted with the obscurity of the secret wisdom[33] imparted to them as though in an enigma, with their lack of mental power or their immaturity,[34] and therefore must submit to urgent admonitions not to revert to the status of the

---

[30]Cf., for example, Philo, *On the Cherubim* 48 and *On the Sacrifices of Abel and Cain* 60.
[31]Cf. *Barnabas* 9:9, and the parallels assembled by Windisch on this passage in his commentary, p. 356.
[32]Cf. Philo *On the Cherubim* 42.
[33]Cf. the beginning of the *Hermetica* 13. According to Reitzenstein, *Studien zum antiken Synkretismus*, pp. 161ff., this aspect is especially clear in the "Naassene Psalm." There it is stated in Chapter 23 that the "reception of this great and inexpressible mystery is very difficult"—οὐδεὶς τούτων τῶν μυστηρίων ἀκροατὴς γέγονεν εἰ μὴ μόνοι (οἱ) γνωστικοὶ τέλειοι. Cf. the addition to Chapter 25: οὕτως...ἐστὶ πάνυ βαθεῖα καὶ δυσκατάληπτος ἡ τοῦ τελείου ἀνθρώπου γνῶσις [ET: "No one became a hearer of these mysteries except only the perfect Gnostics; thus...the knowledge of the perfect man is very deep and hard to comprehend"].
[34]In the *Shepherd of Hermas* Sim. V, 4:2f., and VI, 5:2, the folly of Hermas scolded as a fool serves as method for disclosing a new revelation. On the "device of misunderstanding" in John's gospel, cf. Bultmann, *The Gospel of John*, p. 127, n. 1. In 17:2, Barnabas holds in reserve what is important and difficult as beyond the comprehension of his readers, and requires a special maturity for its revelation; cf. 6:10.

psychical (ψυχικόν) once they have received the revelation.[35]

From this point of view, the rhetoric already observed in Heb. 5:11ff. is explained. It is not as though this section lacked all substance or expressed a mere rhetorical affectation to be taken lightly. But it is not a mere matter of pure paraenesis here, which in any case would be most clumsily situated within the discussion of the high priest theme. *In this section, the author wakens a familiar Gnostic style to new life.* He does so beyond mere affectation, because he really has the concrete conditions of his recipients paraenetically in mind. And he does so aware of the real significance of this style of revelatory speech, as witness the artistic structure, the use of Gnostic terminology, and the character of this passage as preparation for the τελειότης in Chapters 7ff. His addressees are actually in danger of proving themselves immature, as is evident from the entire letter; and he perceives this danger with special force because of the obscurity of the Christ-Logos he has in mind. But this immaturity also serves to accent more clearly the quality of mystery in the revelation to follow, just as it once served a Gnostic λόγος τέλειος.[36]

Hence we note once again the influence of Gnostic traditions in Hebrews, now of course in direct connection with the concept of high priest. But does the characterization of that concept as a λόγος τέλειος mean that it is dependent on mythical traditions also in respect to content?

[124]

---

[35]Cf. *Hermetica* Chapter 4.
[36]Acquaintance with this Gnostic style is not surprising, given the highly Greek cast of Hebrews.

B. The Religious-Historical Background of the Concept of High Priest

It was supposed that in the transfer of the concept of high priest to the Son of God the "original conception of the author in the true sense" could be seen.[37] This opinion is refuted by the fact that Jesus' high priest title is not at all prepared for, that it is introduced quite abruptly in 2:16, and thus assumed to be well known.[38] And in fact it appears[39] as though this title were known to Hebrews, as well as to the other rare authorities for the title in primitive Christianity, from the liturgy of the community. What leads us to this conclusion is especially the fact that the motif of Christ as heavenly high priest is developed in *I Clement* 36:1; 61:31; 64:1; and in Ignatius' *To the Philadelphians* 9:1, with a modification that cannot simply be derived from Hebrews.[40] This thesis, however, does not yet explain, but merely shifts, the problem of historical background, *for the motif could scarcely involve an original creation of the Christian liturgy*, as the presence of extra-Christian parallels confirms. [125]

The Christology of the Gnostic sect of Melchizedek[41] which has been cited on occasion is of little value in this connection. But this is not for the reason that in Hebrews we could detect "absolutely nothing of the influence of such Gnostic speculations."[42] As was shown, exactly the

---

[37]Thus O. Schmitz, *Die Opferanschauung des späteren Judentums* (1910), p. 280.
[38]Similarly Seeberg, pp. 38, 156, and Gyllenberg, p. 674.
[39]Cf. p. 169f.
[40]Cf. p. 170.
[41]Cf. Riggenbach, p. 180, n. 88.
[42]Strathmann, p. 95.

opposite is the case. And this sect at least yields the possibility that motifs related to Hebrews and its concept of high priest were built into Gnostic systems. But in this case, perhaps, we glean information regarding the origin and scope of the Melchizedek speculation elsewhere documented in Jewish Christian Gnosticism, though we reach no clarity about that vitally significant motif of the heavenly high priest.

We must rather bear in mind *that Philo's λόγος also appears as ἀρχιερεύς*.[43] We may earnestly inquire to what extent it yields a parallel to Hebrews. But any direct dependence of Hebrews on Philo at this point must from the outset be rejected for the reason that Philo's portrayal of the λόγος–ἀρχιερεύς bears only very pallid soteriological, and in essence cosmological, features. Hebrews' signal motif of the heavenly high priest's intercession for his own who still linger on earth is without analogy—to say nothing of the offering of his bloody sacrifice before God. *Here, then, we ask only whether Philo and Hebrews may be pursuing a common underlying tradition, though on divergent paths*. In addition, we should note that in his λόγος–ἀρχιερεύς speculation, Philo unmistakably makes contact with the Gnostic myth,[44] to the extent that his high priest who bears the world as garment[45] clearly enters the heavenly holy of holies in his capacity as ἀρχηγός and πρόδρομος of this world.[46]

---

[43]Schrenk deals very instructively with this aspect in *TDNT* III, 273f.
[44]Cf. Käsemann, *Leib und Leib Christi*, p. 73.
[45]Especially in *Moses* II, 133.
[46]No doubt, only the Logos' Aeon title is at first expressed by this being clothed with the world garment. But since this garment is taken along into the heavenly sanctuary, the motif of the atonement and redemption of the cosmic by the Redeemer as ἀρχηγός does faintly emerge.

The question of a common tradition as a point of departure allows us to look first of all at the area of *Jewish
apocalyptic*. In fact, what we find here are adjoining and
overlapping speculations which are important to a historical investigation of the high priest motif in Hebrews, and
thus were already utilized in the newer commentaries.[47]
In the New Testament, the Apocalypse witnesses to the
universal concept of heaven as a preexistent cultic site.[48]
When *Enoch*[49] refers to the house of the divine community's assembly, this yields a certain correspondence with
the idea of the πανήγυρις in Heb. 12:22. According to
Revelation 4, the angels—and in obvious analogy with
Hebrews 12, functioning as priests—praise God in this
heavenly worship, and according to Rev. 5:8 offer God
the prayers of his faithful people. W. Lueken has produced a wealth of material[50] to support the thesis that this
feature of the angels' intercession for believers on earth is
traditional in later Judaism.

In this material, special rank is given *the figure of the
archangel Michael*, who with six other archangels occasionally appears in the company of the "firstborn."[51] He
is the angel of the people of Israel,[52] gathers the souls of
the faithful who have died, or at times with others allows
them into the gates of the heavenly Jerusalem,[53] and
stands before the divine Lord of judgment as the people's

---

[47]Cf. Windisch, p. 70f., and Michel, p. 98.
[48]On the heavenly worship assembly, cf. Revelation 4. According to 6:9;
8:3ff.; 9:13; 14:18; and 16:7, God's altar is there, and according to 11:19 also
the Ark of the Covenant.
[49]Edited by J. Flemming and L. Radermacher, Leipzig (1901), Chapter 53:6.
[50]Lueken, *op. cit.*, pp. 9ff.
[51]Still other heavenly figures bear this title; cf. Lueken, *op. cit.*, p. 38.
[52]*Ibid.*, pp. 13ff.
[53]*Ibid.*, pp. 44ff.

advocate or as Satan's opponent.[54] As such he is called
Chief of Israel[55] and is named ἀρχιστράτηγος, insofar as
he achieves final victory in the struggle with the Antichrist.[56] Finally, it is of decisive importance that he appears as heavenly high priest and, on the basis of Psalm
110, as Melchizedek.[57]

To be sure, in late Judaism the title of high priest as
messianic predicate was not only assigned to Michael. As
early as the second century B.C., we encounter in the *Testaments of the Twelve Patriarchs*[58] the expectation of a
[127]   high priest of the end time alongside of hope in the Messiah. Here, most likely, we will be able to fix the point of
departure for all later development.[59] Now the *Testaments* have certainly been revised from a Christian perspective. But J. Jeremias correctly assigns this expectation of a high priest of the end time to a pre-Christian
stock of literature, since a Christian would scarcely have
transferred this expectation to other figures in opposition
to the Christology of Hebrews, and could not at all be interested in them.[60] Windisch already alerted us to the
close contact between the description of Levi's ascension
and the Christology of Hebrews.[61]

---

[54]*Ibid.*, p. 22f.
[55]*Ibid.*, p. 47. Most likely, the title of Christ as προστάτης τῶν ψυχῶν ἡμῶν
["guardian of our souls"] in *I Clement* 61:3 and 64:1 is to be understood
from this point of view.
[56]*Ibid.*, p. 27.
[57]Lueken, *op. cit.*, p. 30.
[58]Cf. the *Testament of Reuben* 6; *Simeon* 7; *Levi* 2:8,18; *Judah* 21; *Dan* 5;
Naphtali 8; *Gad* 8; and *Joseph* 19.
[59]Cf. A. von Gall, Βασιλεία τοῦ θεοῦ (1926), p. 393f.
[60]Jeremias, *TDNT* II, 932, n. 30.
[61]Cf. the quotation from the *Testament of Levi* 4:2, in Windisch, p. 70
(Charles II, p. 307): εἰσήκουσεν οὖν ὁ ὕψιστος τῆς προσευχῆς σοῦ τοῦ
διελεῖν σε ἀπὸ ἀδικίας καὶ γενέσθαι αὐτῷ υἱὸν καὶ θεράποντα καὶ

In addition, Strack-Billerbeck[62] and Jeremias have indicated the link between the expectation of the high priest and *the Elijah speculation.* Jeremias derives this connection from a combination of Mal. 3:1, 23f. (ET, 3:1; 4:5-6)—where Elijah is referred to as angel of the covenant—with the covenant of Levi in Mal. 2:4f. Jeremias writes: "This combination caused priestly descent to be ascribed to Elijah, so that he came to be identified with the high priest of the messianic period. The Targumim show how popular was this conception."[63] On the basis of Num. 25:11 (and to the extent Elijah is thought to spring from the race of Levi), the zealot priest Phinehas is identified with Elijah, which allows the latter also to be assigned the title of high priest.[64] If post-New Testament ideas are no doubt involved here, *then Jeremias thinks he may safely set the origin of the expectation of Elijah as high priest of the end time within the New Testament period.* If John 1:21 already proves that the Baptist's priestly lineage was no obstacle to his identification with Elijah, Jeremias draws support for his opinion chiefly from Rev. 11:3ff.

In agreement with customary exegesis, Jeremias refers the two olive trees that Revelation 11 cites from Zech. 4:3, 11-14 to Moses and Elijah.[65] He further maintains that in the original text of the quotation, as well as in   [128]

λειτουργὸν τοῦ προσώπου αὐτοῦ ["Therefore the Most High hath heard thy prayer, to separate thee from iniquity, and that thou shouldst become to him a son and a servant, and a minister of His presence"]. Cf. also the enthronement formula in 5:1: Λευί, σοι ἔδωκα τὰς εὐλογίας τῆς ἱερατείας ἕως ἐλθὼν κατοικήσω ἐν μέσῳ τοῦ Ἰσραήλ ["Levi, I have given thee blessings of the priesthood until I come and sojourn in the midst of Israel"].
[62]Strack-Billerbeck IV, pp. 462ff.
[63]Jeremias, *TDNT* II, 933.
[64]Strack-Billerbeck IV, pp. 462ff.
[65]Jeremias gives convincing proof for this in *TDNT* II, 939f.

its predominantly rabbinic exposition, the interpretation is tied to representatives of the monarchy and the priesthood which could also be true of Revelation 11.[66]

This does not exhaust the evidence for the expectation of a messianic high priest. Here, of course, the *Ascension of Enoch*[67] is of no value, since it merely indicates Enoch's peculiarity as ἀρχηγός and πρόδρομος. But particular importance must be assigned to the essay of B. Murmelstein, "Adam, ein Beitrag zur Messiaslehre."[68] This study proves *that in Christian sources, but also in the Jewish haggadah, Adam appears as bearer of the high priesthood,* with which he combines the offices of king and prophet.[69] "So long as the Tabernacle was not set up, sacrifice was not allowed on the high places, and sacrificial service was performed by the firstborn. For this reason, the Eternal clothed Adam with the garments of the high priesthood, because he was firstborn of the world."[70] Seamlessness as mark of the high priest is characteristic of these garments.[71] Thus Moses as well as Elijah-Phinehas were high priests.[72] Even the Antichrist—naturally in demonic caricature—will appear as king, high priest, and prophet.[73] Like the figures

---

[66]*Ibid.*, II, 933f.; this article gives further evidence of Elijah's title as priest of the end time, and especially from Justin *Dialogues* 8:4 and 49:1.

[67]Cf. Windisch, p. 70, and Michel, p. 98.

[68]*Wiener Zeitschrift für die Kunde des Morgenlandes*, Vol. 35 (1928), pp. 242-275, and Vol. 36 (1929), pp. 51-86. There are somewhat parallel observations in R. Eisler, "Das letzte Abendmahl," *ZNTW* 24 (1925), 177, n. 3.

[69]Murmelstein, Vol. 35, pp. 268ff., and 272ff. Thus Adam's body also originates in the center of the earth, and is formed from the dust of the future temple. Cf. L. Troje, *ΑΔΑΜ und ΖΩH* (1916), p. 28, nn. 2 and 3.

[70]Murmelstein, *op. cit.*, Vol. 36, p. 57.

[71]*Ibid.*, p. 58, according to Josephus *Antiquities* III, 7:4.

[72]*Ibid.*, pp. 59ff.

[73]*Ibid.*, p. 83f.

first referred to, he also can represent the *Urmensch*, that is, from the aspect of the fall, hence not as the sum of the elect, but of the impious.[74]

It will be objected that since Murmelstein's case made use of sources which are obviously so late chronologically, it should be excluded from our consideration. To this we may respond first with an argument from subject matter: *These sources reveal a mythical scheme in which the motifs of Messiah and high priest are fused in an original and logically inseparable unity.* Both predicates are connected to the extent they are predicates of the *Urmensch*. [129] If these titles are also assigned to Moses and Elijah, then this coheres with the idea current in Gnosticism that in various generations various envoys appear as incarnations of the one *Urmensch*-Redeemer. This obviously holds true here for Moses and Elijah, while the Antichrist is also the Anti-Adam, that is, the unredeemable substance of the *Urmensch* personified as demon. Further, the fact that Elijah appears as such an incarnation only in his role as Levi's descendant, and thus as identified with Phinehas, is an assimilation of the tradition to late Jewish orthodoxy.[75] In any case, the apparent result of the above interpretation of Rev. 11:3ff. is that Elijah's title as a priest of the end time is already known to the New Testament.[76] Rev. 11:3 likewise portrays Elijah in the role of

---

[74]*Ibid.*, p. 85.
[75]Contrary to Strack-Billerbeck's assertion, IV, p. 460, that the synagogue never knew a Messiah who was also king and high priest, Murmelstein's and Eisler's documentation are valid at least for heterodox circles.
[76]Does the silence of rabbinic literature regarding Elijah's conflict with the Antichrist and his anointing of the Messiah arise from an anti-Christian polemic, as Jeremias, *TDNT* II, 934, n. 50, supposes?

the one sent from heaven, a "superhuman creature,"[77] thus as furnished with an *Urmensch* title.

Purely by way of allusion, we may add that Metatron is also arranged in this scheme by the late Jewish mystics.[78] In the same way he too is ἀρχηγός of souls,[79] the heavenly high priest interceding for mortals[80] in Michael's stead,[81] and likewise πρωτόγονος of creation, thus *Urmensch*.[82]

Finally, *the Melchizedek speculation* belongs in this context. Strack-Billerbeck cite passages in which Elijah does not appear as Levi's offspring and therefore not as messianic high priest. They add that in these passages an unknown *Kohen Zedeq* appears alongside Elijah, or "strangely enough," that Melchizedek twice appears.[83] But this is no longer strange the moment we note with Murmelstein that the title of messianic high priest is construed by late Judaism as a predicate of the *Urmensch* and

[130] his various incarnations. *No doubt, even Melchizedek was regarded by a certain tradition as such an incarnation of the* Urmensch. F. J. Jérôme[84] has in excellent fashion compiled evidence for this from the various writings concerning Adam. Melchizedek, described as great high priest, officiates at the center of the earth and is buried there,[85] as is true also of Adam, according to ancient spec-

---

[77]Cf. Lohmeyer, *Die Offenbarung des Johannes*, p. 85.
[78]Cf. the summary in Odeberg, *3 Enoch* I, pp. 79-125.
[79]*Ibid.*, I, pp. 113e and 122ff.
[80]*Ibid.*, I, p. 115, 5, and II, p. 41.
[81]*Ibid.*, I, p. 120; cf. Chapter 15B, 1, and Odeberg on II, p. 40.
[82]*Ibid.*, I, pp. 120ff., 83, 104, 5 and II, p. 25f.
[83]Strack-Billerbeck, IV, p. 463f.
[84]F. J. Jérôme, "Das geschichtliche Melchisedek-Bild und seine Bedeutung im Hebräerbrief," *Dissertations-Manuscript*, Freiburg (1920).
[85]Melchizedek fragment in Slavonic Enoch; cf. Jérôme, *op. cit.*, pp. 10ff.

ulation. In the Christian *Adam Book of the East*,[86] this theme is taken up in such a way that Melchizedek does service at Adam's grave, bears Adam's body to Mount Calvary,[87] and as bearer of Adam's body also takes over his high priestly functions and serves as connecting link between the high priest Adam and the third priest, Christ.[88] In the Armenian literature, Shem buries the corpse of Adam at Golgotha.[89]

We note what Murmelstein had already indicated, *that the figures change but the scheme remains.* Even Melchizedek can appear as incarnation of the *Urmensch*, and to that extent as bearer of the title of messianic high priest, as elsewhere Moses, Elijah-Phinehas, Metatron, Shem, or Michael.[90] This suits the role which Melchizedek plays in *Pistis Sophia*, that of πρεσβευτής who carries away what is purified of the lights (i.e. the souls) from the Archons to the Treasury of Light,[91] though here also his high priestly office is not mentioned.

---

[86]*Ibid.*, pp. 13ff.

[87]As bearer of Adam's body he is clearly an incarnation of the *Urmensch* and adopts his role.

[88]Jérôme, *op. cit.*, p. 14f. Melchizedek receives the divine commission from an angel: "He has sent me to you that you might go to the center of the earth with the body of your father Adam and there stand before him, serving and worshipping God." At the opening of the ark containing the body of Adam, a new voice of the Holy Spirit is heard: "Rejoice, O you priest of God, whom he created first in the world," and this voice is heard again: "I am the one who made you a priest and breathed upon you from my dwelling place. You are my righteous priest and worthy to bear the body of Adam which I created and breathed upon from my dwelling, and made a priest and prince and prophet." Finally, at Mount Calvary, thus, according to the early Christian view, at the center of the earth, a final word from heaven speaks of Christ's cross.

[89]Cf. *ibid.*, p. 15, n. 1.

[90]That Melchizedek belongs in this series is still to be demonstrated.

[91]Cf., for example, C. Schmidt ed., *Pistis Sophia*, pp. 81, 87, and passim.

This office is of course only one function of the one sent
[131]   as incarnation of the *Urmensch*. Alongside it the other
function certainly has its place—as appears in the figure
of Michael, angel of the nation—that is, to bring the souls
of the redeemed to their heavenly home.[92]

Now the question unavoidably arises of the relation
between these speculations and Hebrews' concept of the
high priest and of Melchizedek. *The striking parallelism
of these late Jewish sources with the Christology of Hebrews cannot be denied.* Christ also is at the same time
Urmensch-Redeemer, ἀρχηγός, apostle, firstborn[93] and
high priest, and again within the framework of a scheme
already fixed and shaped. This scheme likewise characterizes the late Jewish doctrine of Adam and his incarnations, and does not juxtapose the titles of firstborn, apostle, ἀρχηγός and high priest in more or less arbitrary
fashion, but organically connects them. If the notions of
high priest in Philo and Hebrews could at first be construed as independent and merely parallel, this is not possible where Hebrews and its late Jewish analogies are
concerned. The very thing that appeared to hinder any
direct connection between Philo and Hebrews is missing
here, that is, Philo's cosmology, which links his concept
of the Logos, for example, most intimately with the Stoic
idea of the διοικητής. From a purely soteriological perspective, in Hebrews as in late Judaism, the office of high

---

[92]In Philo, Melchizedek is identified with the ὀρθὸς λόγος; cf. Riggenbach,
p. 178, n. 86. This is an arbitrary modification, but not a total elimination of
the function of the one sent, since also the ὀρθὸς λόγος leads to the heavenly
world.

[93]From this standpoint, the title πρωτότοκος in Heb. 1:6 is especially important because it forms the bridge from the *Anthropos* to the high priest, just as
in late Judaism.

priest is a predicate of the *Urmensch*. And in both instances Melchizedek appears in the context as described.

From this material agreement in train of thought only two possibilities emerge: Either late Judaism appropriated and transferred to its holy men a Christian speculation derived from scripture gnosis about Christ as the firstborn of God or *Anthropos* in the Gnostic sense, as well as the antitype or heir of Melchizedek and the high priest of Psalm 110, or, conversely, the tradition of Hebrews is rooted in the beginnings of that late Jewish tradition which in that case would have had to achieve eminence at least in the New Testament period.

There is no doubt that the chronology of the texts in question speaks clearly for the first assumption, and to such degree that under its influence the close correspondence on either side has till now been scarcely taken seriously. Now, however, after these analogies have become clear, *this first assumption plunges us into a thicket of mounting and inextricable problems*. [132]

1. If the late Jewish texts are to be set only in the post-New Testament period, and in fact not only as touching their final form but also the roots underlying their content, then, given the striking material parallelism with the Christology of Hebrews, their origin can hardly be explained in any other way than as conditioned by anti-Christian polemic. *This polemic would have arisen in opposition to isolated utterances from the Christian liturgy*, provided we do not choose to assume direct reference to Hebrews. The question is whether the wide-ranging and compact mass of the late Jewish store of ideas concerning the high-priest *Anthropos* can actually be constructed on the narrow basis of a polemic against isolated utterances from the Christian liturgy.

2. Should we venture to take this position, *then it is inconceivable that Judaism did not oppose merely one contrasting figure to Christ, the allegedly false high priest.* We cannot reduce the mass of titleholders in Judaism's expectation of the messianic high priest to one original figure, alongside which parallel figures could be set in the course of time. But this mass of representatives in Jewish expectation robs the polemic of its force. It can be understood only on the basis of a slow historical process of development, in the course of which a name turning up at any given time is a mere label for the underlying expectation. Sharp polemic, however, excludes the slow growth of an idea; it contrasts with finality the one real hope to the false one. Only a naively sketched expectation free of polemic can gradually be transferred to various figures. And in fact, the late Jewish concept nowhere allows us to detect anything of an anti-Christian polemic. Accordingly, it was doubtless formed independently.

3. *Further, from the perspective of content, this late Jewish view represents a more original stage than does Hebrews.* Whereas the only outcome in Hebrews is that Christ is high priest, the late Jewish texts also explain why Moses, Elijah, Metatron, Melchizedek, and Michael can be high priests: They are incarnations of Adam, who on the basis of a divine decree as firstborn of the world was likewise high priest. But where we recognize the significance of this Jewish motif, the concept of high priest in Hebrews can easily be subordinated to this tradition, since Christ is also the *Anthropos*.

[133]

4. This materially earlier stage of the Jewish idea is further evident from the fact *that it alone makes clear to what extent the Antichrist can appear as a demonically distorted high priest of the end time.* Here, too, such a

conception is readily and initially facilitated by that *Urmensch* idea constitutive in late Jewish texts, since the Antichrist is at the same time Anti-Adam, the sum of fallen humanity.

5. At this juncture, we must again take up the relation between the statements in Philo and Hebrews concerning the high priest. If to this point only their divergence was stressed, now we must note *that in Philo the concept is directly connected with that of late Jewish texts and can be derived from them.* Lueken already drew attention to the fact that Philo's Logos, like Michael, appears as ἀρχάγγελος and πρεσβύτατος, intercedes with God for humans, but also conveys to them God's commands.[94] Nevertheless Lueken believed he had to separate the high priesthood of Philo's Logos from that of Michael, since in Philo "no connection at all between the title ἀρχιερεύς and the use of angelic elements can be proved," and since "the sanctuary in which the Logos functions as high priest is not in heaven, as is Michael's altar," but is rather this world itself as ruled by the divine Logos or even the human soul. Of course, Lueken continues, the Jewish idea of a heavenly temple served by angels is very likely present in Philo's *On the Monarchy* II, 1, but there again the reference is not to the Logos.[95] Lueken is quite correct. There is no direct route from late Judaism's speculation about angels and particularly about Michael to the λόγος–ἀρχιερεύς of Philo. For this reason, all talk of the heavenly sanctuary in the context of the Logos doctrine is out of the question, since in Philo this Logos also assumes the status of the Stoic

---

[94]Lueken, *Michael*, p. 59f.
[95]*Ibid.*, p. 60f.

διοικητής of the world. Conversely, it can no longer be disputed today that Philo's Logos is equipped with features of the Gnostic *Urmensch*. That he is such especially as high priest derives from the idea of his garment which envelopes all things. This resolves the enigma concerning the origin of the idea of the λόγος–ἀρχιερεύς in Philo. [134] *Those late Jewish texts teach that in one specific tradition the title of high priest belongs to the* Urmensch *as such*. But if we may not credit Philo with awareness of the roots of that late Jewish tradition, then the genesis of his doctrine of the λόγος–ἀρχιερεύς is as impossible to explain as is first the title of high priest in Hebrews.

6. *For this reason, we may deny neither Philo's nor Hebrews' acquaintance with esoteric traditions of the heavenly high priest*, nor find in either evidence only of a pure scripture gnosis derived from Psalm 110.[96] Philo is no original thinker. He rather transmits school traditions of his time which were gathered up from every corner, and he secretes these within the Old Testament to the greater glory of Scripture and the revelation of God imparted to Judaism. This is precisely true also of his doctrine of the Logos, and it is scarcely probable that he should have independently inserted into that doctrine this very high priest speculation, since it clearly reflects Gnostic influence, as the allegory of the high priest's garment indicates. But where Hebrews is concerned, we have noted Gnostic traditions at every step of the way in our investigation. Hence also 7:1—10:18 was announced as a λόγος τέλειος. Should this λόγος τέλειος, and it alone, have resulted without underlying traditions from the learned scriptural exegesis of an isolated theologian?

---

[96]In opposition to almost all the commentaries; last of all, cf. Michel, p. 98.

This question must be answered in the negative, and for two reasons. First, *it is conceded[97] that the predicate assigned Melchizedek in Hebrews 7:2ff. can no more be derived from Genesis 14 than from Psalm 110.* One resorts to construing them as *argumenta e silentio.* And since the Old Testament contains no data regarding the person and lineage, birth and death of Melchizedek, according to rabbinic scripture exposition the inference can in fact be drawn that Melchizedek is an eternal and heavenly creature. At the same time, however, all these predicates correspond to titles which in Gnosticism usually apply to an "Aeon." Is this accidental? We would be inclined to reply in the negative on the basis of Hebrews' quite accurate acquaintance with Gnosticism, and thus confirm Philo's Melchizedek speculation as of a specific [135] Jewish-Gnostic tradition.

Second, we must take note here of that curious *concept of the* καταπέτασμα in Hebrews (cf. 6:19; 9:3; 10:20). To explain this concept it is simply not sufficient to state that καταπέτασμα denotes the curtain at the door of the holy place or the Holy of Holies.[98] In Hebrews this concept is clearly linked to speculation according to which heaven and earth are also separated from each other by an analogous καταπέτασμα (cf. 6:19; 10:20). But this idea, important in the context of the high priest doctrine, cannot be traced, say, to the author's independent scripture

---

[97]Cf. G. Wuttke, *Melchisedek, der Priesterkönig von Salem* (1927), p. 12: "While elsewhere in Hebrews we must guard against overestimating Philo's influence, the model of Melchizedek rests entirely on Philo's doctrine of the Logos." Cf. also Windisch, p. 63: "Nevertheless, the history of the interpretation of Hebrews 7 shows that a portion of scripture gnosis is present in these verses which does not quite harmonize with Hebrews' other doctrines, and is hardly of Christian origin."
[98]Contra Riggenbach, p. 176.

gnosis. It is introduced much too blandly and self-evidently for that. Rather, there is a Gnostic school tradition which deals in similar fashion with the curtain between heaven and earth.[99] The speculation in Hebrews must be derived from this tradition, as will later be made more clear.

7. Finally, there are reasons for assuming that the roots of those late Jewish texts and the synthesis of the *Urmensch* myth and the high priest speculation which they contain actually, and as can be proved chronologically, reach down to the New Testament period. In addition, the last decades of religious-historical research have made sufficiently clear *that the chronological datum for fixing in writing or giving final form to a motif or a tradition may not be overestimated.* The datum is most often accidental because the documents that have come down to us represent only fragments of the original mass of literature. Moreover, religious-historical traditions usually [136] have behind them long developments and meanderings

---

[99]According to the *Unbekanntes altgnostisches Werk* (*G. C. S.*, ed. C. Schmidt, p. 360, 1ff.) the Lord of Glory creates two spheres: On the right, that of life, light, and rest, and on the left, that of death, darkness, and suffering. The two are separated from each other by boundaries and veils. At the latter are watchmen. *Pistis Sophia*, p. 103 and *passim*, refers to the light of the veil before the Treasury of Light. In a secondary expansion, there are veils and gates in front of all the great aeons of the Archons; cf. *ibid.*, pp. 53, 99 and 427. *3 Enoch* 45 mentions the "curtain of Maqom" on which all the deeds of all the races of the earth are written down. In the *Extracts of Theodotus* 38:1ff., to be dealt with later, the veil hangs in front of the Τόπος. Lueken, *Michael*, p. 36, cites *Pirke Eleazar* 4 (the treatise on the heavenly halls), section 7: *Expansum est ante eum velum, et septem angeli qui prius creati sunt, famulantur ei ante velum, quod vocatur aulaeum* [ET: "A veil is spread out before him and seven angels who had been created first serve him in front of the veil, which is called a curtain"]. Lueken likewise notes on p. 98f. that according to some Coptic sources only Melchizedek as high priest enters the curtain to God himself.

before they result in written form, by chance in one corner or another. The baffling range of Gnosticism confirms this fact a hundredfold, and especially at its core,
the myth of the redeemed Redeemer.

*There are, however, palpable grounds for the origin of
the* Urmensch-*high priest speculation in at least the New
Testament period.* They have in essence already been
listed and need only be briefly recapitulated here. Philo's
doctrine of the λόγος–ἀρχιερεύς must first be mentioned, so long as it cannot be explained as having arisen
earlier. We dare to exclude that possibility when we take
into account that his garment clearly characterizes the
Logos-high priest as Aeon and *Urmensch*. Secondly,
traces of a synthesis of the *Urmensch* and high priest already appear in the New Testament. Thus, on the basis
of Rev. 1:13, Lohmeyer[100] altogether correctly assigns to
the Christ portrayed as *Anthropos* the title of heavenly
high priest. Thus, in addition, the idea of Elijah as messianic high priest not only appears in Justin, but probably
also in Rev. 11:3ff., and in fact again equipped with motifs of the Gnostic doctrine of the heavenly man. Finally,
it is clear that only from this point of view does the
Melchizedek speculation of Hebrews, which also trans-
fers monarchy and high priesthood to a heavenly creature, take on a stable context.

We must therefore weigh the possibilities: On the one
hand, the chronology of the late Jewish sources just cited
seems to exclude their use for the interpretation of Hebrews. But then we hit upon a welter of problems touching subject matter which can scarcely be solved, and must
leave obscure the question of the origin of Philo's and

---

[100]Lohmeyer, *Die Offenbarung des Johannes*, p. 15.

Hebrews' high priest doctrine, since in each case school traditions clearly underlie it, at least in part. On the other hand, by assuming that the roots of late Jewish texts reach down to the New Testament period, we gain a coherent whole into which Philo, Hebrews, fragments of a high priest doctrine in Revelation and the Gnostic traditions cited are organically arranged, and in the same way. *Above all, we gain a clear picture of the origin of the total conception*, for which that cardinal idea of the *Anthropos* (decisive also for Hebrews) as well as the title πρωτότοκος (likewise characteristic there) achieve commanding importance. Finally, a few chronological data give a not inconsiderable reinforcement to this thesis.

[137]

Should we concede this thesis for Philo, perhaps, but deny it to Hebrews by objecting that in all its high priestly doctrine the accent falls on the aspect of the offering of the bloody sacrifice on Golgotha, but that this aspect can in no way be derived from or set within the mythical tradition we have assumed, that it rather derives solely from the ceremony transferred to Jesus' sacrifice of the Old Testament and Jewish great Day of Atonement? Should not this very interpretation of the Golgotha sacrifice in terms of that ceremony have urged the idea of the high priest on Hebrews' Christology? This argument in fact deserves notice, insofar as in Hebrews the action of the great Day of Atonement was doubtless not only known but of importance.[101] *But it is not correct to state that mythical speculation on the* Urmensch-*high priest would leave no place for inserting this motif of sacrifice.* Finally, one more curious theologoumenon, preserved in numerous variations, must be set within the focus of our investigation.

---

[101]Cf. especially 13:11ff.

In reference to Jellinek,[102] Lueken[103] had already cited the following passage: "And there in the heaven Araboth stands the great prince Michael, and before him the altar, and on the altar he sacrifices all sorts of souls of the righteous." Murmelstein[104] certifies to the same motif for Elijah-Phinehas:[105] " Rabbi Phinehas said in the name of Rabbi Simeon ben Lakish that Phinehas is Elijah. If he were not, we would have no possibility of life in evil Edom. Our teachers said of him that since the devastation of the sanctuary, he offers two sacrifices daily in order to atone for Israel's guilt, and on their skins outlines the events of each day." And in fact, he sacrifices himself,[106] " since he was zealous for his God and atones for the Israelites' guilt (Num. 25:11)—since he gave his life into death (Isa. 53:12). It does not read 'in order to atone,' but rather 'he atones'—from which it must follow that he had not ceased to this day, but continually makes atonement till the resurrection."[107] The same sacrifice is differently interpreted in the Talmud:[108] " What does he bring as sacrifice? There are no bulls or lambs in heaven! [138] Therefore, he sacrifices the souls of the righteous."[109] Murmelstein summarizes:[110] "Elijah who in the one view sacrifices himself to make atonement, according to our passage sacrifices the souls of the righteous. *The two views are identical when we bear in mind that Elijah as*

[102]Jellinek, *Bet ha Midrasch* III, 137.
[103]Lueken, *op. cit.*, p. 31.
[104]Murmelstein, *op. cit.*, Vol. 36, p. 68.
[105]According to S.A. Wertheimer, *Bothe Midraschoth* IV, p. 32.
[106]According to *Sifre Num.* sect. 131.
[107]Murmelstein, *op. cit.*, vol. 36, p. 68.
[108]*Chagiga* 12b.
[109]Murmelstein, *op. cit.*, Vol. 36, p. 69.
[110]*Ibid.*, p. 69f.

redeemer and as Adam's counterpart is the sum of the righteous souls. We may thus interpolate 'souls of the righteous = Elijah' into the second view, and both views are in agreement that Elijah the redeemer sacrifices himself for the nation's weal."

Moses appears alongside Michael and Elijah-Phinehas: " The death of Moses is an altar of atonement for all Israel.[111] Since his burial, Moses suffers for Israel's sins.[112] The idea is clearer in a view expressed in the *Midrash Tannaim*, p. 224: Moses is not dead; he performs the service from above. And in a Samaritan source we find that Moses sacrifices in the heavenly sanctuary which, as we have just seen, signifies self-sacrifice…. This tradition is very old, for as early as in Philo's *Moses* II, 79, it is stated that Moses learned the regulations of the priesthood in heaven."[113]

Finally, Windisch[114] had already referred to *Metatron* who, according to *Num. R.* XII, 15, sacrifices the spirits of the just in heaven in order to atone for Israel in the days of its exile. From this Windisch inferred that the angels not only intercede and mediate prayers, "but can expiate the sins of the righteous by a special and, of course, unbloody sacrifice in holy and priestly service before God in heaven." This passage, of course, can be fully understood only from the foregoing context which in turn confirms it. Conversely, it is itself again confirmed in *3 Enoch*, which at least gives evidence of fragments from it. According to Chapter 15, B1, Metatron—who may be

---

[111]Midrash on the death of Moses in Jellinek, *Bet ha Midrasch* VI, 78, Cf. R. Eisler, *op. cit.*, p. 177, n. 3.
[112]*Ra'ja Mehemna Sohar* III, 280a, 282a.
[113]Murmelstein, *op. cit.*, p. 70, n. 1.
[114]Windisch, p. 71.

identified with Enoch,[115] just as, according to Odeberg, he also acts for Michael as high priest[116]—goes "in under the Throne of Glory. And he has a great tabernacle of light on high." This must be linked to what is said of the souls of the righteous in 43:2, that they are "flying above the Throne of Glory before the Holy One."[117] We can understand this association of the idea of the heavenly high priest with mention of the altar before the Throne of Glory and the motif of the presence of righteous souls at this altar only from the context described above.

[139]

Now the exact result of this portrayal is first of all that both Michael and Metatron-Enoch belong in the series of Moses and Elijah as heavenly high priests. Secondly, it has become clear in any case that late Jewish-Gnostic speculation on the *Urmensch*-high priest not only can absorb the motif of sacrifice, but also as in Hebrews, can give it organic incorporation. *Actually, a splendid parallel has been found to Hebrews' whole idea of the high priest who offers himself*, and which may claim fullest attention.

What gives this evidence a concrete point is that it already induced Lueken to recall Rev. 6:9.[118] Of course, we will scarcely be able to avoid this reminiscence. There, too, the topic is the heavenly altar of offering and the souls of the sacrificed. But the continuation in 6:10-11 makes clear that these souls await the time of the πλήρωμα, which begins only when the whole number of the righteous have been sacrificed. Indeed, the idea of the

---

[115]*3 Enoch* 4.
[116]On this topic, cf. Odeberg II, p. 40.
[117]Parallel evidences on the passage are cited in Odeberg II, pp. 132ff.
[118]Lueken, *Michael*, p. 91.

heavenly high priest and his sacrifice is missing from these verses, just as from *3 Enoch* 43:2. But it is precisely this parallel which demonstrates the identity of the tradition, *the age of which is in this fashion again shown to extend to the New Testament period.*

From this point we must venture a final step. We must now consider whether or not any light is shed on that strange passage in Heb. 5:5-10, according to which God prepares for Christ a body which he is to offer him as substitute for the Old Testament sacrifices. *Does this passage perhaps supplement Rev. 6:9ff., in terms of the heavenly high priest's self-sacrifice, also affirmed of Elijah and Moses?* It is the body of the *Anthropos* of 2:6 which Christ offers to his Father who prepared it, and likewise for the expiation of the people's sins. That a mystery surrounds this body emerges clearly enough from the text. *As body of the* Anthropos, *it is Adam's body which Christ [140] assumed at his incarnation,*[119] *and which he sacrifices on Golgatha*, just as Elijah and Moses are incarnations of the *Urmensch* and as such sacrifice themselves. This then would establish that Hebrews rests directly on the idea of the self-sacrifice of the heavenly *Urmensch*-high priest as fixed in late Judaism, and that Hebrews' entire high priest doctrine has become intelligible as conformed to this historical assumption.

For the moment, our examination of the religious-historical backgrounds of the concept of the high priest in

---

[119]Cf. the doctrine of the *Pseudo-Clementines*, according to which Christ is the last incarnation of Adam, in Bousset, *Hauptprobleme der Gnosis* (1907), p. 172f., and Reitzenstein, *Das mandäische Buch des Herrn der Grösse*, p. 49. Thus, according to the Elkasaites (cf. Epiphanius, *Heresies* 30:3, and 53:1), Christ put on τὸ σῶμα τοῦ ᾿Αδάμ.

Hebrews can leave this last question open. It poses a special problem, soon to occupy us. For the rest, we venture to have achieved a positive result which clearly and uniformly dovetails with our presentation to this point, that is, *that here, too, the* Anthropos *myth forms the basis for the letter's Christology*. The announcement of a λόγος τέλειος proved significant. Light is shed on the historical origin of Hebrews' motif of the high priest, its relation to Philo is explained, and its connection with the Melchizedek speculation is to be regarded as an index of the tradition described. Though expectation of the messianic high priest may have emerged in the days of the Hasmoneans,[120] *only when Jewish expectation of the Messiah was linked to the Gnostic* Anthropos *myth did the idea appear of the* Urmensch-*high priest who in sacrificing himself atones for the people's sins*. Philo and Hebrews are the first witnesses to this synthesis developed clearly and in entirely fixed written form only in late Judaism.

C. The Installation of Christ as High Priest and His Sacrificial Death

There is an old dispute which accompanies the question whether Hebrews considers only the exalted Christ as high priest,[121] or whether this predicate already belongs to the earthly Jesus,[122] in particular to the one sacrificing

---

[120]Cf. A. von Gall, *op. cit.*, p. 393f.

[121]Thus Bousset, *Kyrios Christos*, p. 358f.; A. Seeberg, pp. 6, 56, and Windisch, p. 42.

[122]Thus Schrenk, *TDNT* III, 276 and 279, where Jesus' earthly way is spoken of according to Heb. 5:1-10 as that of becoming high priest. A similar thought in Riggenbach, p. 63, and Schlatter, *Theologie der Apostel*, p. 466.

[141]   his body on Golgatha.[123] This problem, which at all events
is the task of a careful exegesis to clarify,[124] cannot be
solved by separating the titles of Son and high priest, as-
signing the former to the humiliated one, but the latter
only to the heavenly one as a heightening of the former.[125]
The clear result of the interpretation of 1:5 is that only in
the divine assembly did Christ attain to lordship together
with his title as Son. With Strathmann[126] we will hazard
the opinion *that in conferring the title of Son, that of high
priesthood is implied.* The analogy after which 5:5f. sets
the quotation from Ps. 2:7 (already cited in 1:5) alongside
the other from Ps. 110:4 is unmistakable. Both obviously
belong together as one single fact. It is merely that the
predicate of Son sets forth the result of Christ's earthly
saving work, while the high priest from heaven completes this saving work of Jesus' humiliation and death.[127]
This identification of the Son with the high priest is also
justified by the underlying religious-historical evidence
according to which the exalted *Anthropos*, thus the
Anthropos furnished in Hebrews with the title of Son, is
as such the bearer of the heavenly office of high priest.

This seems to answer the question put at the outset, as
to why only the exalted one possesses the high priesthood awarded him according to 5:5f. *In addition, 5:9 expressly states that this award occurs only in a proclamation*

---

[123]Thus Michel, p. 39, on the basis of Heb. 9:11ff., while he allows only the
exalted Lord to be high priest "in the true sense"; similarly Büchsel, *Die
Christologie des Hebräerbriefes*, p. 66.
[124]Contra Schmitz, *Die Opferanschauung des späteren Judentums*, p. 293,
who rules out the question as inadmissible.
[125]Thus Windisch, p. 42.
[126]Strathmann, p. 86; similarly Riggenbach, p. 128f.
[127]Sonship is not, say, merely absorbed in Jesus' relation to God; it also embraces lordship over the angels and future kingship over the world.

addressed to the perfected one, just as Jesus is only now the αἴτιος σωτηρίας αἰωνίου. As αἴτιος he is neither simply identical with the ἀρχηγός, as is usually supposed,[128] nor has he actually been perfected as αἴτιος, as the clear facts of the text show.[129] His τελείωσις is rather the presupposition for his becoming the "pioneer of salvation." That is, now while in heaven he draws his own after him, whereas on earth he was only their forerunner and leader. In the concept of αἴτιος the idea of ἀρχηγός is heightened. The content of the term indicates what is involved in Christ's high priesthood on behalf of his own: The exalted one, who as completer can now also complete others, appears over against the earthly *Anthropos* and brings the latter's work to a close.

In addition, other passages clearly show that the title   [142] of high priest was awarded only to the ascended Christ. This is true of 6:20—entry into the inner shrine behind the curtain preceded the granting of the title—as well as of 8:1f., according to which Christ as high priest sits at the right of God's throne in the heavenly sanctuary, and finally also of 7:28, where only God's oath appoints the one made perfect as a Son forever.[130] To the extent the appointment of high priests who are mortal and subject to weakness corresponds to this proclamation of the Son—though in earthly fashion and according to law—this passage makes clear the complete identity of the titles of Son and high priest.

In support of the opposite view, that Jesus was already high priest while on earth, there can be no appeal to his

---

[128]Cf. for example Riggenbach, p. 138, n. 63, and Delling, *TDNT* I, 487f.
[129]Contra Kögel, *Der Begriff* τελειοῦν, p. 63.
[130]From this perspective the κατὰ δύναμιν ζωῆς ἀκαταλύτου of 7:16 is to be understood: Christ is high priest where this δύναμις is operative. According to 8:4, his high priestly activity on earth is actually superfluous.

sinlessness and constancy in midst of all his temporal trials.
And it is even more misleading to describe his completion
or sonship and his high priesthood as the result of a process of moral development on earth. [131] In his essay on *Die
Versuchungen Jesu nach dem Hebräerbrief,* [132] K.
Bornhäuser clearly indicated the significance of the
portrayal of Jesus' temptations in our letter (cf. 2:18;
4:15; 5:7f.; 12:2f.). He correctly asserts [133] that these
temptations were not, for example, of a universal human
sort, but bore a quite specific stamp. *That is, they are a
prototype of Christian temptations* [134] which do not consist
in moral perils, but in an enticement to apostasize from
the eschatological hope, [135] to the extent earthly suffering
would repeatedly urge the πρόδρομος as well as his community to abandon the Christian status. [136] Jesus overcame
this temptation χωρὶς ἁμαρτίας (cf. 4:15). He did not
waiver in his faith, as his disciples will always do because
of their human weakness. [137]

In opposition to this interpretation, Windisch has
clung to the universally human character of Jesus' temptations by allowing them to be limited for the most part
and concretely to the temptations of the passion. [138] Deter-
minative for Windisch is that, according to Hebrews, Jesus assumed human nature. But he overlooks the element
[143]   correctly emphasized by Lohmeyer [139] that interest in Je-

---

131Thus Strathmann, p. 87.
132Leipzig, 1905.
133*Ibid.*, p. 73.
134Bornhäuser, *op. cit.*, p 74.
135*Ibid.*, p. 75.
136*Ibid.*, pp. 77f., 83.
137*Ibid.*, p. 84.
138Windisch, p. 38; similarly Riggenbach, p. 60.
139Lohmeyer, *Kyrios Jesus*, p. 79.

sus' human nature serves to equate the Redeemer with his
"brothers," and that it is merely this interest in 12:2f., as
well as in 2:18; 4:15; and 5:7f., which occasions mention
of Jesus' temptations. From his own experience the
ἀρχηγός knows the plight of those who are his, knows
their ἀσθένειαι, thus their temptation to an avoidance
of suffering and, as a result, to weariness and lack of understanding of the ἀγών laid on them. He understands
this situation from his own earthly weakness and temptability, though he did not yield to it and thus make sin
concrete. He rather learned obedience in suffering and
thus realized the presupposition for τελείωσις, not, of
course, in terms of a process of moral development.
Gradual developments are not at issue here, but this decision was obviated when he was removed from the sphere
of temptation; it concerned only the ἀρχηγός who, as
such, still shared the same existence with his brothers.

   *The question of Jesus' entry upon his high priestly of-
fice becomes really acute only where we must establish the
closest connection between this event and his death on the
cross.* The reason is that in Hebrews Jesus' death cannot
simply be regarded from the "viewpoint of a precondition for his present position of honor."[140] It is
Gyllenberg's great service to have made this clear. That
is,[141] he noted a dual train of thought in the understanding
of Jesus' death and sought to interpret it on the basis of a
polarity characterizing Christ's saving work. He correctly showed *that two ultimately unconnected tasks fall to
this saving work—the atonement for sins and the conquest of death.* Just as Hebrews leaves these two tasks in

---

[140]Contra Bousset, *Kyrios Christos*, p. 358f., and A. Seeberg, p. 107.
[141]Gyllenberg, p. 677f.

deepest and unresolved tension, so their fulfillment occurs at two different stages of the way of Christ. That is,
if the expiation for sins occurs as it were from above
through the heavenly high priest, the conquest of death
occurs from below through the earthly forerunner and
saving leader.[142] We already encountered this tension
from another aspect in the exegesis of 2:14ff. It is actually
[144]   characteristic of the entire letter "that the author clings to
these two points of view without attempting to derive
them from or assimilate them to each other."[143]

*The religious-historical tradition of Hebrews already
furnished the reason for this curious state of affairs.* The
myth knows only one hindrance on the way toward
God, that is, the deathly power of matter, while the
Christian doctrine of salvation can give certainty only
where it also recognizes that the power of sin is broken.
Hence, the tension characteristic of our letter, and its
overlaying of tasks belonging to Jesus' saving work, derive from the fact that Hebrews borrows from the mythical pronouncement of the annihilation of death's power
through the ἀρχηγός, but must also supplement and correct this tradition in terms of the purging of sins. This latter aspect has no original counterpart in the activity of the
Gnostic redeemer. It is expressed only through expansion of the Gnostic idea of the ἀρχηγός, as Hebrews in
fact adopts it, orienting it to the activity of the heavenly
high priest. *But in so doing, Hebrews highlights Jesus'
death in a contradictory fashion.*[144] That is, in that death
two lines of thought converge. First of all, in accord with
the Gnostic tradition of the ἀρχηγός, Jesus' death is the

---

[142]*Ibid.*, pp. 678, 681f.
[143]*Ibid.*, p. 689.
[144]*Ibid.*, p. 681f.

penetration of matter's deathly power. Second, it is the appointed starting point for the high priest's atoning work. To this is added yet a second dialectic, duly accented by Lohmeyer:[145] Christ is the heavenly high priest interceding for those who are his, and also the sacrifice offered by him to God. Thus we simply cannot fail to recognize that Jesus' death is not merely attached as "precondition"[146] to his heavenly atoning work, since the blood shed in this death is at the heart of his heavenly worship.

This assertion is proved beyond dispute when we continue our religious-historical analysis of Hebrews' doctrine of the high priest. Gyllenberg gives to this analysis its point of departure by observing *that in Hebrews the idea of the heavenly sanctuary is no more uniform than that of Jesus' death* and his work of salvation. That [145] is, the divine world is the prototype to which everything earthly is opposed as a mere copy. But another view also emerges, for example, in 9:12,24, according to which the Holy Place is identified with the heavenly sanctuary, while the earthly sanctuary appears as forecourt. Hence the heavenly καταπέτασμα is not a prototype of the curtain in the earthly tabernacle, but the boundary or dividing wall between earth and heaven.[147] In fact, it is necessary to include this observation in our context and, in particular, to pursue somewhat more closely the idea of the heavenly καταπέτασμα as expressed here.

---

[145]In *Kyrios Jesus*, p. 81, he stated that there is a connection between the early Christian doctrine of the Son of Man and the Jewish concept of sacrifice.
[146]It is hardly fortunate when, on p. 683, Gyllenberg also speaks of Jesus' death as a "suprahistorical, metaphysical, cosmic fact." His death is such, in any case, if we choose to use terminology to describe the supernatural significance of the redemptive event.
[147]Gyllenberg, p. 675.

The religious-historical backgrounds of this idea have already been uncovered, but the interest of our letter in this strange concept has not yet been sufficiently explained. It is clear that there must be such a material interest. But we must not assume that mere delight in symbolism induces Hebrews to transfer the institutions of the Old Testament temple to the area of the cosmic. We are led further here by Strathmann's remark[148] that the heavenly curtain denotes a "hindrance" on the way toward God, just as Gyllenberg had described it as a "boundary or dividing wall." In fact, this aptly paraphrases the task of the curtain, as the Gnostic parallels[149] earlier cited[150] also confirm.

But then the καταπέτασμα *in Hebrews occupies the place taken by the* μεσότοιχον τοῦ φραγμοῦ[151] *in Eph. 2:14 and by the heavenly or demonic dividing wall in the*

---

[148]Strathmann, p. 119.

[149]Cf. in addition the *Extracts of Theodotus* 38:1ff. There the fiery Τόπος has a curtain, ἵνα μὴ ἐκ τῆς προσόψεως ἀναλυθῇ τὰ πνεύματα. μόνος δὲ ὁ ἀρχάγγελος εἰσέρχεται πρὸς αὐτὸν, οὗ κατ' εἰκόνα καὶ ὁ ἀρχιερεὺς ἅπαξ τοῦ ἐνιαυτοῦ εἰς τὰ ἅγια τῶν ἁγίων εἰσήει. ἔνθεν καὶ ὁ Ἰησοῦς παρακληθεὶς συνεκαθέσθη τῷ Τόπῳ, ἵνα μένῃ τὰ πνεύματα καὶ μὴ προαναστῇ αὐτοῦ καὶ ἵνα τὸν Τόπον ἡμερώσῃ καὶ τῷ στέρματι δίοδον εἰς πλήρωμα παράσχῃ [ET: "in order that the spirits may not be destroyed by the sight of it. And only the archangel enters it, and to typify this the high priest every year enters the Holy of Holies. From thence Jesus was called and sat down with the *Topos*, that the spirits might remain and not rise before him, and that he might subdue the *Topos* and provide the seed with a passage into the *Plērōma*"]. Here, then, the curtain is the dividing wall between the *Plērōma* and the sphere of the *Topos* which threatens and hinders the ascent of souls. But Jesus as keeper of his own makes possible this ascent, just as he is called ὁ τῶν ἐπιγείων φύλαξ ["guardian of beings upon earth"] in the *Acts of John* 112f. (Bonnet I, 212; H.-S., p. 257).

[150]Cf. p. 209.

[151]For a detailed treatment of this concept, cf. Schlier, *Christus und die Kirche*, pp. 19ff. He also gives evidence of the alternation of images for the celestial dividing wall. So there is nothing to prevent a Jewish Christian Gnosticism from using the image of the curtain here.

Gnostic myth. The latter also hinders the free ascent of souls to God. But above all, this understanding sheds light on the enigmatic identification[152] of the curtain with the σάρξ of Jesus in 10:20. In Gnosticism the dividing wall between heaven and earth encompasses the sphere of matter and in essence is nothing else than the ban of the material world which humans cannot break. Just as at his incarnation the Redeemer submitted to this ban, so at his ascension he creates a breach in the material world by once more liberating himself from the body of flesh he had assumed. This finds clearest expression in the *Odes of Solomon* 17:8ff. There, after symbolizing the ban of the material world by means of the image of "bars of iron," it is said of the ascending Redeemer that "my own iron(s) had grown hot and melted before me."

[146]

If this Gnostic tradition aided our interpretation of 2:14ff., now it proves indispensable and thus confirms our earlier interpretation. *The identification of Jesus' σάρξ with the hindrance of the curtain before the heavenly Holy Place, and the significance of Jesus' entry through his σάρξ as an εἴσοδος τῶν ἁγίων (10:19) for those who are his, takes on meaning only where Jesus' flesh, like the fleshly body of the Redeemer in Gnosticism, is assessed as a component of the material world as such.* The objection will be raised that the Gnostic Redeemer's body of flesh has demonic power and is derived from the demonic world of matter, while according to Heb. 10:5 Jesus' body is prepared by God. It will be further objected that this difference in origin of the body from the outset excludes transference of the Gnostic motif to Hebrews, and

---

[152]Contrary to the clear evidence of the text in Heb. 10:20, A. Seeberg, p. 113, rejects the identification of the curtain with the σάρξ of Jesus, in order to combine ὁδός and σάρξ into his human nature.

renders impossible any assessment of Jesus' body as a component of the material world. By contrast, in 2:14ff., Jesus' incarnation is in fact described as an entry upon the sphere of demonic power. Further, the objection reads, we should note *the remarkable alternation in Hebrews between Jesus' σῶμα and σάρξ.* Christ's earthly body is described as "flesh" when it signifies the hindering of access to God. Of course, it cannot be denied that this is sometimes the case. But this only subjects the body of Jesus—according to 10:5 prepared by God—to a strange dialectical evaluation, intelligible only from the Gnostic background of the idea. It is called "body" to the extent it serves to effect Christ's self-sacrifice, and for which purpose—hence for that of death—it was prepared by God. But it is "flesh" to the extent it is attached to the sphere of the earthly, and consequently does not allow access to God so long as it is borne. *Both assertions conjoin in the fact that as* Anthropos *Jesus assumed the body of Adam.* Jesus' assumption of the existence of the *Urmensch* and his entry into its corporeality correspond to God's will. But, conversely, God's will in turn destines this corporeality of the *Urmensch* (which in Gnosticism represents the ban of the material world) for death alone, since flesh has no access to God. To this extent Jesus' σάρξ is the precondition for his redemptive work which cannot occur without the incarnation, as well as the curtain which hinders ascent and entry into the heavenly Holy Place. Its destruction completes the work of redemption on earth, frees Christ for his return to the Father, and as breaking the ban of the material world also effects the ἐγκαινίζειν[153] of the ὁδὸς πρόσφατος καὶ

[147]

---

[153]According to Behm, *TDNT* III, 454, this term also means "to make a way which was not there before," as well as "to use a way for the first time."

ζῶσα for his own.[154] Thus 10:19f. is related organically to the context of Hebrews 10 and further to the entire Christology of Hebrews. Once again, the propriety of the thesis of Gnostic influence on our letter has been confirmed and has illumined one of the most difficult passages.

It is clear that 6:19 is also to be interpreted from this perspective. In this passage, the curtain again appears as a hindrance on the way toward heaven. ἐλπίς penetrates it as an anchor,[155] since Jesus the πρόδρομος has already broken through it.

This passage also fixes the point at which the idea of the ἀρχηγός converges with that of Jesus' atoning sacrificial death.[156] This returns the investigation just made to its starting point. We were concerned to show that in Hebrews Jesus' death is not only construed as a "precondition for his present position of honor as high priest," but that as a sacrificial death it must be assigned the high priest's heavenly work of reconciliation. Now we may state *that this very sacrificial death in which Jesus offers his fleshly body to God is both entry through the obstructing κατἀπέτασμα as well as the εἴσοδος to heaven.*[157]   [148]

---

[154]This is a variation on the Gnostic motif of the Redeemer as a way for his own, an idea which is also in the background here insofar as Jesus' body as sacrifice opens up the εἴσοδος.

[155]On the topic of hope as anchor, cf. Windisch, p. 59, who duly accents that the anchor is finally Jesus himself.

[156]Strathmann, p. 119, denies that 10:20 may be interpreted analogously with 10:10, so that "through his flesh, that is, through the offering of his body, and thus through his sacrificial death, Jesus has opened the way" for us. He writes that the διά denotes penetration of an obstacle. This is correct, but the text remains obscure so long as its religious-historical background is not recognized.

[157]This identification of the sacrificial death with the ascension is the reason why Hebrews does not reflect on Jesus' resurrection. Heb. 13:20 only means that the ascension, just as the sacrificial death according to 10:5ff., corresponds to God's will.

To this extent Michel rightly comments that "Good Friday and ascension become Christianity's great Day of Atonement."[158] It is the ἀρχηγός of Chapter 2 who enters the curtain. But since this curtain represents Jesus' own σάρξ offered by him to the Father according to God's will, the ἀρχηγός is at the same time the one who offers himself, as conversely the sacrificial death is also the entry into the Holy Place.[159] *But only the high priest walks into the Holy Place, so that from this standpoint we must allow Jesus' entry upon his high priestly office to begin with his sacrificial death.*

In support of this argument constant reference has also been made to Heb. 7:27 and 9:11ff., which can scarcely be understood in any other way[160] than that "his office comprises both the advancing movement of his saving action and the sublime rest of his now constant benefaction."[161] Further, it would be intolerable if that ἐφάπαξ characteristic of Hebrews (cf. 7:27; 9:12; 10:10) were continually to set the deed of the cross at the center of the saving work[162] and redemption, and yet this truly redeeming act were to represent a mere "precondition" within the framework of the whole. On the other hand, it would be just as intolerable if Jesus' high priestly office were to derive its content merely from the remembrance of his earlier occurring death.

---

[158]Michel, p. 112.

[159]The idea of the καταπέτασμα in 10:20 naturally clashes with 9:11, according to which Jesus passes through the σκηνή, that is, the lower regions of heaven, only after his death, as is stated in 4:14. The idea of the heavenly sanctuary is not even uniformly executed; cf. Gyllenberg, p. 675. Interpretation by all the Greek fathers of the σκηνή as Christ's body, cf. Riggenbach, p. 259, n. 16, will hardly suit.

[160]Cf. finally Gyllenberg, p. 676, and Michel, p. 39.

[161]Schrenk, *TDNT* III, 276.

[162]*Ibid.*

Finally, *parallels from the Gnosticism adjacent to Hebrews* indicate that Jesus' sacrificial death was actually understood as a priestly act. So, for example, the *Acts of Peter and Paul* 30 reads: ἱερεὺς γὰρ ἐν τῷ σταυρῷ γέγονεν, ἡνίκα τὴν ὁλοκάρπωσιν τοῦ ἰδίου σώματος [149] καὶ αἵματος ὑπὲρ τοῦ κόσμου παντὸς θυσίαν προσήνεγκεν.[163] The *Passion of Andrew* 8 refers to the θυσιαστήριον τοῦ σταυροῦ,[164] and in Ignatius' *To the Philadelphians* 9:1 the idea of the ἀρχηγός and ἀρχιερεύς converge: "The priests likewise are noble, but the High Priest who has been entrusted with the Holy of Holies is greater, and only to him have the secret things of God been entrusted. He is the door of the Father, through which enter Abraham and Isaac and Jacob and the Prophets and the Apostles and the Church." Christ is the "door" in his function as ἀρχηγός, just as he is elsewhere described as the "way." And, in fact, he becomes the "door" through his death, just as in *To the Ephesians* 9:1 the cross appears as the μηχανή which lofts the believers to heaven.[165]

There can thus be no doubt that in a certain layer of the tradition the idea of Jesus' sacrificial death has been most closely connected with that of his high priesthood. And this layer of the tradition of course takes its special

---

[163]Lipsius, p. 192 [ET: "For he became a priest by the cross at the time when he brought the whole burnt offering of his own body and blood on behalf of the whole world"].

[164]Bonnet I, 13 [ET: "mercy seat of the cross"].

[165]We may refer in addition to the *Extracts of Theodotus* 27:1-6. There the high priest's passing through the curtain into the Holy of Holies and the laying aside of his πέταλον is used as an allegory for the ascent of the soul and the laying aside of its σῶμα. This passage, interesting also in other respects, thus contains an exact parallel to Hebrews' idea of the high priest and is certainly connected with it historically.

stamp from the fact *that it can achieve this connection only on the basis of the Gnostic* Anthropos-ἀρχηγός *speculation.* The same situation was reflected in the Jewish-Gnostic tradition of the self-sacrifice of the heavenly high priests, Michael, Metatron, Elijah, and Moses, whose trail led to Rev. 6:9ff. Following our clarification of that curious idea of the καταπέτασμα in 10:20 and 6:19f., it should be certain that Hebrews is aware of and assumes this tradition. There is absolutely no historical explanation as to how Jesus' death can denote his exaltation as well as his entry upon the high priestly office than from this Gnostic tradition of the heavenly *Urmensch*-high priest who offers himself to atone for his people. The Jewish idea of the Passover or Day of Atonement sacrifice does not suffice, since it does not indicate the identity of the sacrifice with the one who offers it.

A further element is of importance here. Our investigation till now appears to have ended in a crass contradiction. On the one hand, Jesus' high priestly office is an express function of the heavenly Christ, just as the proclamation concerning the high priest occurs in the divine throne assembly. On the other hand, Jesus' entry upon his office already occurs before that proclamation in his *earthly* sacrificial death. The contradiction is to be resolved by distinguishing Jesus' entry upon his office and the proclamation as separate acts. We may draw this distinction because the proclamation describes only the juridical acknowledgment of Jesus as high priest and his public confirmation in the presence of the angels. Thus also the proclamation of Jesus as Son is only one such pronouncement of the mystery of sonship already existing in the Godhead. Conversely, these separate acts may not be sundered, since the sacrificial death as entry

[150]

of the ἀρχηγός through the earthly sphere at the same time initiates Jesus' ascension and therefore—and only therefore—is also his entry upon the high priestly office. Jesus' high priesthood is a heavenly function. *The existence of the one who dies is already penetrated by the glory of the exalted one, since his dying also denotes his exaltation*, and Jesus, as Seeberg[166] correctly acknowledges, draws near to God by his death. In other words, *Hebrews no longer regards Golgotha as an essentially earthly fact, but as the beginning of Jesus' ascension. For this reason alone the sacrificial death is already a component of the heavenly high priesthood.*

It is clear that this interpretation of Jesus' death cannot be historically understood from purely Jewish presuppositions—thus, for example, from the Passover or Day of Atonement sacrifice—but only on the basis of the Gnostic concept of the ἀρχηγός and the related motif of the heavenly *Urmensch* and high priest who sacrifices himself. Where we do not recognize this fact, we remain trapped in contradictions and enigmas, while conversely we gain a historically transparent and materially uniform picture of Hebrews' doctrine of the high priest, as now becomes clear once more in regard to the question of Jesus' entry upon his high priestly office.

We must, therefore, broaden our earlier assertion that Gnosticism has no real interest in the conquest of sin's power, that to this extent Hebrews must allow for a heightening of the Gnostic concept of the ἀρχηγός which it used in the first part of the letter. This assertion is unqualifiedly true only of the great mass of Hellenistic Gnosticism. But just like Hebrews, Jewish mysticism is

---

[166]Seeberg, p. 102.

also aware of the insufficiency of such a doctrine of redemption which does not take seriously the fact of sin.
For this reason, it wove into the framework of the Gnostic doctrine of the ἀρχηγός and *Anthropos* the motif of
the heavenly *Urmensch*-high priest and his self-sacrifice.

[151] Hebrews profits by this process, without abandoning the
basis for its other statements. But by adopting a generally
unfamiliar, special Jewish-Gnostic tradition in order
from that point to declare to the Hellenist the central
Christian message of the forgiveness of sins, the epistle
can with full right describe the presentation of this
message as a mystery and clothe it in the garment of a
λόγος τέλειος.

D. Christ's High Priestly Office

Our investigation has now developed to the point
that its individual strands may be combined and surveyed
in final form. Before doing so, one more factor deserves
special consideration.

*Christ's high priestly activity is described in 2:17f. and
4:15f. under the aspect of* ἔλεος. Kögel regards these
passages as furnishing the "constitutive element of the
high priesthood as such."[167] With ἔλεος the terms
βοήθεια[168] and συμπαθῆσαι (4:15) run parallel. Despite
its relative infrequency, this terminology is not a little in-
dicative of the origin of Hebrews. Actually, it is only in
the two passages cited above that the terms are applied in
pregnant Christological fashion. With regard to these

---

[167]Kögel, *Der Sohn*, p. 96, n. 1.
[168]Cf. 4:16; βοηθεῖν in 2:18, and βοηθός in 13:6.

terms, we may (as Büchsel has recently done in connection with βοήθεια[169]) safely speak of a conscious reserve on the part of the New Testament, since they express a doctrine of atonement basically alien to Christianity.[170]

The concept of ἔλεος should be understood from its context, a concept which elsewhere in the New Testament harks back to Old Testament roots and has salvation-historical and eschatological significance,[171] but here, instead, makes room for a Hellenistic nuance.[172] Christ has become a merciful high priest and helper of [152] those who are his by becoming like them in his humiliation, sharing their condition of πειράζεσθαι, consequently earning a full understanding of their situation

---

[169]Cf. Büchsel's reference to Schlatter, "Wie Sprach Josephus von Gott?," p. 66, who sees in the use of this concept the approaching danger of the Hellenistic "synergism of rational piety," *TDNT* I, 629.

[170]συμπαθῆσαι is a Stoic term. On βοήθεια, cf. in addition the parallels in *Hermetica* I, 22, already cited by Windisch, p. 25: παραγίνομαι αὐτὸς ἐγὼ ὁ Νοῦς τοῖς ὁσίοις καὶ ἀγαθοῖς καὶ καθαροῖς καὶ ἐλεήμοσι (καὶ) τοῖς εὐσεβοῦσι, καὶ ἡ παρουσία μου γίνεται βοήθεια [ET: "I, the Mind, myself am present with those who are holy and good, pure and merciful, those who are devout. (To such) my coming becomes an aid"].

[171]Cf. Bultmann, *TDNT* II, 477ff.

[172]In Hellenism ἔλεος is the emotion of compassion; cf. Bultmann, *TDNT* II, 482 on Philo. Thus, Philo *On the Sacrifices of Abel and Cain* 42 reads that apart from his compassionate mercy, God would have to condemn everything: ἐν γὰρ τῷ τοῦ θεοῦ ἐλέῳ τὰ πάντα ὁρμεῖ ["for on God's mercy...all things rest"]. Thus also Philo *On the Unchangeableness of God* 74 plainly speaks of the σωτήριος ἔλεος ["saving mercy"], or in Chapter 76 reads that οὐ μόνον δικάσας ἐλεεῖ, ἀλλὰ καὶ ἐλεήσας δικάζει ["He tempers His judgement with mercy which He shews in doing kindness even to the unworthy"]. And thus, according to *On the Sacrifices of Abel and Cain*, even the φαῦλος would perish without the λύτρον of the wise man who compassionately and thoughtfully cares for his preservation; cf. Chapter 121. Gnosticism continues this line: Christ is the ἐλεήμων, cf. *Acts of John* 107 (Bonnet I, 205f.; H.-S., p. 255), and for that reason is father of his own, cf. *Acts of Thomas* 67 (Bonnet II, 184; H.-S., p. 479.), while the demons lack ἔλεος, *ibid.*, 75 (Bonnet II, 190; H.-S., p. 483).

and now putting it to practical use in his συμπαθῆσαι from heaven. It is obvious *that ἔλεος here glides over into the meaning of sympathy which has firsthand knowledge of the brothers' weakness and helps them.* Only in this way can it be compared, in especially characteristic fashion, in 5:2 with the μετριοπαθεῖν of an earthly priest. But μετριοπαθεῖν is "a genuine Greek virtue, which not even the Greek Old Testament once names by name."[173] We need not ignore the fact that, even here, the mercy of Christ remains a free act of divine love and does not appear as expression of a moral doctrine. But it is still characteristic that the eschatological note retreats almost entirely and is clearly replaced by a strong affective coloring. Here, as in Hebrews' motif of discipleship, Hellenistic influence makes itself felt, an influence which dominates the entire letter and which emerges again and again.

Hebrews, as few other writings of the New Testament, makes clear *what the Christian gospel has to say to the Hellenistic-Gnostic environment.* This is true from two points of view: Since the preaching of the gospel does not occur in a vacuum, but addresses concrete individuals in their concrete situation, intrinsic to the event of the Logos become flesh is that in every new historical situation the gospel enters into new historical contexts. Set in the age of Hellenism dominated by the Gnostic myth, it did not simply reject the attempt to adopt the mythical ideas of this period. Rather, it took this risk both, of course, for the sake of the clarity of its language and for the sake of explaining its content. Christ stands at the end of the myth as well as at the end of the law. Conversely, the gospel allows neither the myth nor the law to

---

[173]Büchsel, *Die Christologie des Hebräerbriefes*, p. 32, n. 1.

enlarge or abbreviate its message. It actually makes an
end to both insofar as Christ is not the result of human
piety but the "Son." For this reason, further, redemption
is not described as a cosmic event, but as an announce- [153]
ment of the sovereign, loving will of God. Finally then,
in no way, however secret or inward, does the individual,
of himself, have title to eternity. Quite the reverse, in
himself as mortal and as sinner the individual belongs
only to the material world, to death, and to the one who
has "power over death." Only Christ the high priest
gives surety of attaining the heavenly homeland.

*Because Hebrews is ultimately concerned with the
question of this surety, the entire letter is directed toward
the message of the heavenly high priest*, and this message
appears in the form of a λόγος τέλειος. There is good
reason why the proclamation of the resurrection almost
totally retreats in the face of this message. From this perspective of the myth, humanity's enslavement to the material world and to death is at once obvious, and the possibility of conquering humanity's fear of death is the all-
decisive question. Here, then, the message of the risen
Christ by itself no longer needed to contain any offense,
as it did for Judaism. The Gnostic acts of the apostles give
evidence of the fact that one could only too easily falsify
this message in the Hellenistic sense and misinterpret it
from the metaphysical doctrine of the immortality of the
preexistent soul. The gospel had to defend itself against
this misunderstanding, just as it had to disclose existence
to the Hellenist more deeply than the Hellenist understood it in the myth. Both occur in Hebrews' doctrine of
the high priest. In this doctrine, earthly existence is set
forth as fallen into sin, and the power of sin is witnessed
to as the final hindrance to access toward God. At the

same time, Christ's resurrection is secured from the myth's control *and the risen one is revealed as the one who purges sin.* Redemption now is no longer a cosmic event which self-evidently and universally embraces everyone, and of which one may be just as self-evidently and universally certain. On the contrary, what is proper to it is the concrete reality of forgiveness, which can only be concretely grasped and by the individual. Christ now is no longer just the πρόδρομος and model of humanity in general, but Lord of his community freed by him from sin. Only where he, as such, has acted toward it may it follow his example. And only then does it see in him its πρόδρομος and ἀρχηγός.

This also reveals the offense of the cross. Jesus' death is now no longer a mere stripping away of his fleshly body and an intermediate stage in his ascension, as in [154] Gnosticism, but it is both in such a way *that it appears primarily as a sacrificial death. In this sense it forms the content and midpoint of Christ's high priestly activity.* It is such by itself as the ἐφάπαξ in 7:27; 9:12; and 10:10 indicates, yet in an alignment that is articulated in a two-fold manner: Just as Jesus' death as a once-for-all event[174] effected a fundamental λύτρωσις (9:12, 15) in the καθαρισμὸς τῶν ἁμαρτιῶν,[175] so on the basis of this once-for-all event the high priest accomplishes an ever new sanctification of his own.[176] His death was such that

---

[174]Cf. μία θυσία or προσφορά in 10:12,14, and the ἅπαξ of 9:26,28.

[175]Heb. 1:3. As a setting aside of sins (cf. 9:15,28), this purification, according to 10:10, 29, is at the same time a sanctification, and according to 10:14, a perfecting. And, of course, this holds true—by virtue of an eschatological universality—of all the transgressions committed under the first *diathēkē*; cf. 9:15 and 26.

[176]Cf. 10:14 and the σῴζειν εἰς τὸ παντελές of 7:25.

he also entered heaven, and now he lives and in the power of indestructible life intercedes "for us" there (9:24; 7:25). But with this once-for-all, eschatological ἀϑέτησις of the "power of sin,"[177] Christians are not yet removed from their historical temptability and weakness. Hence, every yielding to this weakness requires new sanctification. But this does not occur automatically, so that the individual could by oneself dispose of the power of Jesus' sacrificial death. Our salvation is not bound to a historical datum of which we might take possession. Rather, it is grounded in the living Christ himself and in his activity which always actualizes itself anew and is effective in his free act of mercy. On the other hand, Jesus' heavenly activity is not a myth humanly conjured up, since it is an intercession on the basis of the blood[178] shed on Golgotha, and consequently points again and again to the historically revealed reality of the sacrificial death. *Jesus' death and his heavenly activity are a mutual safeguard. That is, the death secures the high priestly office against being dissolved by the myth, and the high priestly office secures the death against misinterpretation by way of a historically rigid dogmatism.* Thus the intimate connection of the two—derived at first in purely religious-historical fashion[179]—fulfills a needed task in Christian proclamation.

---

[177]ἐπὶ συντελείᾳ τῶν αἰώνων, 9:26.

[178]Cf. 9:12,14; 10:19,29, and 13:20. Further, Jesus' blood has no independent significance in the pietistic sense. It rather represents the concrete act of the sacrificial death and of the sacrificed Christ himself; cf. Schmitz, *Die Opferanschauung des späteren Judentums*, p. 295.

[179]Religious-historical inquiry is indeed not an end in itself, but serves to penetrate the historical problematic of the New Testament, which consists of continually new reflection on subject matter and theological formulation of the question.

[155]   The effect of Jesus' high priestly activity consists in *the purification of conscience* (9:14; 10:22). This formulation is curious enough to undergo thorough examination. The individual has a συνείδησις insofar as he was aware of God's will. For this reason, conscience also registers transgressions and then becomes a συνείδησις πονηρά (10:22) or ἁμαρτιῶν (10:2), which by this means is also aware of its separation from God. To abolish this separation, the evil conscience now drives the individual to strain toward ἔργα νεκρά (9:14). But since these works do not abolish the συνείδησις ἁμαρτιῶν and can only effect a sarkic cleansing (9:10), an actual λατρεύειν θεῷ ζῶντι (9:14) does not result. On the contrary, it is precisely that evil conscience, with its attempts at placating God through works, which more and more powerfully imprisons the individual in the sarkic-cosmic sphere. In fact, only Christ's sacrificial death sets aside the "power of sin" and thus most profoundly redeems where the separation from God was most clearly seen, that is, in the conscience.[180] Since this is now no longer a συνείδησις ἁμαρτιῶν, and as a result is no longer compelled to perform dead works, it has been freed for a true worship of God (cf. 13:18).

The debate with the nature of Jewish sacrifice obviously and necessarily had to be carried out from this perspective. On the basis of the revelation in the first *diathēkē*, Judaism was preferred to the myth insofar as it knew of sin as hindrance on the way toward God, and had to derive sin's bondage from more than the index of its fear of death.[181] To that extent it could attempt a purg-

---

[180]Cf. the κατὰ συνείδησιν τελειῶσαι in 9:9.
[181]Thus also from the religious-historical perspective it is not accidental that

ing of sins by way of sacrifice and priesthood. In this attempt of the Jewish cultus, humanity's actual situation, as well as the need for God's reconciliation resulting from it, is correctly seen. Thus it may be valued as an omen of the eschatological future of Christ. But this attempt was made only with cosmic means and possibilities, and for this reason had no power actually to purge sins and purify the conscience. So it is in fact the prime example of human striving to achieve a right relationship with God on its own and by dead works. Accordingly, the debate with the Jewish cultus demonstrates the absoluteness of the revelation of Christ for a Hellenistic world in possession of the Old Testament.

For the Christian community itself, the message of the [156] *high priestly activity of the exalted one spells the certainty of salvation even in face of its* ἀσθένιαι. It is in need of παρρησία to complete the wandering begun in faith. A new παράκλησις should restore to this community, shaken by various concrete temptations, this original confidence. Mere paraenesis, as it preponderates in the close of the letter, does not suffice for this. Objective strengthening in hope is needed and is actually offered, first, by showing the necessity of discipleship through the example of Christ as ἀρχηγός, then by portraying the certainty of the goal through a vision of the heavenly high priest. Since Christ has broken through the power of death and accomplished the ἀθέτησις of sin, he is guarantor of a new covenant and announces it through his unremitting intercession for his own before God. For God's wandering people on earth, this fact contains suffi-

---

Hebrews' doctrine of the high priest derives solely from the sphere of Jewish Gnosticism.

cient reason for παρρησία. Now it can continue and conclude its wandering confidently and certain of its goal.

Finally, this has again made clear *that all the utterances in Hebrews culminate in the description of Christ's high priestly office, but take their basis, which supports and purposefully articulates the individual parts, from the motif of the wandering people of God.*[182]

---

[182]So we may surely consider whether the symbolic interpretation of the letter's superscription as represented by Schiele in the *American Journal of Theology* 9 (1905), 290-308, by V. Monod, *de titulo epistolae vulgo ad Hebraeos inscriptae* (1910), and cited by Windisch on p. 7, is really altogether misleading: "῾Εβραῖοι are the homeless who wander over this earth, the pious who seek their heavenly homeland; cf. Gen. 14:13, where the Septuagint reads ῎Αβραμ ὁ περάτης for אברם העברי; 1 Sam. 13:7, where the Septuagint reads οἱ διαβαίνοντες διέβησαν for עברים עברו; Philo *On the Migration of Abraham* 20f., p. 439; Chapter 141, p. 458, and Eusebius *On the Preparation for the Gospel* VII, 8:14f.''

Bibliography

Behm, Johannes. "γεύομαι," *TDNT* I, 675-677.

_____. "διατίθημι, κτλ.," *TDNT* II, 104-134.

_____. "καινός, κτλ.," *TDNT* III, 447-454.

Bornhäuser, Karl. *Die Versuchungen Jesu nach dem Hebräerbrief.* Leipzig, 1905.

Bousset, Wilhelm. "Eine jüdische Gebetssammlung im siebenten Buch der apostolischen Konstitutionen," *Nachrichten der königlichen Gesellschaft der Wissenschaften zu Göttingen, Philologisch-historische Klasse.* Berlin, 1916, pp. 435-489.

_____. *Hauptprobleme der Gnosis.* Forschungen zur Religion und Literatur des Alten und Neuen Testaments 10. Göttingen, 1907.

_____. *Jüdisch-christlicher Schulbetrieb in Alexandria und Rom; Literarische Untersuchungen zu Philo und Clemens von Alexandria, Justin und Irenäeus.* Forschungen zur Religion und Literatur des Alten und Neuen Testaments. N.F. Heft 6. Göttingen, 1915.

_____. *Kyrios Christos: A History of Belief in Christ from the Beginnings of Christianity to Irenaeus,* translated by John E. Steely. Nashville, 1970.

Büchsel, Friedrich. "βοηθέω, κτλ.," *TDNT* I, 628-629.

―――. "ἐλέγχω, κτλ.," *TDNT* II, 473-476.

―――. *Die Christologie des Hebräerbriefes.* Beiträge zur Förderung christlicher Theologie XXVII, 2. Gütersloh, 1922.

Bultmann, Rudolf. "ἀλήθεια, κτλ.," *TDNT* I, 232-251.

―――. "ἔλεος, κτλ.," *TDNT* II, 477-487.

―――. & Rengstorf, Karl Heinrich. "ἐλπίς," *TDNT* II, 517-535.

―――. *The Gospel of John: A Commentary,* translated by G. R. Beasley-Murray et al. Philadelphia, 1971.

Burggaller, E. "Das literarische Problem des Hebräerbriefes," *Zeitschrift für die Neutestamentliche Wissenschaft* 9 (1908), pp. 110-131.

Delling, Gerhard. "ἄρχω, κτλ.," *TDNT* I, 478-489.

Dobschütz, Ernst von. "Rationales und irrationales Denken über Gott im Urchristentum; Eine Studie besonders zum Hebräerbrief," *Theologische Studien und Kritiken* 95 (1923/24), pp. 235-255.

Dölger, Franz J. *Sphragis; Eine altchristliche Taufbezeichnung in ihren Beziehungen zur profanen und religiösen Kultur des Altertums V, 3-4.* Paderborn, 1911.

Drews, Paul. *Untersuchungen über die sogen. clementinische Liturgie im VIII. Buch der apostolischen Konstitutionen.* Tübingen, 1906.

Eisler, Robert. "Das letzte Abendmahl," *Zeitschrift für die Neutestamentliche Wissenschaft* 24 (1925), pp. 161-192.

Flemming, J. & Radermacher, L. *Das Buch Henoch.* Der Kirchenvätercommission der königlich-preussischen Akademie der Wissenschaften. Leipzig, 1901.

Foerster, Werner & Herrmann, Johannes. "κλῆρος, κτλ.," *TDNT* III, 758-785.

Gall, August von. *ΒΑΣΙΛΕΙΑ ΤΟΥ ΘΕΟΥ. Eine religionsgeschichtliche Studie zur vorkirchlichen Eschatologie.* Heidelberg, 1926.

Grundmann, Walter et al. "ἁμαρτάνω, κτλ.," *TDNT* I, 267-316.

Gyllenberg, Rafael. "Die Christologie des Hebräerbriefes," *Zeitschrift für Systematische Theologie* 11 (1934), pp. 662-690.

Hanse, Hermann. "ἔχω, κτλ.," *TDNT* II, 816-832.

Horst, Johannes. *Proskynein. Zur Anbetung im Urchristentum nach ihrer religionsgeschichtlichen Eigenart.* Gütersloh, 1932.

Jellinek, Adolf, ed. *Bet Ha-Midrasch I-VI. Sammlung kleiner Midraschim und vermischter Abhandlung aus der älteren jüdischen Literatur.* Leipzig, 1853-77.

Jeremias, Joachim. "Ἡλ(ε)ίας," *TDNT* II, 928-941.

———. *Die Briefe an Timotheus und Titus.* Das Neue Testament Deutsch 9. Göttingen, 1936.

Jérôme, F. J. *Das geschichtliche Melchisedek-Bild und seine Bedeutung im Hebräerbrief.* Dissertations Manuscript. Freiburg, 1920.

Käsemann, Ernst. *Leib und Leib Christi. Eine Untersuchung zur paulinischen Begrifflichkeit.* Tübingen, 1933.

Kittel, Gerhard. "ἀκολουθέω, κτλ.," *TDNT* I, 210-216.

Kögel, Julius. *Der Begriff ΤΕΛΕΙΟΥΝ im Hebräerbrief im Zusammenhang mit dem neutestamentlichen Sprachgebrauch.* Leipzig, 1905.

_____. *Der Sohn und die Söhne; Eine exegetische Studie zu Hebräer 2, 5-18.* Beiträge zur Förderung christlicher Theologie VIII, 5-6. Gütersloh, 1904.

Lidzbarski, Mark, ed. *Das Johannesbuch der Mandäer II.* Giessen, 1915.

_____, ed. *Ginza. Der Schatz oder das grosse Buch der Mandäer.* Quellen zur Religionsgeschichte XIII, 4. Göttingen-Leipzig, 1925.

_____, ed. *Mandäische Liturgien.* Abhandlungen der königlichen Gesellschaft der Wissenschaften zu Göttingen, Philologisch-historische Klasse. N.F. XVII, 1. Berlin, 1920.

Lietzmann, Hans, gen. ed. *Handbuch zum Neuen Testament Erganzungsbund: Die apostolischen Väter.* I: *Die Lehre der zwölf Apostel. I & II Clemensbriefe,* edited by Rudolf Knopf. Tübingen, 1920; III: *Der Barnabasbrief,* edited by Hans Windisch. Tübingen, 1923.

Lipsius, R. A. & Bonnet, M., eds. *Acta Apostolorum Apocrypha I, II: 1, 2*. Leipzig, 1891, 1898, 1903.

Loew, Wilhelm. "Der Glaubensweg des Neuen Bundes. Eine Einführung in den Brief an die Hebräer," *Die Urchristliche Botschaft, 18*. Berlin, 1931.

Lohmeyer, Ernst. *Kyrios Jesus; Eine Untersuchung zu Phil. 2, 5-11*. Sitzungsberichte der Heidelberger Akademie der Wissenschaften, Philosophisch-historische Klasse. XVIII, 4. Heidelberg, 1928.

_____. *Die Offenbarung des Johannes*, Handbuch zum Neuen Testament 16. Tübingen, 1926.

_____. "ΣΥΝ ΧΡΙΣΤΩ," *Festgabe fur Adolf Deissmann*. Tübingen, 1927, pp. 218-257.

Lueken, Wilhelm. *Michael; Eine Darstellung und Vergleichung der jüdischen und morganländisch-christlichen Tradition vom Erzengel Michael*. Göttingen 1898.

Michel, Otto. *Der Brief an die Hebräer*. Kritisch-exegetischer Kommentar über das Neue Testament, 13. Göttingen, 1936[7].

_____. "Die Lehre von der christlichen Vollkommenheit nach der Anschauung des Hebräerbriefes," *Theologische Studien und Kritiken* 106 (1934/35), pp. 333-355.

Monod, Victor. *De titulo epistolae vulgo ad Hebraeos inscriptae*. Montalbani, 1910.

Murmelstein, Benjamin. "Adam, ein Beitrag zur Messiaslehre," *Wiener Zeitschrift für die Kunde des*

Morgenlandes 35 (1928), pp. 242-275; 36 (1929), pp. 51-86.

Norden, Eduard, *Die Geburt des Kindes; Geschichte einer religiösen Idee. Studien der Bibliothek Marburg.* Leipzig-Berlin, 1924.

Odeberg, Hugo. *3 Enoch or the Hebrew Book of Enoch.* Cambridge, 1928.

Pascher, Joseph. "Η ΒΑΣΙΛΙΚΗ ΟΔΟΣ, der Königsweg zu Wiedergeburt und Vergottung bei Philon von Alexandrien," *Studien zur Geschichte und Kultur des Altertums XVII, 3-4.* Paderborn, 1931.

"Pistis Sophia," *Nag Hammadi Studies Vol. IX: The Coptic Gnostic Libary,* edited by R. McL. Wilson; translated by Violet Macdermot. Leiden, 1978.

Preuschen, E. & Bauer, W. *Griechisch-deutsches Wörterbuch zu den Schriften des Neuen Testaments und der übrigen urchristlichen Literatur.* Giessen, 1928[2].

Procksch, Otto. "ἅγιος, κτλ.," *TDNT* I, 88-115.

Reitzenstein, Richard. *Das mandäische Buch des Herrn der Grösse.* Sitzungsberichte der Heidelberger Akademie der Wissenschaften, Philosophisch-historische Klasse. X, 12. Berlin, 1919.

———. *Hellenistic Mystery Religions: Their Basic Ideas and Significance,* translated by John E. Steely. Pittsburg, 1978.

———. & Schaeder, H. H. *Studien zum antiken Synkretismus aus Iran und Griechenland.* Leipzig, 1926.

Rengstorf, Karl Heinrich. "ἀποστέλλω, κτλ.," *TDNT* I, 398-447.

Riggenbach, Eduard. *Der Brief an die Hebräer.* Kommentar zum Neuen Testament 14. Leipzig-Erlangen, 1922[2-3].

Sasse, Hermann. "αἰών, κτλ.," *TDNT* I, 197-209.

Schiele, Friedrich M. "Harnack's 'Probabilia' Concerning the Address and the Author of the Epistle to the Hebrews," *American Journal of Theology* 9 (1905), pp. 290-308.

Schlatter, Adolf. *Der Glaube im Neuen Testament.* Stuttgart, 1927[4].

_____. *Die Theologie der Apostel.* Stuttgart, 1922[2].

Schlier, Heinrich. "βέβαιος, κτλ.," *TDNT* I, 600-603.

_____. "γάλα," *TDNT* I, 645-647.

_____. "δείκνυμι, κτλ.," *TDNT* II, 25-33.

_____. "ἔλαιον," *TDNT* II, 470-473.

_____. *Christus und die Kirche im Epheserbrief.* Beiträge zur historischen Theologie, 6. Tübingen, 1930.

_____. *Religionsgeschichtliche Untersuchungen zu den Ignatius-Briefen.* Giessen, 1929.

Schmidt, Carl, ed. *Koptisch-gnostische Schriften I. Die Pistis Sophia. Die beiden Bücher des Jeû. Unbekanntes alt-Gnostisches Werk.* Die Griechischen christlichen Schriftsteller der ersten drei Jahrhunderte. Leipzig, 1905[2].

Schmitz, Otto. *Die Opferanschauung des späteren Judentums und die Opferaussagungen des Neuen Testaments; Eine Untersuchung ihres geschichtlichen Verhältnisses.* Tübingen, 1910.

Schrenk, Gottlob. "γράφω, κτλ.," *TDNT* I, 742-773.

―――. "δίκη, κτλ.," *TDNT* II, 174-225.

―――. "ἱερός, κτλ.," *TDNT* III, 221-283.

Schniewind, Julius. "ἀγγελία, κτλ.," *TDNT* I, 56-73.

―――. & Friedrich, Gerhard. "ἐπαγγέλλω, κτλ.," *TDNT* II, 576-586.

Scott, W. & Ferguson, A. S., eds. & tr. *Hermetica I-IV.* Oxford, 1924ff.

Seeberg, Alfred. *Der Brief an die Hebräer.* Evangelisch-theologische Bibliothek. Leipzig, 1921.

Stählin, Gustav. "ἀσθενής, κτλ.," *TDNT* I, 490-493.

Strack, H. L. & Billerbeck, P. *Kommentar zum Neuen Testament aus Talmud und Midrasch III-IV.* München, 1926, 1928.

Strathmann, Hermann. *Der Brief an die Hebräer.* Das Neue Testament Deutsch 9. Göttingen, 1935.

Troje, Louise. "Sanbat," in: Richard Reitzenstein, *Die Vorgeschichte der christlichen Taufe.* Leipzig, 1929, pp. 328-377.

―――. *ΑΔΑΜ und ΖΩΗ; Eine Szene der altchristlichen Kunst in ihren religionsgeschichtlichen Zusammenhängen.* Sitzungsberichte der Heidelberger Akademie der Wissenschaften, Philosophisch-historische Klasse. VII, 17. Heidelberg, 1916.

Weiss, Bernhard. *Der Brief an die Hebräer*. Kritisch-exegetischer Kommentar über das Neue Testament 13. Göttingen, 1897[6].

Wrede, William. *Das literarische Rätsel des Hebräerbriefes*. Forschungen zur Religion und Literatur des Alten und Neuen Testaments 8. Göttingen, 1906.

Windisch, Hans. *Der Hebräerbrief*. Handbuch zum Neuen Testament 14. Tübingen, 1931[2].

Wuttke, Gottfried. *Melchisedek, der Priestkönig von Salem; Eine Studie zur Geschichte der Exegese*. Giessen, 1927.

Index of Passages Cited

Other Ancient Authors and Writers